P9-CKQ-711

SECOND CHOICE

SECOND CHOICE

Michael V. DiSalle

in collaboration with

Lawrence G. Blochman

HAWTHORN BOOKS, INC. / *Publishers*

New York City

SECOND CHOICE

 This book was completely manufactured in the United States of America and published simultaneously in Canada by Prentice-Hall of Canada, Ltd., 1870 Birchmount Road, Scarborough, Ontario. Library of Congress Catalogue Card Number: 66-15240.

First Edition: October, 1966
Second Printing: December, 1966
Third Printing: October, 1967

2621

PREFACE

This book makes no pretense of being a survey of American history. Nor is it a biographical study of all our Vice-Presidents. Its purpose is to trace the evolution of the vice-presidency from the original clumsy second-choice machinery of the electoral college to the specifications of the recent Twenty-fifth Amendment. For this, it seems to me, there is no better vehicle than the stories of the eight Vice-Presidents who have fortuitously achieved the presidency through the deaths of their predecessors.

The Vice-President has traditionally, throughout American history, occupied the back seat. His driving capabilities, so to speak, have been unknown, unless he has been one whom fate has actually put behind the wheel. The sudden transition from powerless obscurity to the position of chief executive of a great nation has always been a challenge to the Vice-President, as well as having created a series of problems for the country. Not all second choices have measured up to the possibilities of the office, while some have outshone their forerunners. Whether they have failed or succeeded has depended upon their comparative backgrounds—educational, political, and economic—and upon their personalities.

We will examine here the reasons for their selection for the vice-presidency, and the climates of the political conventions that chose them. The selection process is often the result of the unrelated efforts of hundreds of people and incidents. (In Chapters 9 and 10 we have tried to give an accurate picture of those pertinent incidents of which we have personal knowledge; however, it is possible that, even where we were closely involved, we may have been unaware of many other persons who rendered services leading up to the nomination of President or Vice-President.) We will also compare campaign techniques of the candidates against the varying background of the contemporary state of the union.

The relationship between an accidental President and his predecessor while alive, his sympathy with his predecessor's policies, his rapport with the inherited Cabinet, his changes in policies and personnel—these are all factors which have affected the history of the United States and made the matter of second choice one of first importance. That is why this book was written.

CONTENTS

SECOND CHOICE

1

"THE MOST INSIGNIFICANT OFFICE . . ."

As late as 1912 the vice-presidency of the United States was considered of such little importance that 3,483,922 Americans voted for a dead man: James Schoolcraft Sherman.

Sherman, an ex-mayor of Utica and for twelve years an obscure congressman from upstate New York, had been Vice-President under William Howard Taft since 1909. When Theodore Roosevelt bolted the 1912 Republican national convention in Chicago to accept the presidential nomination of the Progressive party meeting across town, the stunned Republicans renominated Taft and Sherman.

James Sherman died on October 30, 1912, at the age of fifty-seven. With the election only a few days off, there was no time to find a substitute candidate. Yet the Republican electors could not be allowed to vote for a man who would be six weeks in his grave by the time the electoral college met to cast its ballots. When prominent Republicans approached Nicholas Murray Butler, president of Columbia University, seeking his permission for Republican electors to cast their votes for him on the Taft ticket, Dr. Butler agreed, "as long as there is no chance of my being elected Vice-President." Dr. Butler did not have to worry. Both Woodrow Wilson and Theodore Roosevelt ran ahead of the Taft ticket, which won only eight electoral votes.

Dr. Butler's estimate of the vice-presidency had many precedents.

John Adams, the first Vice-President of the United States, characterized his job as "the most insignificant office that ever the invention of man contrived." Daniel Webster, when offered the nomination in 1848, commented: "I do not propose to be buried until I am really dead." Benjamin Franklin is quoted as calling the Vice-President "His Superfluous Excellency." Woodrow Wilson, in *Congressional Government—A Study in American Politics,* written while he was professor of political science at Bryn Mawr in 1885, declared: "There is very little to be said about the Vice President. . . . His importance consists in the fact that he may cease to be vice president."

Most Americans have long regarded the vice-presidency with either indifference or derision, a matter of serious interest only to professional politicians every four years, and even then more for the good of the party than that of the country. Deals and power maneuvers have too often obscured the evaluation of a man's fitness to occupy, if it so happens, the world's most important elective office. However, the recent realization that, of the seven men immediately preceding Lyndon Johnson into the White House, three had died in office has aroused both the public and Congress to the importance of the succession. The fact that, because of such deaths, the nation has been without a Vice-President for a total of more than forty years in the less than two centuries of its existence is rather a shocking one.

Except for the ones who became President, the Vice-Presidents between John Adams and Hubert Humphrey are remembered by few except historians, though many have been able men. Thomas Marshall, Woodrow Wilson's Vice-President, is known chiefly (if at all) for his expressed opinion that the greatest need of the nation was a good five-cent cigar. Calvin Coolidge's running mate, Charles Dawes, is probably better known for his upside-down pipe than for his plan to enable a bankrupt Germany to pay World War I reparations. It is interesting to note that Dawes refused to attend Cabinet meetings because he believed a Vice-President did not belong there. Monroe's Vice-President, Daniel Tompkins, spent more time in New York raising troops for the War of 1812 and seeking reelection as governor than he did in Washington ("Anyone can preside over the Senate."). Millions know Dallas as the place where President Kennedy was assassinated, but few remember that Dallas was named for President Polk's Vice-President—George M. Dallas of Pennsylvania.

Until fellow-Texan Lyndon Johnson sought his advice on accepting the vice-presidency in 1960, many people had forgotten that John Nance Garner, had he not broken with Franklin Roosevelt, might have succeeded to the presidency. Instead, he had gone home to Uvalde declaring that the vice-presidency was not worth a warm pitcher of—and we must use a euphemism here—what the Japanese call *shōben.*

The popular image of the vice-presidency reached its most picturesque stage of caricature during the last years of the Hoover administration (anyone remember Charlie Curtis?), when the musical satire *Of Thee I Sing* won the Pulitzer Prize for drama. In this Kaufman-Ryskind-Gershwin opus Vice-President Alexander Throttlebottom was pictured as a likable nonenity who had to join a guided tour to get into the White House.

Some of our Vice-Presidents have indeed been political hacks, as have been some of our Presidents. The fact that so many of our second choices have been ignored or forgotten is due, however, more to the character of the office than to that of the men who have occupied it. The limited functions of the Vice-President are defined in the United States Constitution. Article I, Section 3, reads, in part:

> The Vice President of the United States shall be President of the Senate, but shall have no vote, unless they be equally divided.

Article II, Section 2, reads, in part:

> In case of the removal of the President from office, or of his death, resignation, or inability to discharge the powers and duties of the said office, the same shall devolve on the Vice President. . . .

In other words, aside from standing in the wings ready to replace the President in case of emergency, the Vice-President's only constitutional duty is to preside over the Senate—a function which would seem to belong to the legislative rather than the executive branch of government.

Elbridge Gerry, one of the signers of the Declaration of Independence, felt so strongly about this provision that he refused to sign the Constitution. Article I, Section 3, he felt, violated the principle of the separation of powers. "We might as well put the President himself at the head of the legislature," he said. Despite his opposition to an executive-branch "spy" in the Senate, Elbridge Gerry himself became Vice-President during Madison's second term. And Gerry's name has entered the language, but not because he was fifth Vice-President of the United States, nor because he was the second Vice-President to die in office. Gerry happened to be governor of Massachusetts in 1812 when the state legislature redrew the election districts of Essex County (to favor the "ins") in such a way that the outlines resembled a salamander. As a result, a Federalist editor coined a verb to describe the process: "gerrymander."

Despite the efforts of recent Presidents to enlarge the role as defined by the Constitution, the vice-presidency is still completely overshadowed by the White House. Hubert Humphrey, Lyndon Johnson's second choice, at the Atlantic City convention, defined the office: "The vice president will be and is what the president wants him to be . . . a loyal, faithful friend and servant." Faithful friend and servant he may well be, but, regardless of what else the President wants him to be, there are many areas in which the Vice-President, by the nature of his office, cannot serve. Heads of state, domestic political figures, senators and vital members of Congress who feel they outrank the Vice-President (because they have the vote and the influence on legislation needed by the President) will deal only with the White House. While the President may delegate to the second choice such relatively pleasant tasks as crowning cherry-blossom queens, attending historical pageants, speaking at state political conventions or fund-raising dinners, and making goodwill trips abroad, the ultimate responsibility for important decisions is his alone. He is commander in chief of the armed forces. He has the last word on foreign policy. Harry Truman used to illustrate this responsibility with a sign on his desk reading: "The buck stops here."

No matter how closely a President has tried to incorporate his Vice-President into his administration, no second choice can ever know the full meaning of the presidency, with all its trials, problems, and responsibilities, until he has occupied the office in his own right.

Actually some of the second-choice men who have succeeded to the presidency have proved superior to the first-choice men from whom they inherited the office. A 1962 symposium of seventy-five historians, arranged by *The New York Times Magazine* and analyzed by late Harvard historian Arthur Schlesinger, Sr., ranks two accidental Presidents among the ten greatest of all our pre-Kennedy chief executives: Theodore Roosevelt and Harry Truman.

Skipping William Henry Harrison and James A. Garfield because of the brevity of their terms, and John F. Kennedy because he was then incumbent, this poll of historians ranked the other thirty-one Presidents in five categories.

Listed as "great" Presidents were Abraham Lincoln, George Washington, Franklin D. Roosevelt, Woodrow Wilson, and Thomas Jefferson—in that order.

Ranked as "near great" were Andrew Jackson, Theodore Roosevelt, James K. Polk, Harry S Truman, John Adams, and Grover Cleveland. Roosevelt and Truman, it may be noted, were elected to the White House on their own after having served as accidental Presidents. John Adams was the first (and the only "near-great") to have been, after serving as Vice-President, subsequently elected to the presidency without having first filled out the term of a preceding President. Thomas Jefferson and Martin Van Buren were the only others to do this.

The third category—"average"—included Madison, John Quincy Adams, Hayes, McKinley, Taft, Van Buren, Monroe, Hoover, Benjamin Harrison, Arthur, Eisenhower, and Andrew Johnson.

Rated as "below average" were Zachary Taylor, John Tyler, Millard Fillmore, Calvin Coolidge, Franklin Pierce, and James Buchanan.

The final category—"failures"—contained only Ulysses S. Grant and Warren Harding.

Of the second choices, it is interesting to note that Chester Arthur, who succeeded the murdered Garfield, is rated ahead of twenty-second-place Dwight Eisenhower. Andrew Johnson, who inherited the Reconstruction crisis from first-ranked Lincoln and was nearly driven from office, was placed only one rung lower than Eisenhower. Millard Fillmore, who succeeded Zachary Taylor when the Mexican War hero succumbed to typhus during his second year in office, although grouped with the "below-average" Presidents, still outranked Coolidge. And, while nobody has suggested that Calvin Coolidge was a great President, the historians classed him five steps ahead of Warren Harding, who bequeathed him the White House by dying in office.

Although fate decides which second-choice men are to be elevated to the top echelon, the character of the Vice-President himself must determine whether or not he is capable of rising to the challenge. Usually he has been equal to the occasion. More often than not he has been faced with problems that would not have been his had he been the first choice. Not only does he inherit the White House, but he inherits a ready-made Cabinet, the members of which have been made closer to presidential policy and to the presidency itself than has the Vice-President. Most of them consider themselves superior to the vice-presidency, a job which each probably tells himself privately that he would have spurned. Thus the new President finds himself considered an outsider by the men supposed to be his closest advisers. In addition, his ready-made cabinet may contain personalities to which he is violently allergic. Lyndon Johnson, for example, inherited a Cabinet containing Robert Kennedy, then Attorney General, who is certainly an able, and to many an attractive, person. He had such an effect on the Johnsonian blood pressure, however, that the President felt compelled to describe for newsmen how Bobby Kennedy gulped when told he would not be considered for the vice-presidential nomination in 1964.

An "accidental" President also inherits established policies which he may not have approved, because the vice-presidency is not a policy-making office. He may inherit commitments of which he had no prior knowledge, even an impending crisis which may have been building up in the secret arcades of high policy to which the Vice-President does not always have access. He also becomes leader of a party which had not originally chosen him to lead.

When a cerebral hemorrhage killed Franklin Roosevelt at a critical moment of World War II, Harry Truman had to make the decision on history's first atomic bomb, a weapon he did not even know existed before death struck at Warm Springs. Should he, or should he not, as the new commander in chief of the armed forces of the United States, loose this monstrous unknown force upon Japan—and upon the world?

Millard Fillmore, the nondescript politician who had previously failed even to be elected governor of New York State, was picked as running mate to Zachary Taylor, not because he was considered potential presidential timber, but because the big Whigs thought he could rally the dissidents and restore unity to a Whig party as badly split as were the Republicans in 1964. When Taylor died, however, Fillmore turned out to be a dissident himself, and espoused the Clay-Webster-Douglas compromise bills, which Taylor almost certainly would have vetoed. The fact that he was the last of the Whig Presidents was due largely to the fatal schism in the party that Fillmore could not or would not heal.

Chester Arthur, a compromise second choice to Garfield, had the reputation of being a tool of the spoils politicians of New York State. Yet, when he became President after Garfield's assassination, he sponsored the establishment of the civil-service system for a fair and uncorruptible recruiting of federal employees.

When the assassin's bullet struck down Abraham Lincoln in Ford's Theater, a man who had never been to school became President of the United States in one of its most crucial periods. Democrat Andrew Johnson, who learned to read and write from his wife, loyally followed Lincoln's policies toward the defeated South, therefore winning the bitter enmity of the newly formed Republican party—Lincoln's party—and came within one senatorial vote of being impeached. I have often wondered what would have happened if Lincoln had lived to face the opposition engendered by his program. Would he have suffered the same living martyrdom that broke Johnson's heart? Or would he still have triumphed to become as much of a hero as history has made him?

As for the other Johnson—Lyndon Baines—except for the deadly aim of a deranged ex-Marine in Dallas, he might have been remembered chiefly as the Vice-President who invited a Pakistani camel driver to come up to Washington and see him some time. On the other hand, he might have been the man to break into a Kennedy dynasty after eight years. But who could have foreseen that the Great Compromiser, the deep-in-the-heart-of-Texan, chosen in part because he was a "true grits-and-drippin's Southerner," would, upon inheriting the presidency, infuriate the professional Southerners by becoming as uncompromising, eloquent, and passionate a champion of Negro rights as his brilliant young predecessor?

The leadership, ability, strength, and courage of our Presidents can best be determined by judging them against the background of the times in which they lived. Each has seemed equipped with the ability to meet the demands made upon him. How the men originally relegated to second choice by their fellow Americans were able to meet those demands on being advanced to the highest office could well be one of the most important secrets of the strength of American democracy. The records of the Vice-Presidents who succeeded to higher office have been examined by many historians, some of whom had a jaundiced eye focused on a preconceived thesis that the second-choice men were second rate, and that their second-rate decisions were responsible for national embarrassment, if not calamity. There have certainly been errors made by accidental Presidents, but no more than have been made by duly elected Presidents.

It has always been an American tradition (and privilege) to second-guess a quarterback who has elected to pass, instead of punting, on a fourth down and had his pass intercepted, or to scream at a baseball manager who has yanked his pitcher with the bases full, only to have a clutch hitter slam the first pitch of the new left-hander for a four-run homer. It is a great advantage, however, not to have had to make these decisions in advance. Hindsight is as easy as it is self-satisfying.

Instead of decrying the caliber of the second-choice men who inherited the White House, we might more profitably examine the responsibility of the electorate as demonstrated by the wisdom—or lack of it—of their choices. Historians would have been spared the anguish of Millard Fillmore's stewardship as President-by-accident had the voters chosen the competent Lewis Cass—governor of Michigan Territory, Secretary of War, minister to France and United States senator—instead of war hero Zachary Taylor. Economists might not have needed to shake their heads over Calvin Coolidge's sins of omission, which led to the depression of the thirties, had the electorate chosen the eminently respectable and able James M. Cox, three times governor of Ohio, rather than that other Ohioan Warren G. Harding, who soon found himself neck-deep in the most odoriferous scandals since the Grant administration.

The nation may well ponder whether an individual's inability to win the presidency might not on occasion have deprived a great and growing country of a great and willing statesman—a man like Cass or Horace Greeley, Cox or Adlai Stevenson, all of whom were the right candidates at the wrong time. But the nation should also consider, the next time it chooses, not only whether it has chosen the President wisely but whether it has been equally wise in the second choice.

The vagaries and vicissitudes of our thirty-eight Vice-Presidents, the motives and manipulations of the professionals who engineered their nomination, the disappointment or fulfillment of the electorate that elevated them to within a heartbeat of the White House—these constitute a neglected phase of our history. The Vice-Presidents who rose to near-greatness when the occasion demanded, those who failed, those who changed our history, those who remained in the shadow of an obscure office: theirs are all human stories which deserve to be retold in these pages.

2
WHOSE CHOICE?

If the machinery originally devised by the Founding Fathers for choosing the President and Vice-President of the United States had still been in force in 1964, we might have seen Lyndon Johnson in the White House and Barry Goldwater as second choice.

Fantastic? No more so than the ill-assorted tandem chosen by the electoral college just before George Washington stepped down. The electoral vote was John Adams, 71, and Thomas Jefferson, 68. As the Constitution did not call for the electors to vote for President and Vice-President separately, but merely to vote for two men, one of whom must not have been from the same state as the elector, the high man was named President and the runner-up Vice-President. Thus in 1797 we had as President an obstinate, autocratic New Englander, representative of the landowners and capitalists, a Federalist who advocated strong, centralized government, and who championed the Alien and Sedition Laws giving him the power to banish "dangerous foreigners" and to curtail the freedom of the press when critical of officials or official acts. And as heir-apparent we had one of the founders of the Democratic Republican (soon to be known simply as the Democratic) party, author of the Declaration of Independence and its self-evident truth "that all men are created equal," and a champion of a free press and states' rights as expressions of democracy with a small *d*.

It was an impossible team—just as impossible as a Johnson-Goldwater team would have been in 1964—and it demonstrated the imperfections of the electoral college system which had not been apparent in the previous two unanimous elections of George Washington. But no attempt was made to overhaul the system until 1800, when the electors split 73–73 between Jefferson and Aaron Burr. This time both candidates were of the same party, but they had totally differing characters. The election was thrown into the House of Representatives, where, according to Article II, Section 1, a two-thirds majority would break the tie, with each state having only one vote. After thirty-five ballots, neither candidate had the required two-thirds vote. Alexander Hamilton, Washington's Secretary of the Treasury, although of the opposing Federalist party, finally intervened to keep Burr, whom he considered an unprincipled, ambitious adventurer, from the White House. Jefferson became President, and Burr never forgave Hamilton. In 1804 he killed him in a duel fought on the Palisades, along the Hudson River in New Jersey. He was indicted for murder, but never stood trial.

In 1804 also, the Twelfth Amendment to the Constitution was ratified by sufficient states to become effective, and in December of the same year Thomas Jefferson was reelected President, the first man to be chosen by the electors under the new provision allowing separate ballots for President and Vice-President. The first Vice-President to be chosen thus was George Clinton, a former governor of New York and the father of DeWitt Clinton. He had the further distinction of being the first Vice-President to die in office.

Except for the Twelfth Amendment, the electoral college has creaked along in the same old aboriginal way for more than a century and a half. The theory of the electoral college seemed logical enough for the thirteen United States of 1789. Communications were sketchy, transporation was slow and uncertain, newspapers were few and poor. The population of some four million was largely rural. There were only five "cities" with more than twelve thousand inhabitants—Philadelphia, New York, Boston, Charleston, and Baltimore—and the largest of these, Philadelphia, could boast of only forty-two thousand. It seemed unlikely that the far-flung voters could make an accurate judgment on the qualifications of the best man for President, so the responsibility was passed on to the electors, who were assumed to be men of wide knowledge, political experience, and sound judgment.

The people had no direct voice in the nomination of the candidates or the choosing of the electors. In most cases both functions were performed by the state legislatures or by party caucuses in Congress. There is no complete record of a popular vote for President and Vice-President until the election of 1824, when the total was only three hundred and fifty thousand. And it was not until 1845 that Congress voted to create a national election day for the electors of President and Vice-President: the first Tuesday following the first Monday in November. The provision insuring the intervening Monday was to favor religious voters who would not travel on Sunday—in the horse-and-buggy age many voters were a day's distance from the nearest polling place.

Despite the warning by George Washington in his farewell address against the "baneful effects" of political party rivalries, the parties had begun to evolve even before the Constitution replaced the unworkable Articles of Confederation in 1789. The Federalists, favoring a concentration of power, included Washington himself, John Adams, Alexander Hamilton, and John Jay, the first Chief Justice. The opposition group, the anti-Federalists who favored limited sovereignty for the states and were originally against the Constitution, became the Democratic Republican party in 1792. It was the party of Jefferson, Madison, and Monroe.

The issues, simple at first, became more complicated as the United States went through an apprenticeship in national self-government. The Federalists believed in government by a professional ruling class that retained some of the trappings of aristocracy. The Democratic Republicans wanted an ever-broader base of authority, and a widening of the popular electorate. The Federalists wanted a protective tariff and a central bank of the United States. The Jeffersonians did not.

As the issues multiplied, the parties changed. The Federalists disappeared during Monroe's second administration. The Democratic Republicans split in 1828, the followers of Andrew Jackson calling themselves Democrats, and the cohorts of Henry Clay and John Quincy Adams adopting the name "National Republicans." The National Republicans merged with several minor parties in 1834 to become the short-lived Whig party.

During the salad days of American politics, the parties were largely the private property of the professionals. Although voter influence was constantly growing, there was little direct popular participation in the evolution of the party system. Candidates were proposed by state legislatures or regional meetings. And there was little coordination on a national level. In 1822 the Tennessee legislature nominated Andrew Jackson for President of the United States, and the Kentucky legislature nominated John C. Calhoun. A few years later Jackson was nominated for the presidency by a Pennsylvania Democratic convention. In 1831 Clay was nominated for the presidency by a convention of the National Republicans meeting in Hartford. A public meeting in New York City a little later nominated Calhoun for President. Nowhere, however, had there been any attempt to give these nominations a national character, nor had there been any attempt to formulate a platform of party policy.

Curiously, it was a small and little-remembered group that held the first truly national party convention with delegates from most of the states. The Anti-Masonic party is supposed to have sprung up as the result of the abduction and ritual murder of a man who had threatened to reveal the secrets of Freemasonry. Actually it was probably the reaction against a secret society's being a part of national politics: nearly half of American Presidents have been members of the Masonic order. In any event the Anti-Masonic party held the first national convention in United States history on September 26, 1831, in Baltimore, Maryland. Thirteen states sent delegates, and the convention nominated William Wirt for President. Wirt, the biographer of Patrick Henry, was John Quincy Adams' Attorney General.

The Anti-Masons set off a chain reaction. In December of the same year the National Republican party held a national convention, also in Baltimore, and nominated Henry Clay for President and John Sergeant, a Pennsylvania congressman, for Vice-President.

And the following May the Democratic party also came to Baltimore to hold its first national convention, and to nominate General Andrew Jackson for a second term as President. John C. Calhoun, the able, ambitious South Carolinian who was elected Vice-President with Jackson for his first term, had resigned his office to occupy the Senate seat vacated by Robert Young Hayne when he became governor of South Carolina. Calhoun, although he never ceased to covet the presidency, evidently preferred the other end of Pennsylvania Avenue to the vice-presidency. There were giants in the Senate in those days—Clay, Webster, Benton—and Calhoun felt more at home among them. So Martin Van Buren was nominated for second choice by the Democrats in their first national convention.

Jackson won handily over Clay, 219 electoral votes to 49. Wirt, the Anti-Mason, won only Vermont's 8 electoral votes, and his party soon became part of the Whig party, which was formed shortly thereafter.*

Once the party convention had become national, the next step in broadening the popular base for making a first and second choice was the primary election. In 1903, Wisconsin held the first statewide one, but the process has been slow in spreading on a national level. For choosing the President, fewer than half the states have adopted the direct primary, whereby the voter may choose between slates of delegates pledged to certain candidates for nomination, in the way he may vote for electors committed to a party ticket in a general election. The majority still send delegates to the national party conventions as a result of state party conventions or party caucuses.

Nevertheless the primaries are traditionally supposed to indicate regional trends, so the major candidates always lavish time, effort, money, and thousands of painful handshakes campaigning in key primary areas. Only too often the key areas unlock nothing. New Hampshire, which kicks off the presidential (and vice-presidential) primary season, has proved singularly uninformative. In 1952, when the President of the United States entered the New Hampshire primaries to prove to a free-wheeling presidential candidate that he was still cock of the Democratic walk, he was soundly whipped by Senator Estes Kefauver of Tennessee. Yet when the same Harry Truman appeared at the Democratic national convention in Chicago later that year and indicated that he would like to see Adlai Stevenson as the presidential nominee, Kefauver could not even win the vice-presidential nomination. And in 1964, when Barry Goldwater launched his campaign for the Republican presidential nomination by entering the New Hampshire primary, he was defeated by a last-minute write-in campaign to name Henry Cabot Lodge. Goldwater lost the Oregon primary to Governor Rockefeller of New York, but he won California—and the Republican nomination.

In November 1965 the Columbia Broadcasting System televised a program on the rights and duties of citizenship. One of the questions asked the viewers was, "Would you favor a national presidential primary?" While an overall average of sixty-five percent voted in the affirmative, a special group of viewers composed solely of congressmen

* The story of the rise and fall of the Whig party will be told in the following two chapters.

and their wives turned thumbs down. The reason is self-evident. Professional politicians are aware of the many difficulties that would make a nationwide presidential primary impracticable. The physical strain and travel fatigue that the actual candidates for the two high offices now undergo during the presidential election campaign is sometimes almost unbearable. If a nationwide primary campaign were to be added to this burden and multiplied by the X number of aspirants for the nomination, only young athletes in the pink of condition would be able to make the race. What's more, the expense of putting on a successful national primary campaign would be astronomical.

We believe that the convention system, with all its tomfoolery, its windy bombast and ersatz enthusiasms, its puerile pageantry and backstage maneuvers, represents a fairly accurate cross section of a political party, and in most cases produces candidates acceptable to a consensus. Furthermore, we feel that, since television has brought the proceedings into everybody's living room, there will be an increasing tendency to streamline the institution by reducing the banal, the boring, and the baroque.

We also believe that a national primary would make the choice of a vice-presidential candidate extremely difficult. Although the national interest is becoming more and more the primary factor in choosing such a candidate, party considerations and the vote-getting abilities of the prospect still carry considerable weight. The man with the big name, the also-ran who needs to be rewarded for his party loyalty, the man whose geographical origin might help the ticket in parts of the country where his support is uncertain—all these are second-choice material.

Although Bricker enabled Dewey to carry Ohio in 1944, and Lyndon Johnson's name on the ticket did win Texas for Kennedy in 1960, the geographical gambit does not always work. Tyler, as Harrison's running mate (and successor), could not carry his own Virginia. Despite the Democratic landslide of 1940, the late Henry Wallace failed to swing Iowa for Franklin Roosevelt, nor could popular Senator McNary win Oregon for Wendell Willkie as his running mate in the same year. Ex-Governor Earl Warren could not carry California for Dewey in 1948. And Estes Kefauver found it impossible to deliver Tennessee to Adlai Stevenson in 1956. In fact, since the Civil War, the second-place candidate on a losing ticket has failed to carry his own state in seventeen out of twenty-four elections.

In truth, the selection of a vice-presidential nominee on the basis of bolstering the presidential candidate in some trouble area is a practice that is on its way to being acknowledged the myth that it is. Again television is the instrument of imminent change. The little electronic box that gives nearly every American a close-up look at the candidates, together with the jet plane that makes coast-to-coast personal appearances possible, enables the voter to make his own judgment of each candidate's personality. It thus becomes less and less likely that an entire region will approve of a party ticket on the basis of local pride, if the majority of the voters are disenchanted with the candidate for President.

It may soon be possible for a party to nominate two outstanding men from adjoining states and, provided that an intelligent presentation of their personalities convinces the electorate that the nation will best be served by them, put them in office.

Political theorists have come up with many suggestions to improve the method of nominating the vice-presidential candidate, each of them, in my opinion, seeming wilder than the other. One of the wildest, reported in all seriousness,* was that the delegates to the convention nominate their vice-presidential candidate *before* they pick their top standard-bearer. I can just see a sudden epidemic of diffidence breaking out among hopefuls who think they have a real chance at the top spot, as they refuse to be stuck with the second place. I can also see rival factions within the same party hoping to get rid of a rival by making him second choice *first*—the Goldwater supporters, for instance, supporting a Scranton or a Rockefeller to reduce the field for the presidency.

Another suggestion is a constitutional amendment allowing the Vice-President the privilege of "moonlighting." He would keep his job in the Senate, for instance, or as governor of his state, and act only as a standby. This would leave him without an insight into policies and issues from the executive point of view, as well as make him less, rather than more, aware of the nature of the job he may inherit.

A third suggestion would restrict the choice of the vice-presidential candidate to the three front runners in the presidential race. This occasionally happens now, but to make the pattern compulsory could embarrass the presidential nominee by forcing him to accept an incompatible running mate with divergent views on policy. The principle of

* *Hats in the Ring,* by Malcolm Moos and Stephen Hess (New York: Random House)

allowing the presidential nominee to designate his own second choice has been generally accepted during the past half century. One notable exception was made by the Republican national convention of 1920, which nominated Senator Warren G. Harding of Ohio for the presidency.

Senator Harding himself was too surprised by his own nomination to express any personal preference for a running mate, but the clique of Republican senators seeking a genial, complacent administration had definite ideas. First they sought able Governor Frank Lowden of Illinois, whom they had snubbed for the top spot and who now refused to play second fiddle to Warren Harding. Senator Hiram Johnson, a former governor of California, laughed off the proposal of second place—bitterly. The kingmakers in one of the smokiest smoke-filled rooms in history came up with the name of Senator Irvine Lenroot of Wisconsin. Harding was willing. Lenroot was willing. But the delegates suddenly developed a distaste for predigested decisions. They wanted the man who had made headlines within the year, the man who, as governor of Massachusetts, had broken the strike of the Boston police. They nominated Calvin Coolidge on the first ballot.

Actually, in three out of four conventions the vice-presidential candidate has been nominated on the first ballot. The choice of a presidential candidate, on the other hand, has taken as many as 103 ballots. The Democrats were quite deliberate in reaching a compromise on John W. Davis in 1924. Inasmuch as there is statistically almost one chance in four that the man chosen Vice-President will inherit the presidency, we (as well as the delegates to national conventions) should devote more than second thoughts to our second choice.

3
TIPPECANOE AND WHO TOO?

WILLIAM HENRY HARRISON, MARCH 4, 1841–APRIL 4, 1841.
JOHN TYLER, APRIL 6, 1841–MARCH 4, 1845.

The first American Vice-President to enter the White House by inheritance was John Tyler, who succeeded President William Henry Harrison in 1841. A Virginia aristocrat with neither a great talent nor an overwhelming desire for the presidency, Tyler owed his high station, at least indirectly, to a man who would have given his right arm to be President: Henry Clay, onetime wild-eyed congressman, Speaker of the House at thirty-four, senator from Kentucky, Secretary of State, and founder (with Daniel Webster) of the Whig party.

Although Clay once said that he would rather be right than President, his record indicates that he was probably given to hyperbole. No major party candidate, not even William Jennings Bryan, ran for President of the United States so many times—and unsuccessfully. Historians may differ over how right he was in such matters as the protective tariff, the Bank of the United States, the War of 1812, and the censure of President Jackson, but there is no doubt that he was dead wrong when he thought that, if he backed John Tyler for second choice, the first choice would be Henry Clay.

Clay was dead right, however, when he judged the time ripe for the six-year-old Whig party to elect a President of the United States in 1840. The Martin Van Buren administration had fallen flat on its face, and the country was anxious for a change. Van Buren, who had been vice-president in Andrew Jackson's second term, was a Democrat who subscribed to Jackson's policies. He was considered an artful politician (he had been governor of New York), but he apparently lacked the vision to perceive the dangers lining the labyrinthine primrose paths down which Old Hickory's program was headed.

When Van Buren took over from Jackson in 1837, the nation was debt free and prosperous, but a strong inflationary tide was running. The Treasury had shown a surplus since 1835, and Jackson, after having killed Clay's pet Bank of the United States, deposited public funds in private banks throughout the country. In the eight years preceding 1837, the number of banks grew from 329 to 788, and the circulation of bank notes increased from forty-eight million dollars to one hundred and forty million dollars. The speculation, questionably secured loans and other hair-raising practices of the new banks must have caused a seismic disturbance in New York's Trinity Churchyard where Alexander Hamilton is buried.

The Federal Land Offices were doing a land-office business, much of it with syndicates set up by speculators. As the pioneers moved west, looking for public land on which to settle, they found that the best sites had already been staked out by the intrepid hunters of the quick dollar. In the last two years of the Jackson administration the sale of government lands rose from four million acres to fifteen million and the Treasury receipts from land sales increased from less than five million dollars a year to nearly twenty-five million dollars. The Treasury deposited these funds in private banks, which in turn lent the money to speculators to buy more land. Jackson finally stopped this dizzy pyramiding by refusing to sell public lands for bank notes. Only gold or silver coin would be legal tender.

Congress, however, swelled the inflationary current by lending surplus funds to state governments. The states used the money to build roads, canals, and other public improvements, as well as to underwrite the building of new factories in order to attract new industries within their borders.

Easy money and bulging wallets whetted the appetite for luxuries, most of which had to be imported from Europe. When imports exceeded exports, an unfavorable dollar balance—a phenomenon not unfamiliar to more recent federal administrations—added to the economic woes of the nation.

Two months after Van Buren was inaugurated, the economic life of the country was paralyzed. Depression set in. Prices rose alarmingly. Between March 1835 and March 1837, the cost of flour soared from $5.62 a barrel to $12, of pork from $10 to $18. During the same period the wholesale price of coal jumped from $6 a ton to $10.50. Rents rose and employment fell. Rioters in New York attacked and pillaged grain and flour warehouses. As distress spread, the sufferers sought someone to blame, and the obvious target was the Administration. The winds of change were blowing, and Henry Clay set his sails for a Whig victory.

The trouble with the Whig party was that it was a party in name only. When its national convention met in Harrisburg, Pennsylvania, to nominate candidates for President and Vice-President in December 1839, the delegates represented a strange variety of interests and geographical areas. They were united in only one thing: they were *against* the policies of Jackson and Van Buren. There was nothing, however, they were all *for*. Their interests were so divergent, in fact, that they could not agree on a platform.

The Whigs tried to be all things to all men. The cotton planters fuming against the protective tariff were Whigs, and the New England industrialists howling for protection of their growing young industries were also Whigs. The Eastern bankers who hated both Jackson and Van Buren for destroying the Bank of the United States were Whigs. So were the states' rights Southerners and the ubiquitous men of substance who shared a common fear of government interference in the economy. So, too, were the cane planters of the Gulf states who screamed for government interference with the import of underpriced Cuban sugar. The farmers of the Anti-Masonic party had also become Whigs. And a young man from Illinois, an ardent admirer of Henry Clay, the dedicated Mason, was also, at that time, a Whig. His name was Abraham Lincoln.

The name on every delegate's tongue, however, when the Whig national convention was called to order in Harrisburg, was that of Henry Clay. The Kentucky Hotspur was so confident of the presidential nomination that he did not bother to go to Harrisburg that December of 1839. He remained in Washington with a decanter of good Kentucky bourbon, which he attacked with gusto as the voting began.

The first ballot gave Clay 103 votes—a plurality, but not a majority. He was surprised at the strength of the second candidate—94 votes were cast for William Henry Harrison, an old soldier who had been the unsuccessful Whig candidate against Van Buren four years before. Another old soldier, General Winfield Scott, was third with 47 votes.

The voting continued for three days without result, and Clay's decanter went back to the barrel many times in the interim. The party strategists had decided that a Whig victory must not be jeopardized by a candidate as controversial as Clay. The Kentuckian had been in public life for thirty years, and a strong-willed, opinionated, outspoken, and uninhibited man like Clay can accumulate an astronomical number of influential enemies in that time. Moreover, in the House and in the Senate, Clay had never made a secret of his political views, so he could not be presented as a compromise candidate to the fence-straddling delegates. In the House he had spoken for two days in favor of increasing the protective tariff—not an oration calculated to please the cotton-growing Whigs of the South. He believed that the question of slavery should be left to the individual states—not a point of view that would endear him to the Whigs of New England. And Clay's Masonic affiliation would hardly be expected to appeal to the rural Anti-Masons who had recently been gathered into the Whig fold.

The big Whigs, while acknowledging their debt to Clay as a founder of the party, decided that the party could best be served by nominating a figurehead and letting the Kentuckian run the country from the Senate. A military hero, with no strong political opinions, would be the ideal candidate, particularly if his knowledge of government were greatly inferior to his war record. Two names came immediately to Whig minds: William Henry Harrison and Winfield Scott. Both were generals and heroes of the War of 1812. Harrison was known as the victor over the Indians, led by Tecumseh, at the battle of Tippecanoe Creek, a somewhat less than crucial engagement. Scott, although he would not achieve heroic proportions until the Mexican War, was such an able commander—probably the best of the American forces in the North—that the fact of his having been sent to Charleston with a naval force as Jackson's answer to Calhoun's "nullification" proclamation for South Carolina could be overlooked. The preliminary stages in the cooking of General Scott's goose were helped along by the Machiavellian machinations of Thaddeus Stevens, the Vermonter who was at that time congressman from Pennsylvania, a Whig, pending the formation of the Republican party as it is today.

Both General Harrison and General Scott were native Virginians, although Harrison had long been a resident of Ohio, and the Virginia delegation at Harrisburg was split in its allegiance. The rift was healed in favor of Old Tippecanoe by Thaddeus Stevens' gift for collecting (and publicizing) indiscreet letters written by political figures. Stevens had somehow come into possession of a conciliatory letter that Winfield Scott had written to Francis Granger of New York, trying to explain a Virginian's thinking on the slavery question so as to mollify the antislavery sentiments of New York. Granger was an important political figure in New York. Gideon Granger, his father, had been Postmaster General under Jefferson and Madison, and Francis himself was to become Postmaster General in President Harrison's Cabinet. The evidence that General Scott had tried to woo New Yorkers by implying that he was less than an out-and-out champion of slavery had a chilling effect on the Virginia delegates. They cast their next ballot for General Harrison.

Thaddeus Stevens, apparently, also had a letter from Harrison, promising him a Cabinet appointment if Harrison should be nominated and elected, but Stevens' name did not appear on the Cabinet list. He never again spoke to Daniel Webster, whom he blamed for the double cross.

It was the switch of the New York delegation, headed by Thurlow Weed, that clinched the nomination for Harrison. Weed was an upstate editor (the Rochester *Telegraph* and the *Anti-Masonic Enquirer*) who, when he moved to the state capital as editor of the Albany *Evening Journal* in 1830, became a driving force in New York politics. When New York gave a push to the Harrison bandwagon, the three-day stalemate was over. Final score: Harrison, 148; Clay, 94; Scott, 16.

When the courier reached Washington with the news that the Whigs had bypassed the father of their party to nominate an aging nonentity from North Bend, Ohio, Henry Clay erupted fire and brimstone.

"My friends are not worth the powder and shot it would take to kill them!" he cried. "I am the most unfortunate man in the history of parties: always run by my friends when sure to be defeated, and now betrayed for a nomination when I, as any man, would be sure of election."

He was consoled, however, by the thought that, with a bewildered sixty-eight-year-old hero in the White House, the country could be conveniently run from the other end of Pennsylvania Avenue—by Senator Henry Clay of Kentucky.

The matter of second choice had been practically settled earlier in the same year of 1839. The Virginia legislature was about to elect a United States senator. John Tyler, who had previously resigned the seat over Jackson's dispatch of Winfield Scott to South Carolina, now wanted it back. But Tyler was still nominally a Democrat, and Henry Clay wanted the seat for William Cabell Rives, who had announced Whig sympathies. To break a deadlock, Clay promised Tyler his support for the Whig vice-presidential nomination if he would withdraw from the Senate race. Tyler agreed, and the delegates at Harrisburg nine months later ratified the deal by making Tyler the second choice.

General Harrison was not a total stranger to politics. His wealthy father had been a member of the Continental Congress and a governor of Virginia. He himself had been born in Virginia, attended Virginia's Hampden-Sidney College, and studied medicine in Philadelphia, but he soon responded to the call of the old frontier—in those days Indiana and Ohio. Under Mad Anthony Wayne he fought the Indians, and under a mandate from Jefferson and Madison he traded whisky and blandishments for millions of acres of Indian lands in the Northwest to be made available to American settlers from the East.

As governor of the Indiana Territory, Harrison had made a deal with a number of Indian chiefs at Fort Wayne whereby several tribes ceded claim to lands west of the Wabash. The operation aroused the ire of Tecumseh, chief of the Shawnees, who declared the commitment was illegal because it had not been ratified by all the tribes involved. He proceeded to organize the Creeks, the Choctaws, and other tribes to resist the encroachment of the land-hungry pioneers. Tecumseh's brother, known as the Prophet, gave a mystic aura to what was to be a crusade. Harrison sent messages to the Miami, the Delaware, and other tribes, urging peace. The Prophet also sent messages, urging unity against the white man. Harrison decided a show of force was necessary. He demanded that the Indians give up all braves who had been guilty of murdering settlers. The Prophet proposed a council. In November 1811 Harrison moved on the Indian settlement at the junction of Tippecanoe Creek and the Wabash with scarcely more than a regiment. During the rainy, moonless night of November 6, the Indians surrounded Harrison's camp. A sentry's shot aroused the soldiers, and the battle was on, with Harrison in the thick of it. Before dawn, the Indians had been routed, and the Prophet discredited because his magic had failed to deflect the white man's bullets. It was a short and relatively minor engagement, but it affected an election for the presidency of the United States nearly thirty years later.

A few months after Harrison's victory at Tippecanoe Creek, Tecumseh concluded an alliance with the British. In the War of 1812 he rallied a dozen Indian tribes to the British side, and fought bravely as long as the British were winning. After Perry's victory on Lake Erie, however, the British forces under Proctor began to withdraw from Fort Malden. Tecumseh remained behind, wearing a sash given him by the British general Brock—to meet Harrison again. Harrison, now a major general, routed the Indians near Chatham on the Thames in Ontario, and Tecumseh was killed. The date was October 5, 1813.

The Thames River battle was a much more important victory than was Tippecanoe, for it was fought on enemy soil; broke the Indian power; ended Tecumseh's inspired leadership, which might have ultimately created a dangerous federation; and established General Harrison as a military commander of real stature. "Thames," however, does not have the ring or rhythm of "Tippecanoe," so the battle of Chatham was soon forgotten.

Harrison retired to his farm at North Bend, Ohio, a dozen miles west of Cincinnati. His neighbors, however, soon sent him to Washington for a term as their congressman. On his return he was elected to the Ohio senate, then sent back to Washington as United States senator from Ohio.

Whether his farm and whisky distillery were proving unprosperous or he was just growing restless on the banks of the Ohio, 1828 found him in Washington again, seeking the just rewards of an old soldier who has done his duty well. President John Quincy Adams reluctantly made him minister to the new South American republic of Colombia. His diplomatic career was not greatly advanced by his undiplomatic utterances suggesting that Simón Bolívar, the hero who had liberated and was still President of Peru and Venezuela as well as Colombia, was practically a dictator. Harrison managed to avoid being declared persona non grata, however, and survived as an envoy until Andrew Jackson and his spoils system brought him home.

When nominated for the presidency Harrison was moonlighting as clerk of the Court of Common Pleas of Hamilton County (Cincinnati), Ohio. The only other candidate who vaulted to the presidency from such a lowly office in such a short time was Grover Cleveland. In the span of four years Cleveland raced through the offices of sheriff of Erie County, New York, mayor of Buffalo, and governor of New York—to the White House.

Since the Whig party had no platform in 1840, Harrison's campaign could scarcely be fought on the issues. In fact, Nicholas Biddle, the Jackson-hating president of the defunct Bank of the United States, no doubt recalling the old soldier's undiplomatic utterances in Colombia, had advised that "he say not one single word about his principles or his creed. Let him say nothing, promise nothing. Let no committee, no convention, no town meeting ever extract from him a single word about what he thinks now, and what he will do hereafter. Let the use of pen and ink be wholly forbidden."

Tyler was also kept under wraps. He had no great desire to cast them off. His few speaking engagements were noncommittal, calling attention to the fact that both he and Harrison were native Virginians—not a violation of the Constitution, which required the President and Vice-President to be "inhabitants" of different states. After all, Harrison was at this time a long-time inhabitant of Ohio.

The campaign, despite the lack of issues, was one of the most spirited in presidential history. The technique was certainly the forerunner of what Madison Avenue would describe a century later as "the saturated treatment in the region of greatest susceptibility." Harrison, the war hero of 1811 and 1812, was the victor of Tippecanoe. Tyler was the professional Virginian. But having declared himself (before his vice-presidential nomination) as a "firm and decided Whig," Tyler soft-pedaled his Democratic background. When questioned, he pointed to the record, as did a Democrat named Al Smith nearly a hundred years later. Nobody looked at the record either time.

The ballyhoo of the 1840 campaign was a masterpiece of glorification of the irrelevant. The slogan "Tippecanoe and Tyler Too" exploited an elderly hero whose military exploits were mossy with age, and a virtually unknown professional Southerner who did not dare flaunt his real Jeffersonian ideas in most of the Whig country.

The Democratic nominee, Martin Van Buren, on the other hand, tried to conduct a logical campaign on his record as a successor of Andrew Jackson. Curiously, he had no second choice. The Vice-President of his first term, Richard M. Johnson, had run into a little Washington-wife trouble during his four years in office, and the national convention declined to renominate him. This did not deter him from running as an independent, however.

Richard Johnson—no kin to the two Vice-President Johnsons who came later—was regarded as an eccentric by his fellow Kentuckians and particularly by uxorious Washington politicians. The fact that he favored a mail delivery on Sunday was one of his lesser idiosyncrasies. For that he claimed constitutional backing—the First Amendment, barring state religious practices. However, he offered no excuses, legal or moral, for his sexual mores. He made no secret of the fact that he liked to share his bachelorhood with women of African origin. His first Negro mistress, a slave he had inherited from his father, left him with two beautiful mulatto daughters when she died. The second ran off with an Amerindian chief, and was sold for her infidelity. The third, together with his illegitimate daughters, he insisted on introducing to Washington society. A certain lack of enthusiasm greeted this early attempt at integration. However, the story (never actually substantiated) that Colonel Richard Johnson had with his own hands killed Tecumseh in the Battle of the Thames, scene of General Harrison's great victory, apparently cancelled out his trifling with the moral code, for his independent race for the vice-presidency in 1840 won him all but one of Virginia's electoral votes, whereas John Tyler, the Virginian, expected to carry the South for the Whigs, got none.

The Whig campaign was a whirlwind of slogans, songs, parades, torchlight processions, and a completely fictitious image of the presidential candidate. "Old Tippecanoe" was represented as a rough-and-ready product of the West (his Virginia birth was never mentioned), who lived in a log cabin, tilled the soil of his own farm with his own hands, and drank nothing stronger than hard cider. Actually, his Ohio River farmhouse was a fairly sophisticated affair, and the product of his distillery compared favorably to the whisky produced across the river in Kentucky and was certainly appreciated by Old Tippecanoe himself. But the floats in the parades featured cabins made of buckeye logs, and there were always farm implements and jugs of hard cider prominently displayed. Beside the cabin door hung strings of buckeyes—the large, burred, nutlike seeds of this variety of horse chestnut—which gave national circulation to Ohio's nickname, the Buckeye State. The manufacturers of such souvenirs as miniature log cabins, cider barrels, and plows, and of "Tippecanoe and Tyler Too" handkerchiefs and campaign buttons amassed small fortunes.

The campaign songs were directed at Van Buren's high life in the White House in contrast to the simple ways of the old soldier. Instead of cider, Van Buren, the squire of Kinderhook, drank only the finest French champagne from expensive crystal glasses, and ate exotic viands from plates of fine Dresden china. One of the Whig campaign songs attacking Van Buren's alleged extravagant way of life ran as follows:

> Let Van from his coolers of silver drink wine
> And lounge on his cushioned settee.
> Our man on his buckeye settee can recline;
> Content with hard cider is he.

The Whigs started several papers to popularize the plebeian image of Harrison and picture his opponent as effete—"Van, Van, the used-up man." The most prominent of these was the *Log Cabin*, edited by Horace Greeley, then a protégé of New York Whig Boss Thurlow Weed. It was Weed who persuaded Greeley to start the New York *Tribune* in 1841 so that the Whigs could reach the workers through a penny newspaper. But in 1840 Horace Greeley was publishing such little gems as:

> Farewell, dear Van,
> You're not our man;
> To guide the ship
> We'll try old Tip.

The Democrats did fight back. In fact, they succeeded in immortalizing the initials standing for Van Buren's nickname, "Old Kinderhook." In April 1840 *The New Era*, a New York daily, coined a phrase that was to echo in Democratic meetings until election day, then to pass into the language: "We will say to Martin Van Buren, O.K., you can remain at the White House for another four years." The voters, however, seemed to prefer Old Tip to O.K.

While most of the press was favorable to Harrison, Tyler, and the Whigs, an occasional voice was raised in protest. The Philadelphia

Ledger, for one, called the Whig campaign a disgrace and a "national drunken frolic." The worst part of it was, complained the *Ledger*, that many ladies went to the open-air meetings, cheered lustily for the Whig candidates, "drank hard cider from gourd shells, and devoured baked beans with their fingers from barrels." Was this the proper sphere of a woman? the *Ledger* demanded to know. Was this appropriate to her elevating, refining influence? Did such things improve men? No. They merely degraded women and made men still more degraded than they were before.

Degrading as "such things" may have seemed to the Philadelphia *Ledger*, the voters loved them. The Harrison-Tyler ticket won over Van Buren and Johnson by 234 electoral votes to 60, even though the popular majority was only 146,000 out of a total vote of some 2,400,000.

March 4, 1841, saw the inauguration of the last United States President who had been born a British subject. It was a raw day, with a cold wind whistling out of the north, but Harrison, anxious to preserve the image of the old soldier and rugged frontiersman, rode to the ceremony bareheaded, on a white horse. Like the youngest elected President one hundred twenty years later, the oldest elected President stood hatless to read his speech. The chilly gusts worried his white hair for nearly two hours as he delivered the longest inaugural address on record.

Daniel Webster had sat up most of the night trying to reduce Harrison's flowery rhetoric and flatulent prose to reasonable dimensions. When his landlady remarked on his weary appearance, Webster replied: "Madam, within twelve hours I have killed seventeen Roman proconsuls —dead as smelts, every one of them." Despite Webster's editing, numerous Roman proconsuls remained, as anyone who has waded through the dull, uninspiring text will testify.

Perhaps the most interesting thing about the Harrison address is that it was the first such document to reach the nation's metropolitan press by means of communication faster than a horse-borne courier. The text was carried to Philadelphia by railroad and appeared in the newspapers there the same day. In it President Harrison:

§ Deplored the fact that the Constitution did not bar reelection of a President, and pledged himself not to seek a second term.

§ Promised to use the veto sparingly so as not to invade the legislative province.

§ Characterized as dangerous the presidential power over public finances, and the monopoly of government patronage.
§ Rejected the idea of an exclusively metallic currency.
§ Deprecated the agitation over the slavery question.
§ Expressed profound reverence for the Christian religion, and declared that sound morals, religious liberty, and a just sense of religious responsibility are essential to true and lasting happiness.

Having spoken, the half-frozen President insisted on remounting his white horse and leading the parade back to the White House.

William Henry Harrison's thirty days in the White House were not particularly happy ones. He believed that the separation of powers was a two-way street, and that his pledge to use the veto sparingly called for a reciprocal response from the legislative branch. He had taken Henry Clay's suggestions for Cabinet appointments without a murmur, but he resented Clay's assumption that he had unlimited access to the White House at any time of day or night, and on the slightest pretext. A certain coolness grew up between the two ends of Pennsylvania Avenue when Harrison formally requested the Kentucky senator to restrict his visits to the executive mansion to a strict minimum. On the other hand, while fending off Clay's attempt at domination, Harrison practiced an extremely democratic procedure with his Clay-inspired Cabinet. Instead of laying down the line, or even leading by suggestion, Harrison agreed that policy matters should be decided by majority vote, his own vote counting for no more than the others.

The worst nightmare of Harrison's thirty days, however, was the locust-like plague of job seekers. Eight years of the Jackson spoils system had carried over into the Van Buren administration without losing momentum. The deserving Whigs began swarming through the White House even before Old Tippecanoe had dismounted from his white horse. They pursued him up the stairs and through the corridors, waving petitions and letters of recommendation, into the innermost sanctuaries of presidential privacy. He was so harassed, he complained, that he could no longer properly attend to "the natural functions of nature." The clamor of the supplicants was a physical ordeal for him, and apparently was a contributory cause of his death, for in his final delirium, he cried out: "I cannot stand it. . . . Don't trouble me. . . . These applications, will they never cease?"

A more immediate cause of death, however, was Harrison's failure to realize that at sixty-eight he no longer had the resistance of a man of twenty-five. A frugal man, Harrison liked to get up at dawn and do his own shopping for the White House kitchen. His wife tarried in Ohio, reluctant to take over the duties as First Lady, as she was perpetually sorrowing over the death of eight of her ten children and left domestic responsibilities to Harrison. The President was a stickler for the freshness of his vegetables, and confident that he could always strike a shrewder bargain than his servants. Unfortunately, one of his marketing expeditions was made on a rainy morning, and the President came home sneezing and coughing.

A few days later, on April 4, 1841, thirty days from the day that he had taken the oath of office, William Henry Harrison, ninth President of the United States and grandfather of the twenty-third President, died of pneumonia.

Vice-President John Tyler was absent from Washington when the President expired. Tyler had left the capital for his Virginia plantation immediately after taking the oath of office, expecting to lead the leisurely life to which every previous Vice-President had considered himself entitled. Anybody could preside over the Senate. And in case of a tie vote, they could always send for him. No other emergency had ever arisen.

Now that the ultimate emergency had arisen for the first time, Tyler could not be summoned to Washington by telegraph. (Samuel F. B. Morse's classic first message by wire—"What hath God wrought?"—would not be sent from Baltimore to Washington for another three years.) There was still no railway connecting Washington with Williamsburg, the closest town to the Tyler estate, so a messenger was sent by riverboat to carry the momentous news.

The messenger was a young State Department officer named Fletcher Webster, son of Daniel Webster, Harrison's Secretary of State. Young Webster arrived the morning after Harrison's death to find Tyler playing marbles with his sons. Shocked, as would be most future Vice-Presidents suddenly thrust into the seat of power, Tyler first scurried through the neighborhood trying to borrow enough money for the fare to Washington. A local moneylender who had refused him a loan when he was still Vice-President now offered it to him. Tyler passed him by, and accepted help from a friend.

It was dawn on April 6 when the riverboat from tidewater Virginia docked at Washington, bearing the tenth President of the United States. Tyler had been awake most of the night, pacing the deck as the little craft swung into the Potomac from Chesapeake Bay, and sleeplessness made him look even more gaunt than usual. He was a curious-looking man, high, broad forehead above narrow-set eyes, an eagle-beak nose dominating a small mouth in a long face. His long thin neck emerging from the stylish gates-ajar collar could have been called scrawny.

His accidental accession to the presidency was as much a shock to the nation as it was to Tyler. Deliberately kept from the public eye during the campaign, Tyler was virtually unknown outside of Washington and his native Virginia. Son of a former governor of Virginia and a member of the plantation artistocracy, he was a graduate of William and Mary (class of 1807), and a practicing attorney. At the age of twenty-one he was elected to the Virginia house of delegates. He was sent to Congress at twenty-six, was governor of his state at thirty-five (two terms), and a United States senator at thirty-seven.

Although he was originally a Democrat, his politics were purely personal. He claimed to be a Jeffersonian Democrat, and he agreed with Jacksonian democracy for four years. During Jackson's second term, however, he became a dedicated states' rights man—more Calhounist than Calhoun. When Jackson declared he would use force if South Carolina persisted in nullification of federal laws, Tyler was the only member of the Senate who voted against the President. Even Calhoun abstained. And when the Virginia house of delegates ordered him to cast his vote in favor of expunging the Senate's censure of Jackson from the *Congressional Record,* he resigned his seat. It was at this point that he declared himself a Whig.

There is little doubt that, if any of the big Whigs had thought there was the slightest possibility of John Tyler's becoming President of the United States, they would not have made him their second choice. He was generally considered to be an honest, kindly man of polished manners and self-confident poise. He was also a mediocre lawyer and a narrow-minded politician with a genius for getting elected to offices which he had not the slightest genius for filling.

Yet here he was in a parlor off the crowded noisy lobby of the Indian Queen Hotel in Washington, being sworn in as President of the United States by Chief Justice William Cranch of the federal circuit court. The country had been without a President for more than two days—the longest such period in history—and the deserving Whig job seekers whom the late President Harrison had eluded for a month were clamoring impatiently in the Indian Queen bar and lobby. Tyler, however, although insisting that he was qualified to perform the duties and exercise the powers of the presidency without further oath than that he took as Vice-President, had Judge Cranch certify in writing that "as doubts may arise, and for greater caution," the presidential oath had been administered.

The precaution was well taken. There was no precedent for the succession of a Vice-President, and among those who believed that Tyler was entitled to neither the title nor the emoluments of the presidency was ex-President John Quincy Adams, who, since the end of his term, had been sitting in the House as representative from Massachusetts. The Adams diary records a complaint that "Mr. Tyler . . . styles himself President of the United States, and not Vice-President which would be correct style. It is a construction in direct violation both of the grammar and context of the Constitution which confers upon the Vice-President not the office but the 'powers and duties of said office.' "

The ex-President was prejudiced, of course, for he had previously characterized Tyler as a "political sectarian . . . with all the interests and passions and vices of slavery rooted in his moral and political constitution—with all talents not above mediocrity. . . ." However, there were other critics in Congress who believed that Tyler was no more than "Acting President." Tyler put an end to the controversy by sending a message to Capitol Hill signed "John Tyler, President of the United States." Further efforts in Congress to cut down his rank and salary failed, and the precedent still stands. It was formally confirmed when Congress voted to submit the Twenty-fifth Amendment to the states in 1965 and ratified nineteen months later.

The message, sent within a few days of his being sworn in, served as Tyler's inaugural address. In it he promised a Jeffersonian foreign policy that would "render and demand justice"; a complete separation of "sword and purse"; rigid public economy; cessation of the war between the government and currency; and continuance in office of both Cabinet members and other "faithful and honest officers, except for giving their official influences to the purposes of the party."

The Cabinet which Tyler had inherited from Harrison and which he proposed to keep was composed largely of Henry Clay's yes-men, with a few bows to contemporary politics and the interests of New England Whigs. Daniel Webster, the Secretary of State, was under obligation to Abbott Lawrence, powerful Yankee trader who also financed the late President Harrison. Secretary of the Treasury was Thomas Ewing of Ohio, a Clay man beholden to Nicholas Biddle, president of the defunct Bank of the United States. John Critten, who resigned his seat as junior senator from Kentucky to become Attorney General, was of course a Clay man, as was John Bell, the Tennessee congressman who was Secretary of War. Navy went to George Badger of North Carolina, whose chief claim to the office was his friendship with the Southern bloc in the United States Senate. New York Whigs Thurlow Weed and William Seward were rewarded by having their man, Francis Granger, named chief patronage dispenser—Postmaster General.

At his first Cabinet meeting Tyler showed himself to be a much shrewder political operator than the bumbling hero of Tippecanoe. He made it clear at the outset that he did not intend to be guided by a majority vote of the Cabinet, as had Harrison, and that his proposal to go along with the same Cabinet was not without conditions. "I shall be pleased to avail myself of your counsel and advice," he told the hold-overs, "but I shall never consent to being dictated to. . . . I, as President, will be responsible for my administration. I hope to have your co-operation . . . so long as you see fit to do this, I shall be glad to have you with me. When you think otherwise, your resignations will be accepted."

Tyler immediately found himself in opposition to Clay and the nationalist wing of the party on practically every issue. His southern conservatism, and his Democratic background before he had declared himself a "firm and decided Whig," rendered him suspicious to the northern Whigs, who had made him their second choice in order to balance the ticket and win the election. They had not included him in their plans for the Harrison administration because he was against the protective tariff, against the distribution of receipts from the sale of public lands, against public works for the states at national expense. Furthermore his position on states' rights was uncontrovertibly against federal intervention in the slavery question, and favorable to Calhoun's stand on nullification of incompatible federal laws by South Carolina.

The showdown was not long in coming. Tyler had been President just two months when Clay introduced the Whig program in toto into the

Senate: repeal of Jackson's Independent Treasury Act, forbidding the deposit of federal funds in state or national banks; revival of a central national bank; adoption of a new protective tariff; and authorization for the Treasury to distribute among the states money received from the sale of public lands.

The bill reestablishing a central bank squeaked through the Senate by three votes on July 28, and passed the House a week later. It was promptly vetoed by Tyler. Clay and Biddle revised the bill on advice of Cabinet members who thought they could meet the President's objections. The new bill breezed through both Houses and was vetoed by President Tyler as promptly as had been the first bill.

Two days later, as if on cue, all of President Tyler's inherited Cabinet, with one exception, resigned. The exception was Daniel Webster, who was then in the midst of negotiations with the British ambassador to determine the boundary between Maine and Canada. It may be that Webster actually enjoyed being Secretary of State, undominated by the shadow of Clay. At any rate, he was in no hurry to quit. The rest of the Cabinet resigned on September 11, 1841. The Webster-Ashburton Treaty was signed on August 9, 1842, but Webster did not give up his portfolio until May 8, 1843.

Meanwhile Tyler was read out of the Whig party. The Whig members of Congress in caucus voted to end their political alliance with Tyler, and declared themselves free of any responsibility for the administration of the executive branch of the government. Efforts were made to push legislation through Congress to restrict the President's veto power (Tyler vetoed ten bills). Congressman John Botts of Virginia tried unsuccessfully to start impeachment proceedings.

Clay was sure that Tyler, deprived of political base, would be unable to function and forced to resign through paralysis of his executive departments. However, Tyler managed to find support, even among such New England Whigs as Congressman Caleb Cushing and ex-Governor Edward Everett of Massachusetts. William Rives, who sat at Tyler's old Senate desk, was the President's spokesman in the Upper House. Judge Abel Upshur of Virginia became Secretary of the Navy, and Calhoun succeeded to State.

Tyler got little help from his old love, the Democratic party. He courted Van Buren with the offer of a Supreme Court appointment. When Van Buren said no, he made the same offer to Silas Wright, a good Jackson Democrat from New York, who also declined. He offered a Cabinet post to James K. Polk, the Democratic governor of Tennessee, and got a polite refusal. The Democrats were not quite ready to accept the renegade's return to the fold at face value.

Nevertheless, the Tyler administration managed to stay afloat. The Whig press followed the Clay line and wrote shrilly of "Executive Usurpation," a "vast nightmare over the Republic" because of the machinations of "His Accidency." When an epidemic of flu swept the country, Whig editors called it the Tyler grippe. Despite the abuse in the press and in the Congress, Tyler still managed to keep Clay powerless. At last, after reiterating the main points of the program he had failed to push past the President, Clay resigned his Senate seat on March 31, 1842. Dramatically and eloquently, while his audience wept, he announced that he was retiring from public life. He meant it, too—at least until the Whig national convention of 1844.

Tyler's achievements as President, except for the purely negative ones of blocking a revival of the Bank of the United States and other pet Clay schemes, were negligible. His last official act was to sign a bill admitting Texas into the union—as another slave state.

His personal life had both lows and highs. His first wife, Letitia Christian, daughter of a Virginia planter, had borne him seven children and was in poor health when the Tylers moved into the White House. She died there in 1842.

Letitia's death, although not unexpected, cast a deep gloom over the White House. Tyler, profoundly grieved, tried to forget his loneliness by losing himself in the routine of the presidency, and in his plans for a possible third party to circumvent his virtual excommunication by the Whigs.

Six months later, when his personal life, along with his political life, was at its blackest, a great light flashed suddenly in his private sky. The President was dazzled by twenty-two-year-old Julia Gardiner, vivacious, dark-eyed, wasp-waisted and full-bosomed younger daughter of the Gardiner family of Gardiners Island, East Hampton, and Manhattan, New York.

The Gardiner family was pre-Revolutionary, patrician, plutocratic, and very, very social. Founder of the American branch was Lion Gardiner who bought Manchonake Island, off the twin eastern tips of Long Island, from the Montauk Indians in 1639 for ten bolts of cloth.

He rechristened it Gardiner's Island, but cartographers have since lost the apostrophe.

The squire of Gardiners Island in Tyler's time was David Gardiner, a minor Whig politician who had served two terms in the New York State senate. His wife Juliana followed the social seasons with her two nubile daughters, Julia and Margaret. Their schedule included East Hampton, Manhattan, Saratoga, White Sulphur Springs, Europe, and, when Congress was in session, Washington.

In the winter of 1841–42 the Gardiner girls were presented to the President of the United States, thanks to a young naval officer named Richard Waldron, who was squiring Julia around Washington. It was a rather formal and not very gay occasion, as Letitia Tyler was living out the last months of her existence, partially paralyzed by a stroke, in the family quarters upstairs in the White House. However, the ice was broken; and meanwhile the New York girls found plenty to do. Julia, who was an accomplished flirt, had a field day among all three branches of the government. She cut quite a figure among the nine old men of the Supreme Court. Mr. Justice John McLean, who evidently did not feel old at fifty-seven (considered practically antique at that period), actually proposed marriage. Julia turned him down.

President Tyler himself was fifty-three when he fell in love with Julia. It was in February 1843, five months after the death of his wife, that he singled her out of a White House gathering to play a two-handed game of Old Sledge with him. The day before Valentine's Day he asked the Gardiner sisters to stop by the White House on their way to Daniel Webster's ball, so he could admire their new gowns. At the Washington's Birthday Ball at the White House, the President proposed marriage. Julia said, "No, no, no!" shaking her head so emphatically with each "no" that the tassel on the little red Greek cap she was wearing brushed the long Tyler nose three times. The President persisted. He took Julia to art galleries and concerts. He invited her to bring her guitar to the White House. He wrote sentimental poetry in her autograph album. But it was not until a year later, in the wake of tragedy, that Julia gave in.

President Tyler had invited a large party of friends and dignitaries for a cruise down the Potomac aboard the steam frigate *Princeton*. The ostensible purpose of the cruise was to watch a demonstration firing of the *Peacemaker*, said to be the world's largest naval gun, but below decks there were music, champagne, and an elaborate buffet. At the third firing the *Peacemaker* blew up, killing eight men, among them Secretary of State Abel Upshur, Secretary of the Navy Thomas Gillman, and Senator David Gardiner. Julia, who was not on deck when the gun exploded, fainted when she learned of her father's death. When the *Princeton* docked, the President himself carried her ashore in his arms.

Seven weeks later the President formally asked the widow for her daughter's hand. Juliana Gardiner hesitated. The Tylers were relative newcomers to America. The first Tyler had not reached Williamsburg until 1653, nearly twenty years after the Gardiners had landed. Besides, Juliana wanted to be sure that, when the President's term expired, he would be able to support Julia in the style to which she was accustomed. She finally assented, however.

The marriage was celebrated without prior announcement. Despite Julia's Catholic birth, the ceremony was held at the Episcopal Church of the Ascension on New York's lower Fifth Avenue. When the news became known, all Washington howled with laughter at the romantic posture of the middle-aged Tyler. Ex-President John Quincy Adams indignantly wrote in his diary that he was revolted by "the indecency of the January-May match."

The bride, however, found it all a glorious adventure, and she took seriously the President's declaration that the honeymoon would go on forever. Her mother, Juliana, however, cautioned her that she should confine her lovemaking to the evening hours, when it would not distract the President or interfere with affairs of state. If she found time hanging heavy on her hands by day, her mother wrote, she should do something about the filthy condition of the White House, with its tobacco-stained walls, its peeling paint, and its shabby drapes and rugs—an apt criticism, since Congress, in its feud with the President, refused to appropriate money to renovate the Executive Mansion.

Like Tyler's first wife, Julia bore the President seven children, one of whom, Lyon, became long-time president of the College of William and Mary, his alma mater. As the father of fourteen children, Tyler was thus the most prolific of American Presidents, a fact which apparently carried little political advantage.

When the Whigs met in national convention at Baltimore on May 1, 1844, Tyler was never seriously considered as a candidate to succeed himself. Henry Clay was nominated unanimously. Later that month the Democratic convention also failed to consider ex-Democrat Tyler, although it took three days to nominate James K. Polk. A rump Democratic convention of the President's friends met in Baltimore at the same time and nominated Tyler for the presidency. Less than three months later, however, seeing the hopelessness of his cause, Tyler withdrew.

Facing a dismal political future, Tyler retired to his plantation in Virginia. For fourteen years he took no part in public life. When the Civil War threatened, however, he spoke out for preserving the union. The man who once had cast the only vote in the Senate in support of South Carolina's right to secede now used all his efforts and eloquence to prevent secession.

In February 1861, a peace conference of twenty-one states assembled in Washington at his behest. Seven states had already voted to secede—South Carolina, Mississippi, Florida, Alabama, Georgia, Louisiana, and Texas—but as chairman of the conference he did his utmost to engineer a peaceful settlement between North and South. The conference has been almost forgotten today, although there is a plaque outside the Willard Hotel in Washington commemorating the site of Tyler's peace efforts.

When the dissident states met in Montgomery that same month to form a provisional government, however, Tyler saw that further negotiations would be futile. Returning to Virginia, he cast his lot with the South Carolina, Mississippi, Florida, Alabama, Georgia, Louisiana, and sion. In May 1861 he was sent to the Provisional Confederate Congress and later was elected to the permanent body. He never took his seat as a legislator for the Confederacy, however, for he died in January 1862.

The mantle of anonymity which cloaked John Tyler before he became President shrouded him again in death. For more than fifty years his grave in Richmond went unmarked. Not until 1915 did the federal government erect a monument to the first Vice-President to become President of the United States. Raised in recognition of his long public service, it was also the first memorial voted by the Congress of the reunited states to a man whose heart and convictions had led him reluctantly to side against the union in the struggle with the South.

4

THE DECLINE OF THE WHIGS

ZACHARY TAYLOR, MARCH 5, 1849–JULY 9, 1850.
MILLARD FILLMORE, JULY 10, 1850–MARCH 4, 1853.

The Whigs never learned the primary fact of political life—that no party without principles or platform can long survive—but they did discover a few useful devices for winning elections.

The election of 1840 taught them they could capture the presidency with a noncommittal war hero as a candidate.

The election of 1844, like the campaigns of 1824 and 1832, before the birth of the party, was apparent proof that no candidate as controversial, opinionated, and outspoken as Henry Clay could hope to reach the White House.

When the Whigs assembled in national convention at Philadelphia in June 1848 they were determined to nominate an old soldier again. The kingmakers, again led by Weed and Seward of New York, had already made their choice: General Zachary Taylor, who a little more than a year before had climaxed his nine-month campaign by fighting his way from the Rio Grande to defeat Mexican Generalissimo Santa Anna at Buena Vista. General Taylor was not yet sixty-five, only three years younger than General Harrison had been when elected. Although the latter had been the first Whig President, and the first President of the United States to die in office, the big Whigs had no reason to suppose that the second (and last) Whig President would also be the second President of the United States to die in office. Even if they had, it is doubtful that the delegates at Philadelphia would have given more attention to their second choice.

General Taylor seemed made to order for the Whigs. They did not know where he stood on a single issue—a position which most of the delegates shared. Although five Presidents before him had seen war service, Taylor was the first regular Army man to achieve the presidency. (He has of course been followed by others, from Grant to Eisenhower.) Made a lieutenant by President Jefferson in 1808 at the age of twenty-four, he had a long, brilliant record behind him. For forty years he had fought Indians in the Northwest Territory and Florida, in the Black Hawk and the Seminole wars. President Polk sent him into Mexico to win his way through Monterrey, Saltillo, and Victoria before overcoming Santa Anna at Buena Vista, while Winfield Scott fought his way to Mexico City from a Vera Cruz landing.

General Taylor was one hundred per cent soldier, yet he couldn't have looked less like one. In contrast to Old Tippecanoe's impressive military bearing, "Old Rough and Ready," as Taylor's troops called him, was positively a travesty. Squat and dumpy, with an oversized head on a very thick neck, he wore a built-in scowl and the most outlandishly unmilitary attire ever seen on a two-star general. He did not hesitate to appear before his troops wearing a battered old straw hat and a long linen duster. His legs were so short that his orderly had to help him mount his favorite horse, Old Whitey.

When the Whigs decided that Taylor was to be their candidate, they were choosing a man who knew nothing about the law, government, or politics, and who had never voted in his life. When asked about his politics, he replied that, if he had voted, he supposed he would have voted Whig, but that he was "not an ultra-Whig." He said that he would have preferred to have been chosen by acclamation instead of by a party convention, because, if elected, "I should feel bound to administer the government untrammeled by party schemes."

He appealed to the Whig strategists because the party split between the slave-holding "Cotton Whigs" of the South and the abolitionist "Conscience Whigs" of New England was widening. Taylor had been born in Virginia and raised in Kentucky, and was currently living on a Louisiana plantation near Baton Rouge where he owned several hundred slaves—a fact which could be soft-pedaled in the North in view of his military record and his utterly blank political past. Besides, the general hated President Jackson. He hated all foreigners as well, to the extent that he insisted on his uniforms being made exclusively of American cloth. This made him enough of a Whig to win the support of the New York Whig boss, Albany editor Thurlow Weed.

Weed had a rival in state and national Whiggery in the person of an ambitious Buffalo lawyer-politician named Millard Fillmore, who had been an unsuccessful candidate for the New York governorship. Fillmore was an ardent supporter of Henry Clay, who was making his quadrennial bid for the presidential nomination. Another Mexican War hero, Winfield Scott, was also in the running; and Daniel Webster had never given up hope of being President some day. Weed tried to buy off Webster with the offer of support for second choice. When Webster refused with the now-famous remark about not wanting to be buried until he was dead and in his coffin, thereby throwing away what proved to be an open sesame to the White House, Weed offered the vice-presidential nomination to Fillmore. Weed undoubtedly thought that Fillmore would vanish into the anonymity of the vice-presidency and thus be out of his hair (and New York politics) for four years.

The convention did the bidding of Weed and his fellow strategists. Zachary Taylor and Millard Fillmore were duly nominated. There was consternation in high places, however, when the letter notifying Taylor of his nomination was returned from Louisiana unopened. Did this mean that Old Rough and Ready had changed his mind about becoming a candidate?

It meant no such thing. Although Congress had authorized adhesive postage stamps the year before as a means of prepaying mail costs, postmasters all over the country were still accepting letters for payment by the recipient. The letter to Taylor had been sent collect, and the general, whose mail since his retirement had consisted largely of postage-due letters from old army buddies seeking financial assistance, was accepting none.

Taylor's campaign was stage-managed by Weed, John J. Crittenden, a Clay protégé from Kentucky, and Alexander Hamilton Stevens, a proslavery congressman from Georgia. In the usual Whig manner, they saw to it that the general took no stand on contemporary issues: the Whigs again had no platform. They also tried to keep him from writing letters, for Old Rough and Ready, like some other soldier-Presidents since, fought a continuous and losing battle with English syntax. A young congressman from Illinois, one Abraham Lincoln, was active on Taylor's behalf and organized a "Young Indians Club" in the House. He and his colleagues used their franking privilege to distribute campaign literature.

Of far greater assistance to the Harrison-Fillmore ticket than either of the principals was the rise of a host of splinter parties, and, especially, a Whig-like schism in the ranks of the Democrats. The earliest Democratic cracks appeared in New York, where the two factions were called Hunkers and Barnburners. The Hunkers were the conservative wing, the name apparently derived from the old Scottish verb "hunker," meaning to squat on one's haunches—in other words to sit tight while progress passes by. The Barnburners, who got their name from the fable of the farmer whose favorite method of ridding his barn of rats was to burn down the barn, included the radicals, the reformers, and many abolitionists.

Each faction sent full delegations to the Democratic national convention in Baltimore. A compromise proposal seated both factions and gave each delegate half a vote, satisfying neither side. When the Hunkers refused to vote, the Barnburners walked out. The Hunkers thereupon declared themselves the regular Democratic convention and nominated Lewis Cass, United States senator and former Michigan governor, for the presidency. William O. Butler of Kentucky was their second choice.

A month later the Barnburners reconvened in Utica and nominated Martin Van Buren for President and Henry Dodge of Wisconsin for Vice-President.

Still later—in August 1848—some antislavery Whigs of New England joined with the eight-year-old abolitionist Liberty Party and some adherents of the Barnburners to form a new coalition party—the Free-Soilers. The antislavery group adopted a slogan—"Free soil, free speech, free labor, and free men"—and nominated a slate: Van Buren for President and Charles Francis Adams for Vice-President.

Three or four other splinter groups nominated tickets.

The slavery issue, which both major parties had been industriously trying for years to sweep under the rug, had now been kicked squarely into the middle of the campaign. Neither the Whigs nor the Democrats were very happy about it, particularly as the controversy had already been sharpened on the floor of Congress by the question of the new territories won from Mexico in the war just ended: should they be slave or free?

Not even in the most feverish flush of the Potomac fever he had evidently caught during his four years in Washington could Van Buren have imagined that he would be elected. He did, however, take enough strength away from Cass to give Taylor New York's big block of electoral votes. Had not Van Buren split the Democrats, Cass could very well have picked up enough states to win, as Taylor's majority was not impressive. The final score: Taylor-Fillmore, popular vote, 1,360,099 electoral vote, 163; Cass-Butler, popular vote, 1,220,554; electoral vote, 127. The substantial vote for Van Buren and the Free-Soilers, nearly three hundred thousand, was more than double the difference in the popular vote between Cass and Taylor. Distributed among the right states, it could have made Cass President.

Aside from indicating that slavery could no longer be ignored as a political issue, the 1848 election was notable in other ways. It was the first time in United States history that all states voted for President on the first Tuesday after the first Monday—it happened to be November 7—in accordance with the Act of 1845. It was also the first time that four new states were voting for President. Florida, Texas, Iowa, and Wisconsin brought to thirty the number of states in the increasingly precarious union.

Side effects of the Taylor-Fillmore victory were felt in the unlikely area of American literature. The Democratic owners of the Brooklyn *Eagle* fired their bearded young editor, Walt Whitman, for having aided the Cass defeat by his editorials in favor of the Free-Soilers. Walt Whitman took advantage of his enforced liberty to write *Leaves of Grass,* publication of which in turn got him fired from the job as federal clerk that had been buying his groceries in the interim. And the civil-service sweep that followed the Taylor victory swept Nathaniel Hawthorne out of his cushy job in the Salem, Massachusetts, customhouse, giving him time to start working in earnest on his novel *The Scarlet Letter.*

In Washington, the social tone of the White House reached a new low. Visitors to the executive mansion were startled by the sight of Old Whitey, the President's favorite military mount, placidly grazing on the White House lawn. They never saw the First Lady. Margaret Smith Taylor, daughter of a Maryland planter, had been reluctant to leave Louisiana for Washington. She spent most of her time in the family quarters upstairs, moping and smoking a corncob pipe. Her married daughter Elizabeth, the eldest of five, served the President as official hostess.

As President, Taylor was very much his own man. He disliked factional quarrels, and deliberately worked for national interests, to the dismay of sectional axe grinders. He was as annoyed by the business of patronage as President Harrison had been, particularly after he had found that job seekers had bribed his Louisiana tailor to let them put pleading notes in the pockets of the new clothes ordered for the inauguration. He was glad to let Vice-President Fillmore take the burden of patronage off his hands, and the ambitious Fillmore was equally glad to have it.

Thurlow Weed was not pleased to see Fillmore's influence in Washington growing, however. To counter it, he browbeat the New York legislature into naming ex-Governor William H. Seward to the United States Senate. Once in Washington, Seward, a man of great charm, succeeded in getting at least one of the President's ears away from Fillmore.

Taylor, however, was dominated by neither man. He was suspicious of Henry Clay and his plans for settling the slavery controversy. His Cabinet was made up largely of Whig party hacks and offered no suitable counsel. When it appeared that the Wilmot Proviso, passed by the House but rejected by the Senate during the Polk administration, was about to be revived, Taylor let it be known that he was against it.

The proviso, introduced by David Wilmot, Democratic congressman from Pennsylvania, as an amendment to an appropriations bill, would have forever barred "slavery and involuntary servitude" from the territory acquired from Mexico as a result of the war. Actually the proviso made little sense, as neither the geography nor the economics of California or the territory described as "New Mexico" (but which included all land between Texas and California) was suitable for successful exploitation by slave labor.

Early in the Taylor administration a boundary dispute arose between Texas and New Mexico. Texans claimed that parts of their own state had been included within the borders of the new territory. Feeling ran high, and Texas sent state troops to the disputed line. Taylor's reaction was to denounce southern congressmen who supported the Texas claims as "traitors," to threaten to lead federal troops himself to put down the "uprising," and to "hang the rebels."

Early in 1850 Henry Clay introduced into the Senate a series of compromise resolutions to settle amicably the boundary question as well as "all existing questions of controversy . . . arising out of the institution of slavery." President Taylor did not approve of the idea. He wanted California admitted as a free state, now that the gold rush was on, and the devil with any compromise. However the debate raged for seven months and brought out some of the finest oratory ever heard in the Senate. Clay spoke for two days in eloquent defense of his measures. Calhoun wrote a speech opposing the compromise, and although too weak to deliver it himself—he died a few weeks later—tottered into the Senate to hear it read by Senator Mason of Georgia. Daniel Webster spoke in favor of the compromise. Seward spoke against it as unfair to the North.

In the midst of the great debate Zachary Taylor died.

The old soldier had been out in the hot sun on the Fourth of July and had brought on his own demise, according to the old wives' tales, by eating too many cherries and drinking too much ice water and cold milk. Taylor's final illness lasted five days, and during his agony the malady was variously diagnosed as "bilious remittent fever," typhus, and cholera morbus. The latter was the favorite choice, as cholera was a popular diagnosis in mid-eighteenth-century America—and there actually was an epidemic of Asiatic cholera in 1850 which began on the docks of New Orleans and spread to the north and west. Whether President Taylor actually died of Asiatic cholera or of cholera nostras, a summer diarrheal complaint with almost identical symptoms, will probably never be known, for Koch did not discover the "comma" bacillus, which causes Asiatic cholera, until thirty-four years after Taylor's death.

Second-choice Millard Fillmore was sworn in as thirteenth President of the United States in the presence of both houses of Congress on July 10, 1850. A tall, handsome man, erect in carriage and faultlessly groomed, he was more military in bearing than his war-hero predecessor, although he had never served in the armed forces. His long, silvering hair covered half his ears. His slightly prognathous jaw gave him an aggressive look, but it was contradicted by a kindly expression about his eyes, which slanted downward at a dihedral angle.

As he took the oath of office and listened to the eulogies of the dead President by Daniel Webster and Representative Charles Conrad of Louisiana, both of whom had violently opposed Taylor on the compromise, Millard Fillmore must have thought back over the long road he had traveled in his fifty years of life. He had been born in a log cabin in upstate Cayuga County, New York; and at the age of fifteen he had been apprenticed by his father, an impoverished farmer, to a textile processor. He was paid fifty-five dollars a year, but learned nothing about dyeing or fulling cloth, as his employer set him to chopping wood most of the time. He did learn a considerable amount in the one-room schoolhouse he attended. A redheaded schoolmarm named Abigail Powers, a Baptist minister's daughter, took a special interest in the boy. He made such rapid progress that he was soon teaching school himself. He bought his release from apprenticeship for thirty dollars, read law, and, after he was admitted to the bar, married Abigail, who was only two years his senior.

Fillmore practiced law in Buffalo, entered politics as a New York assemblyman, became a congressman and state comptroller, but lost to Democrat Silas Wright in the race for the governorship. The minister's daughter whom he had married had a great influence on his life and career. He neither smoked, chewed tobacco, nor drank. He would not stay at a hotel which served liquor if there were a temperance hotel in the same vicinity. He boasted that he had not gambled since he had been fifteen, when he had won a turkey in a raffle.

When the Fillmores moved into the White House, Washington gasped. Abigail's changes caused a sensation that would not be matched until Jacqueline Kennedy did her own redecoration more than a century later. General Taylor's horse tethered on the lawn disappeared, of course, as did the talk about the former First Lady's corncob pipe. The real changes, however, were basic. Abigail insisted on installing a bathtub—a White House first! She also assembled and placed the first library the White House had ever known. Before her arrival there was not even a Bible in permanent residence there.

Finding a carriage suitable for the new President of the United States involved another important decision. Fillmore was first offered a bargain rig which belonged to a member of the Seward-Weed Whiggery that the new boss was sweeping out of Washington. The President suggested that it might not be appropriate for the chief executive to ride around the capital in a secondhand carriage. "Why not?" countered old Edward Moran, the veteran White House groom who had dug up the bargain. "Your Excellency is a secondhand President."

The Fillmores' transportation problem was solved in style. A group of

New York ladies raised money to present the First Lady with an elegant wine-colored carriage upholstered in blue silk (two thousand dollars) drawn by two white horses (one thousand dollars each) with silver-mounted harnesses.

The changes inside the White House were insignificant compared to the executive changes in policy. Accidental President or not, Fillmore demonstrated from the outset that he intended to be no mere echo of Old Rough and Ready. He jettisoned the Taylor Cabinet of political hacks in a body. To replace the Weed-Seward men he chose loyal Fillmore supporters, good Whigs all, all favorable to the Clay Compromise, and most of them able. Daniel Webster became Secretary of State. J. J. Crittenden returned to Washington from the Kentucky statehouse to serve as Attorney General. Senator Tom Corwin, the man from Bourbon County, Kentucky, who had become governor of Ohio, took over Treasury. Charles Conrad, the House orator at the Taylor funeral, got the War portfolio. And Nathan K. Hall, Fillmore's law partner in Buffalo, moved in as Postmaster General.

The appointment of Hall as the big Santa Claus of patronage was intended not only to destroy once and for all the Weed-Seward control of the Whig party in New York, but was a definite move toward building national support for the Fillmore nomination and election as President in 1852. Also a bid for national favor was Fillmore's message to Congress in August calling for immediate action on the Clay Compromise in order to forestall a civil war growing out of the unrest of the Texas-New Mexico border.

Congress responded by breaking up Clay's original "omnibus" compromise into five separate bills, then passing them between September 9 and 20. Fillmore promptly signed all five. They provided for:

*The entry of California into the union as a free state.
*Organization of New Mexico and Utah as territories without reference to slavery (the Wilmot Proviso would have required a stand on the issue).
*Redefinition of Texas boundaries and the payment of $10,000,000 to Texas as compensation for territory ceded to New Mexico.
*Strengthening of the Fugitive Slave Act of 1793 by replacing state with federal jurisdiction.
*Abolition of the slave trade in the District of Columbia after January 1, 1851.

The Clay Compromise was generally approved by the nation as a measure to keep the peace and perpetuate a prosperous economy. While it undoubtedly relieved the tension in the Southwest, it did little to accomplish Fillmore's hopes of closing the gap between the Cotton Whigs and the Conscience Whigs. By giving something to both sides, it struck the usual Whig pose of issue straddling, but it did not accomplish the unity that Fillmore needed for renomination and the party needed for survival.

The federalization of the Fugitive Slave Act was extremely unpopular in the North, since it gave slave owners the right, with government protection, to invade free states and seize any Negro they claimed was a runaway from the South. The Chicago city council openly refused to enforce the act. Georgia threatened secession if the North violated the compromise. A Negro mob stormed a Boston jail in defiance of the new law to rescue a fugitive slave named Shadrach. Fillmore called upon Massachusetts citizens and officials to uphold the letter of the law—words intended to please the South, which were followed by federal inaction calculated to appease the North.

When the Whig national convention met in Baltimore on June 16, 1852, the 396 delegates apparently did not approve wholeheartedly of Fillmore's Whiggish behavior. They gave him 133 votes, but they gave that other ambitious old soldier, General Winfield Scott, 131. Daniel Webster, still hopeful at seventy, got 29. Five days and fifty ballots later, there was no material change.

At this point the Fillmore and Webster forces got together and agreed to release Fillmore's delegates to Webster if the New Englander could pick up another 41 delegates. He could not; and Scott was at last nominated on the fifty-third ballot. Having won twice with an old soldier, the Whigs were willing to try a third time—and were to fade away in the manner peculiar to old soldiers.

The Democrats had held their national convention two weeks earlier in Baltimore. They had no old soldiers among their candidates, but they had three elderly hopefuls in the running: Cass of Michigan, who had been defeated four years earlier by Zachary Taylor; William Marcy, Secretary of War in Polk's Cabinet; and James Buchanan, who had been Secretary of State in the Polk Cabinet. There was also a youthful challenger, Stephen A. Douglas, at thirty-nine a promising senator from Illinois, who would be heard of later as the "Little Giant."

For forty-eight ballots the Democrats could not decide. Buchanan led but could not attain a majority. Second place swung back and forth between Cass and Marcy—and gradually the name of Franklin Pierce began to appear. Pierce was a New Hampshire lawyer who had been a Jacksonian Democratic senator, as well as a brigadier general of volunteers in the Mexican War, wounded at Contreras. He was a smiling, personable, well-mannered candidate with a record of offending no one. He agreed with the Democratic platform—the Clay compromise, peace, and union. He was nominated on the forty-ninth ballot, in a bandwagon rush that left Buchanan with no votes.

As second choice the Democrats nominated William R. King, Alabama senator and minister to France, who was dying of tuberculosis. By special act of Congress after the Pierce-King ticket was elected, King took the oath of office in Havana, where he was vainly seeking good health. He died a month after taking office, causing the United States to be, with the exception of that one-month interval, without a Vice-President from the death of Zachary Taylor until the election of James Buchanan—almost seven years!

Franklin Pierce won in a landslide, with 254 electoral votes to Scott's 42. The popular vote was not so one-sided—1,601,274 to 1,386,580.

Why had the Whig victory formula of putting up an apolitical old soldier failed this time, even though General Scott traveled far and campaigned hard while Pierce stayed home? Was it because the Whigs had for once adopted a platform—support of the 1850 Compromise? Was it because the Whigs had failed to nominate for the presidency their previous second choice, originally named for political expediency, but who had actually served as President for nearly three years? Was it, as some newspapers charged, that the voters believed Scott to be a puppet of Senator Seward of New York?

Henry J. Raymond, editor of the infant *New York Times* (the newspaper celebrated its first birthday just six weeks before the election) accused the Whig convention managers of having made a bargain with the South. The Whigs gave the North a New England candidate, said the *Times*, but gave the South a platform containing a stronger Fugitive Slave Act and without the Wilmot Proviso.

There is little doubt that this dichotomy of the Whig party was responsible not only for the loss of the 1852 election, but for the dissolution of the party. Had Zachary Taylor lived, his strong personality and personal popularity might have kept the party alive despite the handicap of his previous political entanglements. Even Fillmore, had he had the courage and political skills to reconcile the dissidents, might have won reelection, saved the party, and forestalled the formation of the Republican party. But the Whig party was unable to outlast Old Rough and Ready and Fillmore too.

Millard Fillmore's disappointment was compounded by the grief of losing his beloved Abigail, who died a month after he had left the White House. His only daughter, Mary Abigail, who had served as his official hostess during her mother's last invalid months, died a year later at the age of twenty-two.

Like many other occupants of the White House before and after him, Fillmore was incurably infected by Potomac fever during his term of office: he could never get used to the idea of being no longer President. When the Know-Nothings, a meteoric third party whose official name was the American party, nominated him for the presidency in 1856, he accepted.

The Know-Nothings had started out as a secret organization, and had earned their nickname by always claiming they knew nothing about the inner workings of the party. They adopted the Whig attitude of solving the slavery question by denying it existed; and they were anti-Catholic and xenophobic to the extent of promising to tighten the naturalization laws making it almost impossible for foreigners to become citizens. To Fillmore's credit, it must be said that he was a little ashamed of the radical nativistic policies of his backers, and was somewhat relieved when the last survivors from the sinking ship of Whiggery met in forlorn convention at Baltimore and endorsed his presidential candidacy and that of Andrew Donelson of Tennessee as second choice.

Fillmore must have realized that his was a hopeless cause, but he campaigned seriously as though he expected to win, as though a new major party had not arisen to replace the impotent, doddering Whigs. He must have been aware of what had happened at Ripon, Wisconsin, when younger, more vigorous men from among the Conscience Whigs, the antislavery Democrats, and the Free-Soilers met to found the Republican party; and at Philadelphia when the first Republican national convention chose as presidential candidate John C. Frémont, explorer, California hero in the Mexican War, and son-in-law of Senator Thomas Hart Benton, the roaring colossus from Missouri. If not, he was rudely brought up to date by the November election results. While the Democratic ticket of James Buchanan of Pennsylvania and John C. Breckinridge of Kentucky won with 174 electoral votes, the Republican ticket of Frémont and William L. Dayton of New Jersey polled 114 electoral votes. Ex-President Fillmore suffered a humiliating defeat. He won only Maryland's 8 votes.

Fillmore retired to private life and his law practice. Two years later he married Caroline Carmichael McIntosh, the wealthy widow of an Albany merchant, thirteen years his junior. A pre-nuptial contract with Mrs. McIntosh demonstrated that the fifty-eight-year-old ex-President had lost neither his skill in the law nor his dislike of games of chance. It gave him complete control of her fortune "without in any way being accountable therefore." All profits and income were his, as was the entire estate, if he should survive her. If he died first, only one-third of his estate would go to the widow.

After his second marriage he bought the largest, finest mansion he could find in Buffalo, and lived there until his death in 1874. The second Mrs. Fillmore died seven years later.

Millard Fillmore was seventy-four when he died, but the age of the Whigs had long since perished in the fratricidal holocaust that they could not or would not prevent. In the two decades between 1840 and 1860 the field of American politics had been, if not barren, at least fallow. The great men who had seen the nation through its formative years had no worthy immediate successors. Washington, Adams, Jefferson, Madison, Monroe, John Quincy Adams, and Jackson were leaders possessed of the rare qualities of loyalty, vision, unselfish dedication, and courage. Fortunately they built our historical foundations so soundly that the nation was able to survive this dubious twenty-year period.

Historians rate Tyler and Fillmore, the first two Vice-Presidents to achieve the White House through the death of their predecessors, as below-average Presidents. Yet the men they succeeded were no better. In fact, with the possible exception of James Polk, our Presidents during those twenty years were of comparatively minor caliber. Theirs was a period of vacillation, equivocation, and political convenience that led inevitably to destructive civil war. It was a period when professional politicians and the selfish interests they served dictated a party's choice of candidates for leadership, and the professionals picked only the men who were vote getters, not those with experience and ability.

The giants in the Senate were passed over. The men with controversial ideas and the courage to take a stand never got their chance to lead. And before the eighteen fifties had run out, Daniel Webster, Henry Clay, John C. Calhoun, and Thomas Hart Benton were dead.

Luckily there was a new generation ready to take over, a generation that was sick to death of fence straddling and retreat, of twenty years which had seen no progress in the nation except a westward territorial expansion resulting from a questionable war.

The people of the United States, on the verge of disunion, were ready for leadership which would lead.

5

UNION AT THE CROSSROADS: MARTYR BY PROXY?

ABRAHAM LINCOLN, MARCH 4, 1861–APRIL 15, 1865.
ANDREW JOHNSON, APRIL 15, 1865–MARCH 3, 1869.

The dynamic young Republican party was ready and eager to take over leadership of the nation in 1860, but the question of whose hands were to hold the reins was not easily answered. Abraham Lincoln did not spring full panoplied from the head of Jupiter—or even of Thurlow Weed. The still-powerful Whig boss who had scurried to the Republican banner when his own party began to fall apart still had the numerous New York delegation behind him. Weed had ambitious plans for his long-time protégé Senator William H. Seward.

Other kingmakers were also open for business in the new party. The Democrats, by their recent compromises and evasions designed to win votes, had succeeded only in widening the gap between North and South. The Pierce administration's sponsorship of the Kansas-Nebraska Act, giving local option to the two new territories in defiance of the Missouri Compromise, alienated many antislavery Democrats. The Buchanan administration bore the blame for the Supreme Court's Dred Scott decision, which declared that a Negro could not bring suit in a federal court, and that the Missouri Compromise was unconstitutional. Furthermore Buchanan could not escape responsibility for the Panic of 1857, with its more than thirteen thousand business failures in three years. It was only natural that many antislavery and Jeffersonian Democrats rallied to the new party, such men as Hannibal Hamlin, Maine governor and United States senator; Salmon P. Chase, Ohio governor and United States senator; David Wilmot, the proviso man from Pennsylvania; Simon Cameron, another Pennsylvania man; Francis Preston Blair, editor of the Washington *Globe,* mouthpiece of two Democratic administrations; and Gideon Welles, editor of the Hartford *Times.* Also hovering in the wings were Free-Soilers, such Conscience Whigs as Senator Charles Sumner of Massachusetts and Senator Benjamin Franklin Wade of Ohio, and literary characters turned amateur abolitionist politicians like poets John Greenleaf Whittier, Walt Whitman, and William Cullen Bryant (who, although known to schoolboys today chiefly as the author of "Thanatopsis," was very much a politician as editor of the New York *Evening Post*).

The log-cabin origins and impoverished youth of Abraham Lincoln are too well known to be repeated here. His political career began inauspiciously. After eight years in the Illinois legislature, he was elected a Whig member of Congress for a term. He had some support as second choice at the first Republican convention in 1856, but was not a serious contender. He was a candidate for the United States Senate from Illinois in 1858, and was defeated by Democrat Stephen Douglas.

The defeat, which would ordinarily have wrecked a political career, actually made a national character of Lincoln. Although his seven debates with Douglas apparently did not impress the Illinois legislature (the legislature was responsible for the choice, as United States senators were not required to be picked by popular vote until the Seventeenth Amendment to the Constitution was adopted in 1913), the homely, pungent common sense of his antislavery arguments struck the popular fancy, and also brought Lincoln to the attention of the Republican party leaders when they were seeking a candidate for the presidency. They liked such phrases as, "A house divided against itself cannot stand," and, " . . . this government cannot permanently endure half slave and half free." Thus, by the time the second Republican national convention assembled at Chicago in May 1860, the communicable sincerity of a gifted phrase maker carried more weight than his mediocre qualities as a politician.

The 1860 convention of the Grand Young Party did not differ greatly from its future conventions as the Grand Old Party, except perhaps in that the whisky flowed more copiously than the oratory. There were no nominating speeches in 1860, but there was plenty of both ballyhoo electioneering and backstage maneuvering. Seward's forces were well heeled and well organized. Thurlow Weed had arrived in Chicago with a brass band and Tom Hyer, the American heavyweight champion, who used to do a little street fighting and barroom brawling on the side for the Know-Nothings against Tammany ward heelers in New York. What he was supposed to do in Chicago is not clear, but he was probably there as a possible backstop for Weed's free champagne and cigars, which were available to all delegates at the Seward headquarters.

Seward got 173½ votes on the first ballot, but Lincoln polled a surprising 102. Cameron, Pennsylvania's favorite son, out-polled Salmon Chase 50½ to 49, while white-whiskered Edward Bates, an ex-Whig from Missouri, got 48. On the second ballot Pennsylvania, Vermont, and several other small delegations switched to Lincoln, giving him 181 to Seward's 184½.

Before the third ballot was taken, Horace Greeley worked hard to dump Seward, whom he disliked personally, and was joined by conservatives of Pennsylvania, New Jersey, Indiana, and Illinois. When the roll call on the third ballot showed Lincoln within one and one half votes of nomination, Ohio shifted four votes to insure a victory for the rail splitter, and the bandwagon began to roll.

Hannibal Hamlin of Maine was the second choice.

Weed wept.

In the November elections Lincoln won over his old opponent Stephen Douglas of Illinois, who had defeated him in a state election just two years earlier. The score: 180 electoral votes to 12. Lincoln was aided by a schism in the Democratic party, when the southern delegates walked out of the convention at Charleston. They met later at Baltimore to nominate John C. Breckinridge of Kentucky for President and Joseph Lane of Oregon as second choice. The Charleston dissidents racked up 72 electoral votes from eleven states. Even the one-shot Constitutional Union party nominees—John Bell of Tennessee and Edward Everett of Massachusetts—representing only a few die-hard Whigs and other conservatives, but pledged to sectional conciliation, captured 39 electoral votes. Everett, incidentally, was such a renowned orator that he was chosen to make the principal speech at Gettysburg—a long and boring discourse since forgotten in the light of Lincoln's brief, incisive eloquence.

Lincoln's electoral majority was impressive. He did not receive a clear majority of the popular vote, but the mandate was certainly antislavery and pro-union.

Before Lincoln's inauguration on March 4, 1861, Georgia troops had seized Fort Pulaski and the United States arsenal at Augusta; Alabama troops had taken the Mount Vernon arsenal and forts Gaines and Morgan on Mobile Bay; Florida state forces had occupied the United States arsenal at Apalachicola; Louisiana had seized the United States mint and customhouse at New Orleans; and Arkansas and Texas had taken over United States arsenals at Little Rock and San Antonio. A month before the inauguration, the Confederacy was born at Montgomery. On Inauguration Day, the United States Army numbered less than fourteen thousand.

Lincoln's principal opponents at Chicago were appointed to his Cabinet. Seward became Secretary of State; Chase, of Treasury; Cameron, of War; and Bates was made Attorney General. Editor Welles of Hartford got the Navy portfolio, and Washington editor Blair's son Montgomery became Postmaster General.

The Administration had been in office scarcely a month before Fort Sumter was fired upon. President Lincoln declared that a state of insurrection existed and called for seventy-five thousand volunteers.

The cruel realities of civil war did nothing to enhance Lincoln's contemporary reputation. As the war dragged on, often with bumbling inefficiency and mistakes by political generals and amateur strategists, as the casualty lists grew and conscription was enacted to replace the dead and wounded, dissatisfaction spread through the North. Not even Lincoln's own party was united behind him. A group of radical Republicans who wanted an immediate constitutional amendment to end slavery, who thought the war was not being prosecuted with sufficient vigor, and who opposed Lincoln's plans for ultimate reconciliation held a rump convention and nominated Frémont for President on a platform that included punishment of the South and confiscation of rebel lands. They found sympathizers in Thaddeus Stevens and Charles Sumner.

The Democrats, too, were split in their attitude toward the war. The peace wing, contemptuously called "Copperheads" by the war Democrats, wanted to stop hostilities on any terms. Leader of the Peace Democrats was Clement Vallandigham, an Ohio congressman, who was arrested for making antiwar speeches and sentenced to prison by a military court, but exiled to the South by Lincoln.

Opponents of conscription did not burn their draft cards. They burned the headquarters of the provost marshal in New York, several armories, a Negro orphan asylum, and various other public and private buildings. The New York draft riots of July 1863 left more than a thousand dead and wounded and caused millions of dollars in damage.

The gold value of federal greenbacks dropped to sixty cents, then to less than half a dollar.

Lincoln was called by hostile newspaper editors an imbecile, a baboon, a misfit, a dictator, and a despot. No name seemed nasty enough, no caricature grotesque enough to satisfy the lunatic fringe, which, it would seem, has been always with us.

Lincoln's enemies in Congress did their best to circumscribe the powers of the executive through trying to run the war by congressional committees, notably the Joint Committee on the Conduct of the War. Ohio's Senator Ben Wade, severe critic of the President's more-in-sorrow-than-in-anger approach to the disloyal states, rode herd on the committee, which often hamstrung able military men and favored political generals.

The Cabinet members were far from unanimous in their appreciation of Lincoln's curious combination of realism and idealism, his basic humanitarianism, his vision, or his persistence in putting first things first: he never wavered in his belief that the primary war aim of the North was to restore the Union; the solution to the complex problem of abolishing slavery was to be accomplished in a deliberate and carefully studied program. Secretary of State Seward, who laughed the hardest of all his colleagues at Lincoln's stories, was author of a monograph suggesting that the President occupy himself largely with matters of patronage and leave the running of the government to a sort of executive Vice-President, who would of course be the Secretary of State. Treasury's Salmon Chase, an ambitious widower, driven by his daughter's passion to be belle of the White House, worked secretly to undermine Lincoln as a candidate to succeed himself. Simon Cameron, who was given the War portfolio to honor an unauthorized promise made by a subordinate at the Chicago convention, proved so incapable that he was shipped off to be minister to Russia. His replacement, Edwin M. Stanton, a War Democrat named by Lincoln to further his goal of a Union party and a coalition government, was an able administrator who spoke contemptuously of the President (behind his back) as "the gorilla." Vice-President Hamlin was more polite but equally critical.

Lincoln ignored the pessimistic predictions of his erstwhile friends that he could not be nominated, let alone elected, to a second term. He took the long-range view of his job. The first stage, the winning of the war, was far from over, but the end was in sight. Lee's invasion of the North had been stopped at Gettysburg. Grant had taken Vicksburg and Farragut's fleet controlled New Orleans and the delta, opening the Mississippi. The Confederates had been driven from Tennessee. The military situation was favorable enough to warrant following up the Emancipation Proclamation with a Proclamation of Amnesty and Reconstruction. The second proclamation offered to pardon all Southerners who would take an oath of loyalty, and provided for conditions under which a Confederate state could organize a loyal government and return to the union.

To broaden his political base, Lincoln planned to make his fusion with the War Democrats a reality by calling the Republican Convention of 1864 a Union party convention, and to favor the nomination of a Democrat for the vice-presidency. Looking further ahead toward eventual reconciliation, he went shopping for a southern Democrat. To this end he sent General Daniel Sickles clumping into Nashville to report secretly on the performance of the military governor of Tennessee, Andrew Johnson.

Dan Sickles was an eccentric character who, when he lost a leg by battlefield amputation at Gettysburg, had the useless bones packed in a miniature coffin and sent to the Army Medical Museum in Washington (they are still there), where they could be admired by his friends. He was a close friend of Lincoln's who admired his sense of humor and trusted his judgment. Apparently his report on Andrew Johnson was favorable.

The National Union party convention opened in Baltimore on a hot and sticky June 7, 1864. Lincoln was obviously more popular in the backwoods than the Cassandras of Washington, New York, and Philadelphia realized, for he was nominated on the first ballot. Only Missouri cast 22 votes for General Ulysses S. Grant, but quickly switched to make the nomination unanimous.

The race for second choice was more exciting, for Lincoln had not given advance notice of his preference. Vice-President Hannibal Hamlin let it be known that he would be available for renomination, and he had considerable strength among the delegates. When word was first passed that, in the interests of unity, the President would like to see a Democrat nominated, the name of Daniel S. Dickinson, a former senator from New York, was mentioned. Lincoln meanwhile had been quietly working backstage with the big-state delegations on behalf of Andrew Johnson. He talked separately with leaders of opposing Pennsylvania factions and got each to give Hamlin a complimentary vote on the first ballot, then switch to Johnson. Seward promised the support of half the New York delegation to block the candidacy of Dickinson, who was backed by the anti-Seward faction.

Johnson polled 200 votes on the first ballot. Hamlin got 150, and Dickinson 108. Pennsylvania shifted to Johnson before a second roll call, and other states followed suit, giving him 494 votes.

The ticket was a perfect setup for attack by both the radical wing of the Republicans and the regular Democrats. The radical Republicans criticized Johnson as a renegade from a rebel province. The Democratic press characterized the Union ticket as "a rail-splitting buffoon and a boorish tailor, both from the backwoods, both growing up in uncouth ignorance." Except for the pejoratives, the description was fairly accurate —and the electorate loved it.

Andrew Johnson was indeed a tailor from the backwoods who had grown up in ignorance. His parents were "poor whites" in Raleigh, North Carolina, where Andy had been born in 1808. His father was a janitor who died when the boy was three; his mother was a hotel maid. Andy and his brother were bound in apprenticeship to a tailor until both should reach the age of twenty-one. The boys fled after a few years, and, when they got home to Raleigh, they found a ten-dollar reward posted for their return. Andrew must have been a good tailor, for, when he set up his own tailor shop at Greeneville, in eastern Tennessee, he prospered. He also acquired a wife. Or rather, as pretty Eliza McCardle used to boast to her giggling girl friends in the little hill town, *she* acquired *him*. Eliza was seventeen and had gone through school. Andrew was nineteen, and had not. Eliza tutored her young husband and read to him as he sat cross-legged and plied his needle.

Johnson was an apt pupil and soon found that he had a way with words. The same words he learned from his quiet, soft-spoken wife changed character when he used them. As they leaped from his strong, willful lips, they roared and fought and grabbed men by the throat to make them listen. His skill with the spoken word made him an alderman at twenty, mayor of Greeneville at twenty-two, and a member of the Tennessee legislature at twenty-eight. He served five terms in the House as representative from his mountainous district of eastern Tennessee, then went home to be elected governor of the state.

In 1857 he was elected to the United States Senate, where he was ostentatiously the champion of the common man—of the simple mountaineer, the small farmer, the people who, like he himself, were not ashamed to earn a living with their hands. He sponsored the first Homestead Act, which opened the public lands of the West to the little man, the American whose resources consisted of a pioneering spirit and a stout heart.

Although a Southerner and a slaveholder, he was at constant odds with his southern colleagues in the Senate, most of them representative of the plantation aristocracy. When one of them, Senator Jefferson Davis of Mississippi, who was later to achieve fame in another role, dared make slurring reference to his lowly origins, Johnson blasted him with the full fury of his explosive tongue:

"I know we have an illegitimate, swaggering, bastard, scrub aristocracy who presume to know a great deal," he shouted, "but who, when the flowing veil of pretension is torn off from it, is seen to possess neither the talent nor the information on which one can rear a useful superstructure."

Johnson had supported Breckinridge and the Democratic ticket against Lincoln in 1860. When Lincoln's election provoked a hysterical demonstration by twenty-one of the twenty-two southern senators, however, the twenty-second, Senator Johnson of Tennessee, arose on the floor of the Upper House to make an angry and eloquent plea for the preservation of the union. While he was condemning the very idea of secession, his colleagues were heaping him with ridicule and branding him as a traitor to the South. The states of the future Confederacy were already preparing to vote on the question of secession.

As Tennessee joined the potential seceders, Johnson hurried home to plead for sanity and union. It was a futile and dangerous mission, for feeling was running close to frenzy, and the once popular senator, now generally regarded as having betrayed his people, was threatened with violence and death. He had the courage of his convictions, however, and he was a practical man: he went about armed. When he faced hostile crowds, roaring menaces and obscenities, he would draw from the hip, brandish his pistol, and roar back: "If any man has shooting to do, let him begin now."

Nobody began.

They listened with grim determination not to be swayed by his usually convincing oratory. They wanted none of him or of this Lincoln, interfering with their way of life, and when they went to the polls on June 8, 1861, they voted better than two to one for secession.

Johnson's original constituents, however, remained loyal. The mountaineers of eastern Tennessee furnished thirty-five thousand men for the Union armies!

When Lincoln called the Thirty-seventh Congress into special session the following July 4 to define war aims and crush the rebellion, Crittenden of Kentucky made the presentation in the House, and Johnson in the Senate.

Declared Senator Johnson, "This war is not prosecuted on our part in any spirit of oppression, nor for any purpose of conquest or subjugation, nor for the purpose of overthrowing or interfering with the rights or established institutions of those states, but to defend and maintain the supremacy of the Constitution and all laws made in the pursuance thereof, and to preserve the Union, with all the dignity, equality and rights of the several states unimpaired. . . ."

The statement did not please the radical Republicans, but it pleased Lincoln, and, as soon as Tennessee was sufficiently cleared of Confederate troops, the President sent Johnson to his home state as military governor. And the National Union convention, at Lincoln's urging, made him second choice on the ticket.

The Lincoln-Johnson ticket did not please the radical Republicans either. Even some of the moderate Republican leaders did not think Lincoln could be reelected. The war seemed to be bogged down again in the summer of 1864. Casualty lists continued to grow. Wartime restrictions were creating a black market. In July the gold value of the greenback dollar dropped to 39 cents. The people were weary of bloodshed and destruction.

Horace Greeley's New York *Tribune* predicted that Lincoln would be defeated, but Greeley wrote, if Lincoln did win, he should immediately begin peace negotiations on any terms—unless the rebellion were crushed by election day. (The logic seems as tortured as that of some current editorials on Vietnam.) A Cincinnati editor wanted a new slate of candidates. Some New York Republicans agreed, calling for a new convention. Thurlow Weed wrote to Seward that Lincoln's reelection was impossible because of his unrealistic and arbitrary insistence on the abolition of slavery as a condition of peace. Henry J. Raymond, who in addition to being editor of *The New York Times* was also chairman of the Republican national executive committee, reported to Lincoln that his chances were bad in nearly all sections of the country.

These gloomy predictions convinced even Lincoln. Apparently he did not realize the importance of the victories at Gettysburg and Vicksburg of a year before. On August 23, 1864, he wrote the following memorandum, which was kept secret until after election:

> This morning, as for some days past, it seems exceedingly probable that this administration will not be re-elected. Then it will be my duty to co-operate with the president-elect to save the Union between the election and the inauguration, as he will have secured his election on such grounds that he cannot possibly save it afterwards.

Lincoln was attributing to his critics a gift of prophecy which they did not possess when he spoke of "such grounds," for the Democratic party would not choose his opponent or adopt a platform until the week after he had written his memorandum. It is true, however, that, when the Democrats opened their convention in Chicago on August 29, the Copperhead wing was in control of the party. Clement Vallandigham, the Ohio Copperhead, who had sneaked back into Ohio via Canada, succeeded in having a plank adopted declaring the war a failure in restoring the Union and calling for a cease-fire and an early convention of the states to restore peace on the basis of a federal union. The convention then nominated General George McClellan (whom Lincoln had relieved as commander in chief) for President, and George H. Pendleton, Ohio congressman, for Vice-President.

McClellan accepted the nomination, but repudiated the platform, saying, "I could not look in the faces of my gallant comrades of the army and navy who have survived so many bloody battles, and tell them that their labors and the sacrifices of so many of our slain and wounded brethren had been in vain."

Lincoln campaigned on a principle that has been used by other candidates since. In a message to the National Union League, he said that it was not best to swap horses while crossing a stream. Swapping Vice-Presidents, evidently, was a horse of a different color.

The Lincoln-Johnson ticket got a tremendous boost from a change in the fortunes of war just as the Democratic convention was adjourning. General Sherman captured Atlanta. Admiral Farragut closed the port of Mobile to blockade runners. General Sheridan cleared the Shenandoah Valley of Early's army and lifted the threat to Washington. And Frémont withdrew from the presidential race.

The Lincoln-Johnson ticket defeated McClellan and Pendleton by 212 electoral votes to 21. Curiously enough, although the popular vote was close, those who could have been expected to disapprove most of further fighting, the war-weary Union troops, voted overwhelmingly for Lincoln over General McClellan, 116,877 to 33,748.

Between election day and inauguration, the military deciding point in the Civil War had already been reached. Sherman's devastating march from Atlanta to the sea had ended in the capture of Savannah, cutting the Confederacy in two. Wilmington, North Carolina, last port open to the South, fell to General Schofield. Peace feelers went out from both sides, encouraged by Lincoln, who promised generous terms.

Vice-President-elect Johnson left Washington right after election to brief his successor as military governor on how to organize a reconstructed Tennessee. He handpicked delegates to a January convention in Knoxville, which framed changes in the state constitution to prepare Tennessee for resuming statehood upon the imminent Union victory. The situation appeared favorable.

In February, however, Senator Sumner, the rabid New England abolitionist, began a filibuster to block recognition of Louisiana, despite its adoption of a new constitution outlawing slavery. Sumner's motivation was two-fold: the constitution had been Lincoln-inspired, and it did not give the freed slaves the vote. Lincoln summoned Andrew Johnson back to Washington. As a loyalist Southerner, he would be of great help in handling a rebellious Congress.

The President's message found the Vice-President-elect recovering from an attack of typhoid fever, and he pleaded to be allowed to remain in Tennessee during his convalescence: there was still work to be done. The President was insistent. He needed Johnson in Washington at latest by March 4, Inauguration Day.

The second inauguration of Abraham Lincoln was a memorable

occasion for three reasons. First, Lincoln's sense of humor was hugely aroused at having the oath of office administered by a man who had wanted the job himself, and who had finally resigned from Lincoln's Cabinet after having tried to undermine him: ex-Treasury Secretary Salmon P. Chase. Chief Justice Roger Taney (of the Dred Scott decision fame) had died the previous October, and Lincoln had waited until after election to name his successor. Salmon Chase wanted the job desperately as the next best thing to being President, but he hesitated at humiliating himself by seeking a favor from a man he had publicly ridiculed and demeaned. Instead he had friends do it. Since Lincoln considered Chase as able as he was ambitious, he made him Chief Justice—and it was his job to swear in the Civil War President.

The high point of the day was certainly Lincoln's second inaugural address, which is without doubt one of the most eloquent, moving, and human pages of all the state papers of the American Presidents.

The low point of the day—but important because it illuminated the Achilles heel of an otherwise courageous and impregnable man whose leadership was to be destroyed by a pack of yapping predatory enemies—was the Vice-President's embarrassing, spectacular, and somewhat drunken inaugural address.

Andrew Johnson had arrived the day before the inauguration and moved into a two-room ground-floor suite just off the lobby of Kirkwood House, at Twelfth Street and Pennsylvania Avenue, then one of Washington's better hotels. He was dropped into the midst of pre-inauguration festivities and feted by all his old friends and colleagues. He arose next morning with a monumental hangover which pursued him to the Capitol, where he arrived in good time for the ceremonies. The debilitation of his bout with typhoid, complicated by his morning-after jangling of the nerves, brought him to the verge of his great office weak and perspiring. He asked his predecessor, Vice-President Hannibal Hamlin, if there was a hair of the dog readily available.

Hamlin, a teetotaler responsible for the enactment of the nation's first prohibition law in his own state of Maine a few years earlier, told his successor that he had stopped the serving of intoxicating liquor in the Senate restaurant, but that he would send out for a bottle.

He did, and Andrew Johnson fortified himself against the imminent ordeal of becoming second choice to Abraham Lincoln—the sixteenth Vice-President of the United States. How much he actually drank has been a moot question for the past hundred years—each time Hamlin told the story the amount increased amazingly—but there is no doubt that the combined effects of the whisky, the night before, the post-typhoid shakiness, and the overheated Senate chamber did a disservice to the new Vice-President.

Johnson was glassy eyed when he advanced belligerently toward the rostrum. All the pent-up resentment at the years of slurs and insults that had been gratuitously flung at him boiled to the surface as the alcohol released his inhibitions. His pride in his plebeian beginnings provoked an aggressive attack on his perennial attackers. The self-made man revealed his feelings of inferiority by reminding the senators, the Supreme Court judges, and the members of the Cabinet present that they all owed their exalted positions to the people—plebeians like the new Vice-President. He then begged the members of the august body over which he would preside to forgive a poor plebeian's ignorance of parliamentary procedure, in case he should make mistakes. After an uncomfortable quarter hour, Johnson somehow got his tongue around the oath of office, kissed the Bible with a sweeping gesture, and retired.

The diplomatic gallery was amused, but the rest of the spectators were either embarrassed or outraged. Lincoln admitted that Andy had "made a bad slip," but insisted that he was no drunkard. Francis Preston Blair, the Bernard Baruch of his day, said that Johnson's speech was not "bad sense, only bad taste." The Tennesseean would never quite live down the moment.

The grotesque interlude only seemed to heighten the dignity of the tall, gaunt figure who arose to follow Johnson in speaking. The curious mixture of tragedy and kindliness that marked the scraggly-bearded face with its deep rictus folds was never more impressive as a mask of greatness, yet it is doubtful that many of those present in the Senate chamber that day recognized the true qualities of the man who stood before them. The second inaugural address which followed was not only a personal expression of Lincoln's humanitarian policy, which, unknowingly, he was bequeathing to Andrew Johnson, but it was a verbal transcription of the Great Seal of the United States. Like the eagle of the Great Seal, he extended both the sheaf of arrows and the olive branch. The ringing phrases are always fresh no matter how often repeated:

> Fondly do we hope, fervently do we pray, that this mighty scourge of war may speedily pass away. Yet, if God wills that it continue until all the wealth piled by the bondsman's two hundred and fifty years of un-

> requited toil shall be sunk, and until every drop of blood drawn with the lash shall be paid by another drawn with the sword, as was said three thousand years ago, so still it must be said, "The judgments of the Lord are true and righteous altogether. . . ."
>
> With malice toward none; with charity for all; with firmness in the right as God gives us to see the right, let us strive on to . . . bind up the nation's wounds, to care for him who shall have borne the battle, and for his widow and his orphan—to do all which may achieve and cherish a just and lasting peace. . . .

Exactly one month later Grant took Richmond, and the following day Lincoln traveled to the abandoned capital of the Confederacy to walk alone in the streets.

On April 9, 1865, Lee surrendered to Grant at Appomattox Court House and the Civil War was virtually over, although there would be sporadic fighting for another month.

On April 14, Good Friday evening, while watching a play at Ford's Theater in Washington, Abraham Lincoln was mortally wounded by a bullet fired by actor John Wilkes Booth.

The Booth conspiracy to avenge the South by wiping out Lincoln and his Cabinet had also marked Vice-President Johnson for death. A Prussian carriage maker named George Atzerodt was assigned to shoot Johnson. On Good Friday, Atzerodt registered at Kirkwood House and was given a room directly above the Vice-President's suite. His instructions were to knock on Johnson's door at exactly ten-fifteen that night, the hour at which Booth would fire his derringer into the presidential box, and Paine, another accomplice, would attack ailing Secretary of State Seward.

Johnson was in his room before ten-thirty. He had refused an invitation to attend the performance at Ford's Theater. He was tired and went to bed early.

Atzerodt, a stupid little man, was terrified of his job. Hiding his large pistol and a bowie knife under the pillow in Room 136, he spent most of the day in the Kirkwood House bar, asking suspicious questions about the Vice-President and seeking courage in whisky. When ten-fifteen came, he had lost his nerve completely. At the first news of the assassination of Lincoln, he staggered drunkenly to where he had tethered his rented horse and fled. He would be captured later and hanged.

When Johnson was aroused by friends with the news, he tucked his shirttails into his trousers and insisted on walking to the President's deathbed. The provost marshal of the District of Columbia tried to dissuade him ("There is murder in the streets"), as did others who feared that the conspiracy was more widespread and better organized than Booth's amateurish cabal actually was. Nobody had ever accused Andrew Johnson of cowardice, physical or moral, and if there were murder in the streets, he was ready to meet it head on. He walked the two and one-half blocks to the Petersen house across Tenth Street from Ford's Theater, to which the stricken President had been moved.

Johnson joined the death watch, stood looking at the dying President for a long moment, went into a back room to exchange a few phrases with Secretary of War Stanton, who was writing dispatches, giving orders, and generally running the country during the emergency, looking like a character from Ecclesiastes with his flowing Old Testament beard and steel-rimmed spectacles. The Vice-President then spoke a comforting word to Robert Todd Lincoln, squeezed the hands of the sobbing First Lady, and walked back to his hotel.

Lincoln died at 7:22 A.M. on the rainy morning of April 15.

A few hours later Chief Justice Salmon P. Chase stopped by Kirkwood House to swear in Andrew Johnson as seventeenth President of the United States. The oath was administered in a parlor adjacent to the hotel lobby in the presence of a few Cabinet members and other officials. It was a solemn ceremony. The perpetual scowl which wrinkled the new President's round, gypsy-dark face seemed more somber than ever, the squinting eyes under the heavy eyebrows narrower than ever. The wavy dark hair which he wore brushed back in what in more recent years would be called a page-boy bob had seemingly acquired new gray streaks overnight, although he was only, at fifty-six, two months older than his dead predecessor. Johnson rose to his full five feet nine as he firmly intoned the oath, then made a brief speech expressing his grief, his humility, and his political creed as the "honest advocacy of the great principles of free government."

Theoretically the Johnson administration should have had smooth sailing. Although originally of different political parties, Johnson and Lincoln, united in the National Union party, saw eye to eye on most issues, and Johnson intended, as he had pledged, to follow Lincoln's policies. He announced at once that he intended to retain the Lincoln Cabinet, which, although only two members were holdovers from the original 1861 Lincoln Cabinet—Seward of State and Welles of Navy—was a fairly accurate cross section of the National Union party.

It was apparent, however, before he had been in office twenty-four hours, that he was in for a stormy passage. The extremists in the Senate, led by Sumner of Massachusetts, Wade of Ohio, and Stevens of Pennsylvania, were determined to destroy Lincoln's plans for the Reconstruction and substitute their own. They called on the new President twice during his first two days in office, singly and in a group, to discuss postwar matters and their desire for Negro suffrage. Johnson listened, but was noncommittal, only repeating that he would follow the essentials of Lincoln's policy. The radical senators must have misunderstood him, for, instead of binding up the nation's wounds, they had every intention of rubbing salt into them.

The war had produced not only deep hatreds, but, as wars often do, a stampede of the avaricious, determined to profit personally at the expense of the prostrate South. They were in no mood for charity, and malice dominated their every motive. The radical Republicans reflected the resolution of these Northerners that the South must be made to suffer for five years' loss of life and property. They actually rejoiced in the death of Lincoln, who had been an obstacle to their objectives. They regarded Johnson as a "poor white" who hated the southern aristocracy (which he did) for its contemptuous rating of him as no better than the slaves they exploited. They saw no sign of Lincolnian nobility in him and expected him to yield easily to suggestions. As Senator Wade expressed it: "By the gods, there will be no trouble running the government now!"

Johnson ignored all suggestions and began immediately to draw up his own program of Reconstruction in the hope that he could complete it before Congress reconvened in December. Thaddeus Stevens, one of the leading rebel haters, wrote to the President asking him to await the approval of Congress. In the interim, he suggested, the South should be treated as a conquered province and ruled by military governors. The President went ahead with his own plans.

Before Congress reconvened, developments in the South further infuriated the radicals. New legislatures in the former Confederate states were passing laws which showed every sign of perpetuating slavery. The vagrancy laws against wandering Negroes and the apprenticeship laws assigning Negro youngsters to guardians for whom they would work without wages seemed to be a deliberate evasion of the Thirteenth Amendment abolishing slavery and "involuntary servitude." The amendment, passed by the Thirty-eighth Congress and signed by Lincoln before his death, was currently being ratified by the states. It was to be proclaimed effective when Congress met again.

The Johnson program was ready by December, and the newly elected senators and representatives from the reorganized southern states were in Washington, waiting to take their seats. The radicals, however, refused to admit them. A radical bill to form a Joint Committee on Reconstruction was pushed through both Houses—and the battle between the Capitol and the White House for management of Reconstruction was on.

The fifteen-man committee, largely influenced by Thaddeus Stevens, assumed the power to inquire into status of the returning prodigal states, and to determine the eligibility of their representatives.

In the second skirmish of the open warfare between a determined President and an equally determined Congress, the radicals drew blood by voting to extend the life of the Freedmen's Bureau, a War Department agency guaranteeing to Negroes certain basic needs, employment, and educational facilities. Military tribunals would enforce provisions of the law. Stanton would be boss. President Johnson vetoed the bill on the grounds that it would make the Negro a ward of the national government, that ample safeguards already existed without resort to military tribunals, and that the expedient of military tribunals constituted a danger to democracy. Johnson's veto was sustained, but the breach between the President and the party he was supposed to lead grew wider, and the anger of the radical Republicans approached the apoplectic.

On the first anniversary of Lee's surrender at Appomattox, Congress passed a civil-rights bill granting suffrage to the Negro. It was instantly vetoed by Johnson, for reasons which were and are still debated. Some believe he was following the Lincoln policy: that the primary aim of the Civil War was to preserve the Union; that the Emancipation Proclamation was a war measure and did not guarantee voting rights; that the illiterate slaves should be granted the franchise as they became educated to the civic duties, as well as the rights, of free men. Others say that Johnson was merely a bullheaded states' righter and that his love for the common man did not extend quite as far as the Negro. In any event, the radicals had by this time gained sufficient strength in both Houses to override the presidential veto.

Had there been such a thing as a public-opinion poll in 1866, Johnson probably would have discovered little national support for his conciliatory postwar program. Moreover, his enemies were well organized, aggressive, politically shrewd, unscrupulous, and relentlessly determined to destroy him. Johnson, on the other hand, was outspoken to the point of bluntness, honest, politically naive, with strong convictions and the courage to fight for them. His fingers were apparently insensitive to the pulse of the people. A hothead, he attacked his adversaries frontally. He would harangue a crowd from the steps of the White House and lose support by his intemperate language.

During the mid-term election campaigns of 1867, he traveled to Chicago to lay the cornerstone of a monument to Stephen A. Douglas, and took the long way home to fill many speaking engagements on behalf of his policies—a serious error, as he found out. Everywhere he spoke—Cleveland, Detroit, St. Louis, Cincinnati, Pittsburgh—his enemies had been there first to set clever traps. Organized groups of hecklers, knowing his weaknesses, would boo him when the audience was supposed to applaud, laugh derisively at his most serious statements, and goad him into losing his temper. Fuming and frothing at the mouth, he would strike back with foolish and extravagant personal insults. The newspapers never failed to recall his drunken performance at Lincoln's second inaugural, leaving no doubt that his intemperate language was caused by the intemperate use of strong spirits. The phrase "drunken tailor" appeared again.

When November rolled around, the radicals won majorities in both Houses of Congress. Henceforth any hope of a conciliatory Lincolnian program for the South was doomed.

On March 2, 1867, Congress passed two bills that hamstrung the executive power of the President, and imposed harsh Reconstruction conditions on the South.

The Tenure of Office Act, in violation of the separation of powers and system of checks and balances provided by the Constitution, destroyed the independence of the presidency by making that office subservient to Congress. It prohibited the President from removing from office any Cabinet officer, or other government official appointed with the consent of the Senate, without the Senate's consenting to the dismissal.

The Reconstruction Act imposed military rule on the ten southern states not yet restored to the Union, and provided that restoration would be conditional upon Negro suffrage and ratification of the Fourteenth Amendment with its guarantee of citizenship rights.

Johnson promptly vetoed both bills, and Congress just as promptly passed them both over his veto.

The President challenged the constitutionality of the Tenure of Office Act by removing Secretary of War Stanton from office. Stanton was an able administrator, but as full of complexes as he was devoid of any loyalty to Johnson. He was generally regarded as a secret agent in the Cabinet reporting to the Stevens-Sumner-Wade axis.

Johnson replaced Stanton with General Ulysses S. Grant, but the Senate refused to confirm the appointment, and Stanton, who had barricaded himself in his office, stayed on the job.

On February 24, 1868, the House voted to impeach President Johnson for "high crimes and misdemeanors in office." The Senate resolved itself into a Court of Impeachment, and the trial of the President began on March 13, 1868, with Supreme Court Chief Justice Chase presiding.

The trial, if it could be called that, pursued its shameful, spectacular, and vindictive course for more than two months. The cynicism with which the oligarchs of Congress pretended that the President of the United States was actually guilty of malfeasance in office on eleven trumped-up charges, when every one knew that the impeachment trial was nothing more than a lynching bee, disturbed even some Republicans. When one of them approached clubfooted old Thaddeus Stevens with the complaint that his conscience bothered him, the seventy-five-year-old arch enemy of Johnson replied: "Conscience! Tell your conscience to go the devil and follow the party line."

Andrew Johnson wisely refused to dignify the kangaroo proceedings with the presence of the President of the United States, second choice though he may have been. While his defense was being ably conducted by Attorney General Henry Stanbery of Ohio and his successor William M. Evarts, destined to become Secretary of State under President Rutherford B. Hayes, Johnson busied himself with packing preparatory to leaving the White House. He also did a little wry historical research into what became of the members of the parliamentary cabal that had railroaded Charles I of England to the headsman's block on charges of treason.

The prosecution was in the hands of General Benjamin Franklin Butler, noted New England criminal lawyer who might have been

Lincoln's second choice in 1864 had he not preferred to remain in the Army. A sawed-off runt of a man, Butler had been called "The Beast" by Southerners when he was military governor of New Orleans, and "Old Cockeye" by his men behind his back. On his return to civilian life he was elected representative from Massachusetts, a post he held when called to prosecute President Johnson. By this time his red hair had been reduced to a fringe, his Hitler-type mustache was graying, and he was developing a paunch, but the rasping voice which had swayed juries and terrified his soldiers was still at its courtroom best.

Butler tore into the President of the United States as though he were prosecuting a petty sneak thief. Johnson had come to the White House, he said, "by murder most foul," and through testimony by Representative James M. Ashley of Ohio he tried to show that Johnson had not been a stranger to John Wilkes Booth's conspiracy—a questionable line of attack, since Johnson himself had been marked for assassination. However, in the emotion-charged atmosphere of the Senate chamber neither fact nor fairness was expected. Even Ben Wade, as President Pro Tem of the Senate, traditionally without a vote except to break a tie, eagerly voted for conviction when the time came.

When Lincoln's death had elevated Johnson to the presidency, leaving the country without a Vice-President, Senator Ben Wade of Ohio had been elected President Pro Tempore of the Senate. Wade was not only one of the bitterest of Johnson haters, but he also saw himself as occupying the White House on Johnson's impeachment. It was generally believed that he had already picked his Cabinet and written his inaugural address. Mrs. Wade was also ready to move into the White House. She held daily court in the Senate gallery, surrounded by friends from Ohio who had already selected their gowns for the inaugural ball.

On May 15, 1868, President Johnson dedicated a momument to the memory of President Lincoln. Neither the House nor the Senate had adjourned to pay honor to the dead leader. They were too absorbed in the impeachment proceedings, which would come to a vote next day.

As Chief Justice Chase called the roll, all fifty-four members of the Senate were present, even James Wilson Grimes of Iowa, who had suffered a paralytic stroke a few days earlier and was carried in on a stretcher. It was quickly apparent that the vote would go against Johnson, but there was some doubt that his enemies could muster the required two-thirds majority. The radical Republicans were voting on strict party lines—until the name of Senator William Pitt Fessenden of Maine was called.

"Mr. Senator Fessenden, how say you?" demanded the Chief Justice. "Is the respondent, Andrew Johnson, President of the United States, guilty or not guilty of a high misdemeanor as charged in this article?"

The Maine Republican, who had served as Secretary of the Treasury in Lincoln's Cabinet, stood up and declared in a strong, resonant voice: "Not guilty!"

A murmur of surprise swept over the Senate chamber, followed by a disbelieving hush. The gallery stirred uneasily. The Republican ranks had been broken.

Then Grimes of Iowa, no friend of Johnson's, propped himself up on his stretcher to utter a barely audible "Not guilty." Lyman Trumbull of Illinois, an old friend of Lincoln's, but an enemy of Johnson's, also voted with the Democrats. In all, seven Republican senators—the seventh and deciding vote was that of Edmund G. Ross of Kansas—voted against the impeachment charges, not so much in favor of Johnson personally as to protect the dignity, the power, and the integrity of the executive office.

Only nineteen senators in all voted for acquittal. The vote of thirty-five senators spoke their belief that the President of the United States was guilty of high crimes and misdemeanors.

The total was just one vote short of the two-thirds majority required to remove the President from office.

Secretary of War Stanton thereupon resigned. Johnson had won a narrow victory over the Tenure of Office Act, although the act would not be repealed, in large part, until 1887. It was declared unconstitutional by the Supreme Court in 1926.

For the seven Republicans with enough courage to vote for the independence of the presidency, it was Pyrrhic victory. Their stand for a principle was an act of political suicide. None of them was ever elected to political office again. Ross, the freshman senator from Kansas, was called a skunk and a perjurer. His neighbors no longer spoke to him, and Kansas became untenable for his family. Fessenden of Maine was hounded to an early grave. John Henderson was burned in effigy by fellow Missourians. Peter Van Winkle, West Virginia's first senator, was called by newspapers "the betrayer" of his state. Trumbull was warned to keep off the streets of Chicago lest "the representatives of an indignant people . . . hang him to the most convenient lamppost." Joseph

Fowler, Tennessee's freshman senator, forced into retirement after his only term by the threats and defamation of his fellow radical Republicans, declared: "I acted for my country and posterity in obedience to the will of God."

In his book *Profiles in Courage,* the late President John F. Kennedy agreed with Fowler when he declared that the vote of Edmund Ross "may well have preserved for ourselves and posterity constitutional government in the United States."

Four days after the collapse of the impeachment conspiracy the Republican party met in convention at Chicago, shed the wartime label of National Union party, and nominated the war hero General Ulysses S. Grant for President. For second choice, Ben Wade led for four ballots, but lost on the fifth to Speaker of the House Schuyler Colfax.

The 1868 Republican platform was a collection of inconsistencies. It praised Congress and its Reconstruction program, deplored the untimely death of Lincoln, regretted that Andrew Johnson had succeeded to the presidency only to betray the people who had elected him and the cause he was pledged to support. The delegates were obviously blind to the fact that the man they condoned and the man they condemned were equally opposed to the policies which the radical Republicans glorified.

Grant, as everyone knows, was elected and reelected to make one of the worst Presidents in American history. The *New York Times*-Arthur Schlesinger, Sr., symposium rated the brilliant general with Harding as one of the two failures in the presidency. Nevertheless, the Republican party continued to elect Presidents for the next twenty years. The seeds of hate and vengeance that were planted by self-seeking radical Republicans during the Lincoln and Johnson administrations, however, yielded a bumper crop of long-lasting southern antagonism that created the Solid South, a monolithic Democratic bloc that would not produce an electoral vote for a Republican candidate until 1928.

Whether or not Abraham Lincoln would have survived this poisoned atmosphere of malice, avarice, and corruption which almost destroyed his successor will always be a moot question. Arthur Schlesinger, Jr., the historian of the Jackson, Franklin Roosevelt, and Kennedy eras, has said that Lincoln would have triumphed because he had a superior political sense. This is not so certain, however. The desperately vindictive little congressional cabal which grew into a powerful oligarchy that usurped and nearly destroyed the functions of the executive as represented by

Johnson had already been sniping at Lincoln. The Wade-Davis Reconstruction Bill, designed to remove postwar problems from presidential concern and allow the congressional diehards to punish the South to their own advantage, was vetoed by Lincoln, but the Great Emancipator felt it necessary to issue a lengthy explanation.

Could Lincoln have blocked the later and harsher congressional Reconstruction programs that imposed military governors on the southern states, allowed the carpetbaggers to join forces with unscrupulous southern scalawags to exploit the uneducated but enfranchised Negroes to gain control of the state legislatures? Could he have prevented the resultant corruption and ignorant ineptitude which outweighed the advantage of any legislation designed to benefit the underprivileged? The actual liberation of the Negro, the supposed aim of the radical Republicans, has been delayed a hundred years by the lasting reaction to the bitterness and acrimony generated by Thaddeus Stevens and his hate brigade.

Some historians believe that Johnson brought about his own downfall by his fiery temper, his stubbornness, and his chip-on-shoulder aggressiveness. They say that he lacked the instinctive political acumen which could have capitalized on his proletarian popularity. For instance, had he made an earlier attack on the war profiteers who grew rich on government bonds, he could have won new friends and confounded his enemies. Instead it was not until the last months of his Administration that Johnson lashed out at the money patriots who bought war bonds with depreciated greenbacks and were reimbursed in gold—the new federal-bond aristocracy, as he called them, which had replaced the landed, slave-based elite the war had destroyed.

That even Lincoln's true greatness would have overcome the nasty pettiness of the postwar period, however, and passed unsullied into history will always remain a matter for conjecture. John Wilkes Booth, instead of destroying the man he hated, may very well have enshrined him in martyrdom by sparing him the anguish and political disaster that engulfed the man who, though second choice, tried to continue his policies. Lincoln's policies, his prestige, and his nobility belong to history. So does Johnson's failure.

One of Andrew Johnson's last official acts was in the great Lincolnian tradition. The President's old senatorial adversary, Jefferson Davis, in the interim President of the Confederacy, had been imprisoned in

Fortress Monroe, Virginia, since 1865. After two years, he was released on bond furnished by Horace Greeley, Cornelius Vanderbilt, and former New York abolitionist congressman Gerrit Smith. On December 3, 1868, his trial for treason began before the United States Circuit Court of Virginia.

On Christmas Day President Johnson proclaimed a general amnesty for everyone connected with the rebellion, and the charges against Jefferson Davis were dropped.

Some six years after the impeachment trial, Andrew Johnson had the courage to return to his old seat as senator from Tennessee. When he entered the Senate chamber, he was greeted by applause, a remarkable return for a man who had come within one vote of being the only President ever impeached. Many of his old enemies were still there, but the old vituperation and oratorical invective of the ex-tailor become ex-President were gone. Now in his sixty-seventh year, he had attained a philosophical calm—or perhaps it was resignation. His political beliefs, however, had not changed. When he arose to speak, it was on behalf of reconciliation and union.

"Let peace and unison be restored to the land," he urged in an earnest voice. "May God bless this people and God save the Constitution."

It was his only speech. Four months later, on July 31, 1875, the seventeenth President of the United States, the third second choice to achieve the office by inheritance, was dead.

His death passed almost unmourned at the time, and there have been few monuments to him since.

Andrew Johnson's grave in Greeneville, Tennessee, bears the inscription:

"His faith in the people never wavered."

6

THE STALWARTS AND THE HALFBREEDS

JAMES ABRAM GARFIELD, MARCH 4–SEPTEMBER 19, 1881.
CHESTER ALAN ARTHUR, SEPTEMBER 20, 1881–MARCH 4, 1885.

"Chet Arthur, President of the United States? Good God!"

So exclaimed a friend of Vice-President Chester Alan Arthur on July 2, 1881, when half-demented Charles Guiteau, a frustrated job hunter, shot President James A. Garfield in the back.

Guiteau, still waving his ornate pistol, made a similar declaration to the policeman who arrested him in the Washington, D.C., railway station: "Now Arthur is President of the United States! I am a Stalwart of the Stalwarts!"

Both men were premature. Although shot through the spine, Garfield fought for his life for eleven weeks. When he finally died on September 19, he probably succumbed to medical ignorance as much as to Guiteau's bullet. While Lister had given his first American demonstration of antiseptic surgery in Chicago that year, elsewhere surgeons were still operating in business suits and stropping their scalpels on anything handy.

The long interregnum was embarrassing to Vice-President Arthur because of the political implications of the assassin's wild statements. Although Article II of the Constitution provides that the Vice-President shall assume the functions of the office upon the President's "inability to discharge the powers and duties of the said office," it does not specify who should decide that the President is incapable, or how. The situation had never arisen before, although it would occur several times again before the Twenty-fifth Amendment, outlining the proper procedures, was ratified by the states in 1967.

Garfield and Arthur represented opposite wings of the Republican party, and both were nominated by the 1880 Republican convention at Chicago despite the opposition of the party's kingmakers. The political power of Seward and Thurlow Weed had been passed on to younger men during Grant's first administration. The new Republican boss was Roscoe Conkling, an arrogant, eloquent United States senator from upstate New York. The son of a federal judge, an admirer and protégé of Seward, Conkling was in his twenties when first elected to Congress. After three terms in the House, he went on to the Senate. He was a flamboyant ham with a genius for intrigue. A six-footer with an athletic build, blue eyes, curly hair, and a magnificent blond beard, he loved to strut in fawn-colored trousers and sensational waistcoats, with brilliant foulards around his neck. In Grant's eight years he built a formidable political machine so venal that in comparison the Jacksonian spoils system was like a bingo game in a church bazaar.

Conkling inherited most of the personnel and all of the policies of the radical Republicans. He inherited the hate of the South and the desire to punish the secessionists. His cohorts wanted military and carpetbagger rule of the old Confederacy because of the profits which would devolve from such a continuation of the Thaddeus Stevens policies.

Conkling called his radical wing of the New York Republican party the "Stalwarts." Those who opposed him, the moderate wing, which included Rutherford Hayes, James Blaine, John Sherman, and James Garfield, he called "Half-Breeds," because they were only half Republicans. And they shared in less than half the vast patronage that Conkling would be giving out, because they believed in some sort of civil-service merit system to place federal appointments on a competitive basis.

Although Conkling was nominally boss of only the New York Republicans, he had built up a feudal system which included Stalwart-thinking Republicans in all the big-vote states—General Ben Butler, the Beast of New Orleans, who had a stranglehold on patronage in Massachusetts; the Camerons, father and son, of Pennsylvania; and John Logan, another political general who not only ruled the Republican party of Illinois, but cracked the whip over the Grand Army of the Republic, the American Legion of post-Civil War days.

Conkling and his Stalwarts enriched the Republican campaign chest with kickbacks from federal jobholders, massive raids on the United States Treasury on behalf of generous Republican contractors, and just plain wholesale larceny, the like of which would not be seen for another forty or fifty years. First there was the Railroad Ring: members of Congress got free shares in the Crédit Mobilier, organized to finance (and secure government subsidies for) the building of the Union Pacific. President Grant got a private railway car that would take him anywhere, courtesy of the Erie. Other railways got subsidies in the form of public lands worth millions and millions of dollars. Then there was the Whisky Ring—distillers who paid the excise tax on a small fraction of their product and either used forged revenue stamps on the remainder, or paid no tax at all—except as contribution to the Stalwart campaign funds. There was also the Star Postal Route Ring—a scheme by which mail contracts went to a fraudulent low bidder who later, with the collusion of the Post Office Department, charged huge amounts for purely fictitious extra services. Perhaps the most vicious, and certainly among the most profitable for both the Stalwart coffers and the recipients of Republican patronage, was the Customhouse Ring.

Collectors of the port, during this period, received no salary. They received, however, a percentage of fines collected and half the value of goods confiscated for nonpayment or false declaration of duty. The customhouse at Boston used to produce hundreds of thousands of dollars in fines and confiscations, much of which found its way into party coffers, while some of it went in legal fees to such good Stalwart attorneys as General Ben Butler, the Beast of New Orleans and the prosecutor of President Johnson.

An example of how the system worked was an episode of 1872, when the big metal importers, Phelps, Dodge & Co., risked the confiscation of a shipment worth $1,750,000 because of an erroneous underpayment of duties involving a few thousand dollars. On advice of counsel, Phelps, Dodge settled out of court for slightly more than two hundred and seventy thousand dollars—half of which, according to law, went to pay attorneys' fees (fifty thousand dollars to Messrs. Roscoe Conkling and Benjamin Franklin Butler), and to the top officers of the port of New

York, including Alonzo Cornell (son of Ezra, founder of the university), surveyor of the port, and Chester Alan Arthur, collector of the port.

Chester Arthur, the unsalaried customs officer whose percentages came to some forty thousand dollars a year—not peanuts in an age when eight cents would buy a loaf of bread and a quart of milk, and there was no income tax—was one of Boss Conkling's most important lieutenants. He had more than a thousand customs officers on his payroll, all of whom kicked back a percentage of their pay to the party coffers in gratitude for their appointments. Many of them spent weeks or months far from the waterfront, reminding inland bureaucrats that, although their first duty was to their country, they also owed allegiance (and a small portion of their salaries) to the party which had given them their livelihood.

No more unlikely person could be imagined as a big wheel in an unscrupulous political machine than Stalwart Chester Alan Arthur. The son of a Baptist minister, Arthur was born in Fairfield, Vermont, in 1830. His youth was spent in upstate New York, following his father from one church to another, until he entered Union College in Schenectady. When he was graduated, a Phi Beta Kappa, at the age of seventeen, he struck out for New York City to practice law. He drifted into politics as a way of meeting clients. Party clubhouses, he discovered, were frequented by important men as well as ward heelers.

He found politics a fascinating hobby, and was soon up to his waist in active participation. Although he did not hesitate to work at the precinct level, his aim was always higher. "Gentleman Boss," the boys in the back room called Chester Arthur. They never called him "Chet" to his face, for he disliked the nickname, and was big enough to enforce his prejudice. A well-fed, handsome man with a Gallic deltoid mustache and startling muttonchop whiskers, he dressed with quiet elegance. Married to a Virginia girl, daughter of a naval officer killed in action, he lived in a style to which he had not been accustomed as the son of a country preacher. His apartment on New York's Lexington Avenue was a place where the sophisticated could always be sure of good food, fine wines, and witty conversation. The "Gentleman Boss" was cultured, well read, and endowed with good taste.

For political services rendered, Arthur was commissioned quartermaster general of the New York militia early in the Civil War, a desk job of procurement. Both the job and the rank were withdrawn when a new administration took over in Albany.

Arthur's great services to Senator Conkling, however, were recognized by President Grant, who appointed him collector of the port of New York in 1871.

The accession of the former Ohio governor Rutherford B. Hayes to the presidency in 1877, at the end of Grant's second term, was bad news for both Conkling and Arthur. Hayes was determined to disinfect the reeking mess left behind by Grant's spoilsmen. He abolished the percentage system of compensating the customs service, put the collectors on a straight salary (twelve thousand dollars a year), and fired both Arthur and Cornell as collector and surveyor respectively of the port of New York. Hayes appointed Theodore Roosevelt, Sr., to replace Arthur, but Conkling managed to block senatorial confirmation until Roosevelt's death.

Meanwhile Conkling was doing his political future no good by furnishing the sensational press with a first-rate scandal. For some time gossips had noted that, whenever the golden-bearded Beau Brummel from New York was about to make one of his sarcastic speeches in the Senate, the glamorous Kate Chase Sprague was sure to be in the gallery. The daughter of Lincoln's one-time Treasury Secretary had, when her efforts to make her father President of the United States ended in failure, married Rhode Island's millionaire senator William Sprague. In August 1879 some newspapers reported that Sprague, by reputation an alcoholic, surprised Senator Conkling in his Narragansett home and chased him out with a shotgun.

President Hayes could not quite suppress a note of satisfaction as he recorded in his diary his enemy's discomfiture:

> The Conkling scandal . . . will do good in one direction. It will weaken his political power, which is bad and only bad.

But the President was underestimating Senator Conkling's durability and ingenuity. Just three months after the incident at Narragansett the Stalwart boss had bounced back sufficiently to put over his entire slate in the New York gubernatorial election, including as governor Alonzo Cornell, whom President Hayes had dismissed as surveyor of the port.

Having reaffirmed his domination of the New York Republican party, Conkling began plotting to recapture the national scene. The Stalwarts would nominate and reelect General Grant in 1880. Grant's handlers had sent the two-term President on a world tour so that he could be feted and honored by international leaders and kept out of the country until the lingering effluvia of his maladministration had blown away. When his homesick wife brought him home ahead of schedule, the Stalwart bosses bundled him off again to Mexico and Cuba.

Cameron of Pennsylvania and Logan of Illinois joined with Conkling in the plot to restore Grant to the White House, and the Stalwarts to the trough of federal patronage. The triumvirate arrived at the Chicago convention with more than three hundred delegates pledged to Grant.

There were two other serious candidates in the field: James G. Blaine, senator from Maine and former Speaker of the House, who had barely missed the 1876 nomination; and John Sherman, former senator from Ohio, who as President Hayes' Secretary of the Treasury could claim credit for restoring the nation's economy to stability after the panic of 1873. Both Blaine and Sherman were Half-Breeds and therefore enemies of Conkling and his Stalwarts. There was no love lost either between Blaine and Sherman—Sherman accused Blaine of invading his native Ohio to steal favorite-son delegates—so there was no possibility of a stop-Grant coalition.

As his floor manager, Sherman chose fellow Ohioan James Abram Garfield, a veteran of the House who had mild presidential aspirations himself. Sherman had just persuaded the Ohio legislature to elect Garfield to a vacant seat in the Senate, so Garfield could hardly refuse to make the nominating speech for Sherman.

At the outset of the convention, Garfield showed considerable political skill in rallying the anti-Grant forces to defeat Roscoe Conkling's efforts to adopt the unit rule of voting, whereby an entire delegation's vote would be cast as a bloc in accordance with the majority. Had "Lord Roscoe" put over his maneuver, the nomination of Grant would have been assured. As it was, the Conkling trick enraged the independents, including some in his own New York delegation.

The first ballot gave Grant 304 votes, Blaine 284, Sherman only 93, and the rest to half a dozen favorite sons.

The deadlock continued for two days, with neither Blaine nor Sherman able to gain significant strength. Thirty ballots were taken without result. As roll call followed roll call, the name of James A. Garfield began to appear. A few of his friends, not more than two or three, kept him before the convention with complimentary votes.

On the thirty-fourth ballot the break came. The Wisconsin delegation, solidly for Blaine, switched 16 votes to Garfield—giving him a total of 17.

Garfield immediately arose to a point of order. What he was going to say—was he going to ask that the 16 votes be switched to Sherman?—will never be known, for the chairman ruled him out of order. He sat down.

Roscoe Conkling, white with anger, scribbled a note on a scrap of paper and sent it to Garfield, whom he had been calling "the angle-worm." The note read: "I congratulate you on being the dark horse."

On the thirty-fifth ballot Indiana shifted 27 votes to Garfield. A few scattering delegates brought his total to 50.

The solid-core Stalwarts still gave Grant 306.

There was no television in 1880, but John Sherman, sitting in Washington awaiting the call which never came, could see the handwriting on the wall. He wired Chicago, releasing the Ohio delegation to Garfield.

On the thirty-sixth ballot, Blaine released the Maine delegation to Garfield, and the Half-Breeds were in business. When the stampede was over, the 306 Stalwart votes for Grant had not changed. But Garfield, with 399, was the Republican candidate for President.

The Half-Breeds knew, however, that they could not win without the big-state votes controlled by the Stalwarts. The second choice must therefore be a Stalwart. The nomination was first offered to Levi P. Morton, the poor Vermont farm boy who had become the second biggest banker in New York (after the House of Morgan). Morton was rich enough both to be above suspicion and to bankroll the Republican campaign (his Anglo-American banking firm grew into the Guaranty Trust Company, today merged with the House of Morgan). He wanted very much to run for Vice-President, but Conkling said no. Morton would have to wait eight years to be second choice to Benjamin Harrison.

The Half-Breeds' second choice for the second-choice nomination was Chester Alan Arthur, the "Gentleman Boss" who had never in his life been a candidate for an elective office. Again Roscoe Conkling said no. He would allow no Stalwart to accept crumbs from the Half-Breed table. Besides, he didn't think Garfield could be elected.

Arthur, however, had the courage to defy Lord Roscoe and say yes. He declared that he would accept the distinction even if it were "only a barren nomination."

Conkling sulked, but Arthur quickly became the Republican convention's second choice.

After a sullen summer, the sulking Stalwarts became resigned to their defeat and agreed to join in the campaign. Grant was persuaded to visit Garfield in his country home at Mentor, Ohio, some twenty miles east of Cleveland. Conkling reluctantly agreed to make a few speeches outside New York State.

The Republicans had an attractive candidate in Garfield. He had much in common with his running mate. Both men were tall and well built, both were well educated and gregarious, and both came from humble and religious families. Garfield in fact had seriously eyed the ministry for a while, before accepting the presidency of Hiram College on his way to the Ohio legislature.

Commissioned brigadier general of Ohio volunteers by Ohio governor Dennison, he saw combat in western Tennessee. While in the field, he was elected to Congress from Ohio. He pestered Secretary of War Stanton for a command of his own, but Stanton, already up to his neck in political generals, could offer him nothing better than chief-of-staff to General William Rosecrans. Garfield apparently goaded the usually cautious Rosecrans into recklessness at Chickamauga, and the Union troops were defeated. Garfield, however, was promoted to major general for his part in the battle. When Congress reconvened in December, 1863, he hung up his sword and took his seat in the House. For nearly twenty years he followed the Republican party line, which meant that he voted to pass the Freedmen's Act and the Civil Rights Act over President Johnson's veto—"a thing unprecedented in American History," as he wrote to his friend General David Swaim.

The fact that Garfield had seen combat did not hurt his chances with the Grand Army of the Republic, and the veterans' vote was an important factor in any campaign. Another plus for the Republican candidate was his being born in an Ohio log cabin—the last American President to have that advantage, for the nation was beginning to run out of genuine log cabins for the care and feeding of future leaders. Garfield's managers, to be sure, made as much capital out of the log-cabin birthplace as had the men behind Harrison and Lincoln.

A new element, however, as well as the old favorites, entered this 1880 campaign. American big business was beginning to feel its oats. The big capitalists, the monopolists of finance and industry, instead of making a patronizing contribution to one party or the other in the hope of getting some minor special privilege, were seriously moving in on policy making at the party level. Garfield was aware of this trend, and actually sought the support of such plutocrats as Chauncey Depew (the Vanderbilts and the New York Central), the Rockefellers (Standard Oil), Jay Gould (Union Pacific), and Mark Hanna, the Cleveland coal and iron millionaire. These new peers of the rising American aristocracy of wealth were impressed by Garfield's conservatism during his two decades in Congress, and were inclined to back him.

Whitelaw Reid, who had succeeded Horace Greeley as editor of the New York *Tribune,* was in a position to make many big-money contacts for Garfield, and did so. He did not, however, entirely trust Garfield's judgment, his decisiveness, or his ability to resist the many pressures to which he would be subjected. "I beg you to make no promises to anybody," he advised in a letter to the Ohioan, pointing out that he had seen too many presidential candidates entrapped by hasty pledges. He added: "Please don't make any journeys or any speeches."

Except for a trip to New York to meet the financial barons and to try to make peace with the Stalwarts, Garfield followed Reid's advice, stayed home in Mentor, and carried on a front-porch campaign which some other Ohio Republicans, also fated to die in office, would later imitate. Delegations and single personalities were induced to make pilgrimages to Garfield's front porch—war veterans, editors, political figures—and listen to the general's words of wisdom, which were duly reported in the friendly press.

The Democrats also nominated a Civil War hero for the presidency—General Winfield Hancock, who commanded a corps at Gettysburg. Second choice was Governor William H. English of Indiana.

The Garfield-Arthur ticket won a hair-raising margin of only 9,464 popular votes. The electoral vote, however, thanks to the powerful Stalwart organizations in populous New York, Pennsylvania, and Illinois, was a comfortable 214 to 155.

President Garfield was greatly influenced by James G. Blaine, whom he made Secretary of State, in naming his Cabinet and making other federal appointments. The Stalwarts were frozen out almost completely. Conkling claimed that Levi Morton had been promised the Treasury portfolio, but Garfield offered him the Navy instead. Conkling ordered him to refuse.

The crowning insult to the Stalwarts was Garfield's appointment of Judge William H. Robertson, a bitter political enemy of Conkling, to be collector of the port of New York. Even Vice-President Arthur, who had tried to keep the peace between the Stalwarts and the Half-Breeds, accused Garfield of not having been "square, nor honorable, nor truthful with Conkling," and, under Blaine's influence, of breaking every pledge.

Conkling, in protest at this violation of senatorial courtesy by the President's failure to consult with the New York senators on a New York appointment, resigned his seat. Tom Platt, the junior senator from New York, could hardly do otherwise, although he had been in the Senate only three months. The two Stalwart ex-senators then repaired to Albany, where, Conkling assured his junior, the well-trained New York legislature would vindicate them by reelecting them as a gesture of confidence.

However, things had changed in Albany during the past few months. When the President of the United States dared appoint a bitter enemy of Conkling as collector of the port of New York, a post that had always been the private province of the Stalwart boss, the feeling was that Conkling must be losing his touch. The Half-Breeds in the legislature waged a persistent fight to block the reelection of Conkling and Platt. Even some of the Stalwarts, tired at last of Lord Roscoe's arrogance, dragged their feet. Conkling found himself in the humiliating position of begging for votes instead of ordering them. When the deadlock had gone on for two months, Conkling sent a distress signal to Washington, and Vice-President Arthur hurried to Albany to help lobby for his friends.

The Vice-President's intercession in the cloakrooms of the Albany legislature was a matter of personal loyalty, rather than a political gesture. As he was to demonstrate within a very few months, he had definitely put Stalwart spoilsmanship behind him in deference to the responsibilities of higher office. His rescue expedition on behalf of Conkling and Platt might be compared to Vice-President Truman's flight to Kansas City sixty-odd years later for the funeral of Democratic boss Tom Pendergast, a spoilsman whose spoils had never touched Truman. The fact that both men did not forget old friends did not necessarily mean that each accepted the other's religion.

At the end of June 1881, the Conkling scheme for rehabilitation and reelection collapsed in a gale of Half-Breed laughter when Tom Platt, ex-president of Tioga National Bank, pillar of the church, and paragon of respectability, was surprised in his room at the Delavan Hotel in Albany with a lady of the evening. The Half-Breed press had a field day, Platt withdrew his candidacy, and Conkling would soon go into another political eclipse.

As Vice-President Arthur, on his way back to Washington, got off the Albany night boat as it docked in New York on the morning of July 2, he found that the Platt scandal had been forced from the front pages by more shocking news.

President Garfield had been shot.

Garfield had been on his way to Massachusetts to speak at Williams College, his alma mater. The ever-present Blaine was at his side as he walked through the railway station, holding forth on his favorite subject—the expansion of American trade through the peaceful conquest of the Caribbean and South America. The Secret Service was nowhere, for, despite the fact that it had been organized the year Lincoln was shot, its duties would not include protection of the President's life until after the third presidential assassination, twenty years later.

Apparently nobody noticed the seedy little man following the President and the Secretary of State until he drew his pistol, fired twice, and began shouting incoherently.

Charles J. Guiteau was a minor clerk who owed his job to the New York Stalwart organization. Because he had handed out campaign literature for a ward heeler once, he considered that the Republican party was indebted to him. He bombarded Garfield with letters demanding appointment as a consul to France. When the letters brought no result, he came to Washington and managed to get into the White House—but no consular appointment was forthcoming. To his deranged mind, he was being ignored because the President was a Half-Breed and he was a Stalwart like Vice-President Arthur. He had to kill Garfield, so Arthur could become President.

This political motivation for his act was described by Guiteau over and over again, to the police, in letters he had written before the crime, during his trial, and in a poem he recited from the scaffold. He insisted that God had ordered him to kill Garfield.

Despite the obvious evidence that Guiteau was psychotic, the American people and the American press, like the jury that found him sane and guilty, regarded Garfield as a victim of the spoils system. The real assassin, therefore, was Roscoe Conkling, and his accomplice was the Stalwart Vice-President, Chester Alan Arthur. The indignation was nationwide, as was the sympathy for Garfield in his long agony. There was a universal demand for reforms in government service, and a universal apprehension that Arthur in the White House would mean Lord Roscoe Conkling as the *éminence grise.*

Arthur spent most of the interregnum in his New York apartment, a cheerless place since the death of his wife from pneumonia the previous year. He made no attempt to exercise power under the disability clause, although Garfield was certainly completely out of the picture: he had been taken to a seaside villa in New Jersey to die. Only when reporters told Arthur on September 19 that the President was dead did he go to Washington to take the oath of office as the twenty-first President of the United States.

Arthur remodeled the Administration with caution and deliberation. Over a period of half a year most of Garfield's appointees resigned from the Cabinet. The only permanent carryover was Robert Todd Lincoln, the late President's son, who was Secretary of War in both Cabinets. Secretary of State Blaine resigned in December to go home to Maine, write history, and bide his time until the next Republican convention. His successor, Frederick T. Frelinghuysen, former senator from New Jersey, threw out Blaine's great scheme for a commercial empire in the Caribbean and Latin America, and called off a Pan-American conference that Blaine had arranged.

The expected comings and goings of Conkling through the side door of the White House did not materialize. Conkling was not offered a Cabinet post. At one time Arthur is supposed to have mentioned a Supreme Court appointment, but the ex-senator refused. Relations between the two men deteriorated badly when Arthur refused to demand the resignation of collector of the port Robertson. There is no doubt that Arthur did favor Stalwarts if they were competent, but most of his appointments, even to minor posts, were generally considered sound.

The new President did not act with such caution in establishing himself in the White House, which he found far below his fastidious standards as a residence. He moved out vanloads of the old furniture he found there—Jacqueline Kennedy retrieved some of the historic pieces and moved them back in 1961—and he brought in New York artist Louis Comfort Tiffany to supervise the redecoration. He added to the library and the wine cellar. As his daughter Ellen was only ten when he inherited the presidency, he invited his sister Mary McElroy to come from Albany to be his official hostess—a full-time job, for the White House was the scene of many gay, glamorous, and witty affairs during the Arthur administration.

President Arthur's busy social life was not confined exclusively to the White House. He could be lured abroad by exquisite food, vintage wines, charming women—or political obligations. It may have been the latter reason which secured his presence at an affair which had Washington gasping for many days—the marriage of flamboyant Senator Horace A. W. Tabor, the Bonanza King of Colorado, to Elizabeth Bonduel McCourt of Oshkosh, Wisconsin, better known in Denver and Leadville as Baby Doe.

Tabor, a fantastic character who tossed money about as if the mines of Leadville would keep him a millionaire as long as he lived, built opera houses to bring culture and world-famous artists to the Wild West, and also let fall a crumb or two upon Republican party waters. He had been a mayor and a lieutenant governor of Colorado. And when Colorado's Senator Henry Teller resigned his seat to become Arthur's Secretary of the Interior, Tabor wangled an appointment to fill the unexpired thirty days of Teller's term. It was undoubtedly Secretary Teller who persuaded President Arthur to attend the wedding and reception at the Hotel Willard, one of the most spectacular exhibitions of wealth and bad taste the capital had seen in years.

The groom was in his fifties, wore terrifying black walrus mustaches, and had just divorced his first wife, who had crossed the plains with him from Maine twenty-five years earlier. Baby Doe was blonde, blue eyed, and twenty-two. With her own hand she addressed the wedding invitations, bordered and embossed in solid silver, to the President and other dignitaries. The bride was stunning in her new ninety-thousand-dollar diamond necklace and heavily brocaded white satin gown. She was attended by her father, mother, two sisters, two brothers, and two brothers-in-law, all wearing black: they were mourning another brother-in-law.

The Willard ballroom was smothered in thousands of dollars' worth of flowers worked into the shape of six-foot wedding bells, cupids, hearts, shamrocks, and other appropriate symbols. There were even flowers festooning the champagne buckets. President Arthur stayed until ten forty-five, and, as he wished the bride good night and good luck,* asked her for a rose from her bouquet, which she prettily gave him.

Garfield had been in office too short a time to have left much of a

* Tabor's luck and mines played out simultaneously in the eighteen-nineties, and, facing penury, he was surprised to find that the bread cast upon Republican waters was returned to him. Henry Teller, who returned to the Senate when he left Arthur's Cabinet, used his influence to have Tabor appointed postmaster at Denver a year before his death. Baby Doe Tabor froze to death in the shaft house of one of the abandoned Tabor mines in 1935.

legislative program to his successor. However, he did bequeath to Arthur the nasty job of cleaning up the Star Route post office scandal. Thomas L. James, Garfield's Postmaster General, had unearthed evidence that a half-dozen men had swindled the government out of at least four million dollars in fraudulent Pony Express and stagecoach contracts in the West. The legacy was a particularly disagreeable one for Arthur because one of the chief conspirators was Stephen Dorsey, who had managed the 1880 campaign for the Garfield-Arthur ticket. Only a month before he became Vice-President Arthur had spoken at a testimonial dinner for Dorsey and praised him extravagantly. Another culprit was Assistant Postmaster General Thomas J. Brady, whose job it had been to collect kickbacks from postal employees for the Republican war chest. Despite the old bonds of friendship and politics, the President gritted his teeth and ordered his Attorney General to prosecute "with the utmost vigor."

The first trial of Dorsey, Brady, and six others opened in June 1882. Defense attorneys, led by Roscoe Conkling and Colonel Robert Ingersoll, "the Great Agnostic," attacked the indictments, the judge, the grand jury, and the prosecutors. Confessions were withdrawn, and there were rumors of jurors being offered bribes. After several months, the trial ended with a hung jury. A second trial ended in acquittal.

With a Republican majority in both Houses of Congress, President Arthur could have hoped for the success of a fairly conservative program. The most startling piece of legislation which he asked was the passage of a civil-service act introduced by Senator George Pendleton of Ohio, who had been General McClellan's running mate on the Democratic ticket defeated by Lincoln and Johnson in 1864. The spectacle of a boss spoilsman who had been fired by a former President for his spoilsmanship sponsoring a bill that called for a merit system for federal appointments must have shocked his fellow Republicans into a state of disbelief, for they ignored the recommendation in his first message to Congress. Arthur was evidently sincere in demonstrating that the twenty-first President of the United States was not the same man as the discredited collector of the port of New York, for he made his point again in his second message. This time he got results, for the complexion of the House had been changed by the off-year elections of 1882. The Democrats won a majority, and Congress apparently understood that the electorate was displeased. The lame-duck session passed the Pendleton Civil Service Reform Act on January 16, 1883. The vote was 155–47 in the House and 38–5 in the Senate, with many vacant seats registering the unwillingness of some to stand up and be counted.

The Pendleton Act created the first Civil Service Commission, provided for competitive examinations, prohibited the levying of political assessments on federal officeholders, and ordered a staggered application of the act, beginning at once with post office and customhouse employees. More than fourteen thousand officeholders were affected within the month.

Arthur was less successful with his veto of the eighteen-million-dollar Rivers and Harbors Bill, which he considered a gigantic pork barrel. The bill was passed over his veto.

Congress did give him his appropriation for three armored cruisers and a dispatch boat, the beginning of a steel-clad navy and the beginning of the end of the wooden ship.

In his efforts to revise the protective tariff laws, long a subject of complaint from the agricultural states, President Arthur had appointed a commission of nine citizens to review the current rates and revenue needs. In December 1882, the commission presented to Congress a report that suggested an overall reduction, with a few exceptions, that averaged twenty per cent. The report was greeted with approval by most business leaders, and promptly made into a complete hash by the lame-duck Congress under pressures from increasingly effective lobbies and local special interests. Finally showing increased rates in some categories, it was called "The Mongrel Tariff" by the press.

President Arthur also asked for changes in the presidential succession law. Although the assassination of Garfield was still fresh in memory, and the nation had been without a Vice-President for more than three years of the Arthur administration, Congress took no action.

Arthur's program had been modest, and its realization was even more modest. Yet if his only accomplishment had been the legal beginnings of the Civil Service as against the spoils system which he had once championed, he would have merited the gratitude of his generation and of subsequent generations. In fact, he thought so himself. True, the fine glow of prosperity which had pervaded the country during most of his administration had been somewhat dimmed by the financial crisis that followed the failure of the stock brokerage firm of Grant & Ward. The panic wiped out the fortune of ex-President Ulysses S. Grant and resulted in more than ten thousand American bank failures in 1884. Still, Chester

Arthur thought he deserved to be renominated on the basis of his record.

There seems to be no question that, after a tough start, Arthur definitely established himself as a good President. Many Republicans felt so, for when they flocked to Chicago in 1884 for the national convention, they adopted a platform containing the following paragraph:

> In the administration of President Arthur we recognize a wise, conservative, and patriotic policy under which the country has been blessed with a remarkable prosperity, and we believe his inimitable services are entitled to and will receive the hearty approval of every citizen.

Arthur did indeed have great popular support at the time of the convention, and was a strong contender for the presidential nomination in his own right. However, the Stalwarts had little enthusiasm for their former colleague as a result of his unexpected dedication to responsible duty as President. One of his old cronies had come to see him in the White House to ask a favor, and was turned down.

"Why, General!" exclaimed the astonished Stalwart. "If you were still president of the New York County Republican committee, you would be here asking for the same thing."

"I certainly would," said Arthur, always the gentleman, "but since I came here I learned that Chester A. Arthur is one man, and the President of the United States is another."

Despite the Stalwart foot dragging, Arthur had enough backers to keep him in the running for three ballots. However, there were enough defections to undermine his political base, and James G. Blaine, at long last, won the presidential nomination on the fourth ballot. The convention then made the second choice of one of the old Stalwart triumvirate, General John A. Logan of Illinois, hard-core supporter of General Grant, rumored beneficiary of the Whisky Ring, and political genius of the Grand Army of the Republic.

Arthur took his defeat with his usual urbanity, and pledged his support to the Blaine-Logan ticket. How much support he actually gave to the campaign against the Democratic ticket of Grover Cleveland, honest sheriff, veto mayor of Buffalo, and rotund beer-loving governor of New York, and his running mate Thomas A. Hendricks of Indiana is a matter for conjecture. The chairman of the Republican national committee accused him of contributing neither time, nor money, nor effort toward the election of "the Plumed Knight," as Colonel Ingersoll had called Blaine in his nominating speech in 1876.

Had Arthur been nominated, there is some doubt whether Grover Cleveland would ever have been President of the United States. The campaign between Cleveland and Blaine degenerated into name calling, parades, and singing vilification by both parties. The Democrats paraded singing:

> Blaine! Blaine! James G. Blaine!
> Monumental liar from the state of Maine!
> Burn this letter!

The reference is to letters which Blaine wrote to a stockbroker friend in Boston, supposedly confirming charges that as Speaker of the House Blaine had profited from graft involving the Union Pacific Railway. Instead of being burned, as Blaine had suggested, the letters fell into the hands of the Boston broker's embittered bookkeeper, one James Mulligan, and were published in *Harper's Weekly* a few months before election.

The Republicans campaigned on an equally high level. They sang:

> Ma, Ma, where's my Pa?
> Going to the White House. Ha, ha, ha!

They were rejoicing over the effect the youthful pecadillos of bachelor Cleveland might have on a Victorian electorate. Apparently a widowed friend of Cleveland's, one Maria Halpin, had borne a child registered as "father unknown." Cleveland had assumed the charge, was periodically blackmailed by the mother, who had become an alcoholic, and finally had the child removed from her custody. The expected Victorian revulsion at Cleveland's wild oats was outweighed by the well-meaning Reverend Samuel Burchard's pledge to Blaine that the Protestant clergy would never desert the Republicans for the party of "Rum, Romanism, and Rebellion"—a statement which, when passed over in silence by Blaine, cost him hundreds of thousands of Catholic votes.

How the Arthur candidacy would have fitted into the situation cannot be asserted by hindsight. In any event, Blaine lost to Cleveland by only twenty-three thousand popular votes, but the electoral score was 219 to 182.

Arthur was blamed. The accidental President wrapped himself in the dignity of the office he would hold until the following March and refused to engage in an exchange of invective. He also withdrew his name as a candidate for a Senate seat from New York, for which his friends were grooming him when he should leave the White House.

The infighting, rabbit punching, and arm twisting that he had loved as a brilliant lawyer dabbling in politics as a hobby he hated now that they had come boomeranging back to wound him deeply as a professional. The series of transmutations had come full circle. The amateur machine politician become President of the United States by accident, the wheeler dealer turned honest champion of civil service in government, the party-liner calling for the prosecution of corrupt friends and colleagues, he had reached the pinnacle of his life. He could go no higher, had perhaps already gone beyond his capabilities. He was content to return to the starting place.

When he left the White House, he reverted to his practice of law in New York, his Lexington Avenue apartment with his wife's room the same as the day she died. It was more fun being the gay bachelor in New York than in Washington. He could entertain friends because they were civilized and intelligent or just because he liked them. He did not have to think of the political repercussions of an invitation or lack of one. He could eat and drink what he liked and as much as he liked without having reporters appraising the shade of his naturally florid cheeks to speculate upon his relations with the bottle. It was a good life, even if he was not to enjoy it for very long. He died in November 1886, not quite two years after he left the White House.

Conkling, who had lived in obscurity for some time, outlived him by more than a year. Lord Roscoe was frozen to death while walking home in the Great Blizzard of 1888, when New York transportation was paralyzed.

Tom Platt also outlived Arthur. Moreover he outlived his amorous indiscretion in the Albany hotel room, was reelected to the Senate, and was busily rebuilding the Republican organization in New York to his own specifications before he died.

7

THE PROTECTIONIST AND THE ROUGH RIDER

WILLIAM McKINLEY, MARCH 4, 1897–SEPTEMBER 14, 1901.
THEODORE ROOSEVELT, SEPTEMBER 14, 1901–MARCH 4, 1909.

Theodore Roosevelt is the only vice-presidential candidate in American history whose election campaign made more noise and attracted more attention than that of the head of the ticket. This was only natural. With his first term in the White House tucked safely away in the archives, its success ratified by the Republican party's renomination, President William McKinley wrapped himself in the dignity of his high office and the godlike aloofness ordered by his grand strategist, Marcus Alonzo Hanna, senator from Ohio and chairman of the Republican national committee. There was no reason in 1900 to go chasing around the country in an effort to refute the silver-tongued silver-minded Democratic candidate for President, William Jennings Bryan. Bryan and his coinage issue had been repudiated by the electorate in 1896. Bryan and his free-trade issue had been refuted by nearly four years of national prosperity under a "sound" protective tariff. If the voters had any further questions about the full dinner pail or the American victory in the war with Spain, let them come to McKinley's Ohio home to ask them.

And the voters came in droves, courtesy of Mark Hanna. The wealthy party boss spent thousands of dollars bringing influential Republicans to Canton, where they shook hands with the President on the front porch of McKinley's house (a wedding gift from his banker father-in-law) or trampled his front lawn. They listened while he spoke with quiet charm of the expansion of American trade, of the open-door policy in China (now that the United States had become a world power by defeating Spain), and the possibility of relaxing the protective tariff, since the country's business was in such good shape. The candidate-President's remarks were recorded in great detail by Whitelaw Reid's New York *Tribune* and other loyal Republican papers.

Meanwhile the Republican second choice was barnstorming the William Jennings Bryan circuit with great success. He was a born showman. Colonel Theodore Roosevelt, hero of San Juan Hill, shouted, waved his arms, shook his fist, pounded on tables, and drew large crowds. His listeners were sometimes surprised by the high-pitched voice emanating from his robust and vigorous figure, but they were delighted by the features that endeared Roosevelt to political cartoonists—the pince-nez with the flowing black ribbons, the pugnacious lower lip, the luxuriant red mustache, and the gleaming double octave of white teeth when he smiled. The colorful vice-presidential candidate waved the flag (as would be expected of the man who led the charge of the Rough Riders) and promised a better army and a bigger navy to secure the country against the enemies of her manifest destiny.

McKinley and Roosevelt made strange running mates. Although both were good Republicans, they were poles apart in temperament, background, and political outlook. McKinley came from a more than modest family (his father was an iron worker), but developed politically into an ultraconservative friend of big business. Roosevelt, born to great wealth, was, perhaps because he was more sensitive to the changing climate of the nation, an enemy of monopoly in business and a champion of the emerging forces of organized labor.

McKinley's military career was longer and more professional than that of his successor's. At the age of eighteen, he enlisted in the Twenty-third Ohio Volunteers, in which Rutherford B. Hayes was a major. McKinley advanced in rank as he fought through the Civil War. He was a commissary sergeant at Antietam, won battlefield promotion to captain, and was breveted major in 1865. Returning to Canton, he practiced law only two years before seeking public office. Elected first as prosecuting attorney for Stark County, he later served six terms in Congress as representative from Ohio, and two terms as governor of Ohio (1892–96).

It was in Congress, as a vigorous and articulate champion of the protective tariff, that McKinley attracted the attention of Mark Hanna. The Cleveland millionaire, who had first wet his feet in the turbulent waters of politics during the Garfield-Arthur campaign, had been getting in deeper and deeper in the intervening years, and by 1896 was up to his armpits. He admired McKinley for his political outlook, as a man, and as a vote getter. The admiration was mutual. While Hanna looked up to McKinley as the successful politician he would like to be, McKinley stood in awe of the financial genius who had amassed a huge fortune in iron, steel, and Great Lakes shipping. With the nation's economy in questionable shape during the second Cleveland administration, and with a candidate like McKinley, Hanna saw prospects for a Republican victory in 1896, with himself in the role of kingmaker.

There was considerable unrest in the country. Prices and wages were low; unemployment was high. Strikes during 1894, many of them unsuccessful, involved seven hundred and fifty thousand workers. When the Pullman Company reduced wages by 25 per cent, and the workers struck for a restoration of the cut, the strike spread to the railroads and the Chicago area was paralyzed. Federal troops were sent in over the protests of liberal Illinois governor Peter Altgeld, and the strike was broken. Coxey's "army" of Midwest unemployed marched on Washington to demand public-works and other relief legislation, only to be spurned while Jacob Coxey, their leader, was arrested for walking on the grass. The 1894 congressional elections, reflecting the mood of the nation, foreshadowed the Democratic defeat of 1896.

Mark Hanna began his buildup of McKinley far in advance of the Republican national convention. While McKinley believed that the will of the majority was law, Hanna felt that the will of the majority was whatever he wanted it to be. To make sure that the majority agreed with him on McKinley, Hanna spent a small fortune of his own funds—at least one hundred thousand dollars, according to contemporary estimates—in developing his candidate's pre-convention chances. As McKinley moved across the depression-struck country on speaking engagements, billboards blossomed with huge posters screaming welcome to "the advance agent of prosperity." There was never a doubt about his nomination when the convention opened in St. Louis on June 16.

The convention ignored Hanna's wishes on the platform, however. Hanna wanted no outright declarations on controversial subjects. The delegates voted a gold-standard plank, despite Hanna, and the silverite

Republicans, led by Senator Teller of Colorado, walked out. Other planks favored the protective tariff, Cuban independence, and the building of a Nicaraguan canal.

Garret A. Hobart of New Jersey was nominated as McKinley's running mate.

Three weeks later the Democrats convened in Chicago to nominate William Jennings Bryan for President and listen to him declare: "You shall not press down upon the brow of labor this crown of thorns. You shall not crucify mankind upon a cross of gold." Arthur Sewall, wealthy Maine shipbuilder, was the vice-presidential candidate.

Bryan traveled eighteen thousand miles, making six hundred speeches urging the free coinage of gold and silver at the ratio of sixteen to one, while McKinley stayed home at Canton. The front-porch campaign was Mark Hanna's suggestion, and McKinley rarely turned down a suggestion from the man who had once rescued him from bankruptcy.

The silver-gold issue split even the minor parties, and numerous splinter groups developed, each nominating its own slate. The Prohibitionists, for example, broke into Narrow Gaugers, who opposed free coinage but wanted to restrict the Prohibition platform to a single plank outlawing alcohol, and the Broad Gaugers, who favored the Bryan program, but not Bryan's running mate. A free-swinging campaign developed, with the coinage issue masking the basic differences behind all the excitement. The fight was really between the industrial East and the rural South and West. Anti-Bryan feeling was so strong in the East that employers put printed slips into pay envelopes reading: "If Bryan is elected, don't bother to come back to work on Wednesday. The plant will be closed."

The Republicans called Bryan a revolutionary and an anarchist. The Democrats turned their attention from McKinley to Mark Hanna, whom they called "Dollar Mark."

When the votes were counted, McKinley had 7,111,607 to Bryan's 6,500,052. Bryan carried only the South and the West, with the exception of California and Oregon—eleven states with 176 electoral votes. McKinley had 271.

As the returns came in, William McKinley, a God-fearing Methodist since childhood, knelt with his wife and mother to give thanks for his victory. Putting her arm on her son's shoulders, the elder Mrs. McKinley added a prayer of her own: "O God, keep him humble."

On the surface, it would have been excusable for the new President to have lost his humility. Tariffs were raised, prosperity did materialize, and McKinley and his supporters took full credit. Development of new gold fields in the Klondike, South Africa, and elsewhere, together with improved mining methods, doubled world gold production and made the question of coinage largely academic.

Nevertheless, McKinley would have plenty to worry about during the next four years. First, there was tragedy in his personal life. Following the deaths of his only two children in childhood, his wife had developed epileptoid seizures. She was the object of his constant and tender concern. In the White House, as in the statehouse at Columbus, he would interrupt a Cabinet meeting or an interview with an important personage if he thought his beloved Ida needed him.

Next was the failure of McKinley and most of his backers to sense the ground swell of social change developing in the nation. They were so jubilant over the Republican victory that they did not analyze the meaning of the fact that a million more Democratic votes were cast in 1896 than had been cast for Grover Cleveland four years before. Democratic mayor Tom Johnson of Cleveland, a victim of the Republican tide, described the election as the first great protest of the American people against monopoly. "It was not free silver that frightened the plutocrat leaders," he said. "What they feared then, what they fear now, is free men."

Probably the most worrisome question of the century's final years was that of war and peace. McKinley was elected on a platform favoring Cuban independence, yet he personally was against armed American intervention in the struggle between Cuban patriots and their Spanish overlords. The revolt against the colonial government had been going on for years, and its brutal suppression by General Weyler, the military governor, brought a note of protest from McKinley's Secretary of State John Sherman. McKinley himself had offered his services to Spain as a mediator to stop hostilities, but he was under considerable pressure from several quarters to use force to end Spanish rule in Cuba.

There was widespread moral indignation in the United States aroused by atrocity stories of Spanish mistreatment of the Cubans. The martial spirit was raised to boiling point by a newspaper war in New York. Publishers William Randolph Hearst with the *Journal* and Joseph Pulitzer with the *World* were outdoing each other with sensational headlines, jingoistic editorials, and much beating of the war drums. Hearst sent author Richard Harding Davis and artist Frederic Remington to Cuba to record firsthand impressions of the Cuban freedom fighters and the inhuman Spaniards.

Other instincts besides the American love of liberty governed some of those who clamored for war. American investment in Cuban sugar plantations was estimated at fifty million dollars, and trade with the island was perhaps double that. And there were still others who merely believed the time had come for the United States to show her strength and take her rightful place among the world powers.

Among the men in Congress and the Administration who were determined to make the eagle scream, despite the President's hesitation, was an Assistant Secretary of the Navy. Men of sub-Cabinet rank do not ordinarily have much power in Washington, but, when the Assistant Secretary's name is Theodore Roosevelt, he helps himself to power.

Teddy Roosevelt was in the Navy Department because Tom Platt, now firmly established as New York State's Republican boss, found him too rambunctious to fit into his machine. Two years after his graduation from Harvard in 1880, Roosevelt was elected to the New York assembly. He made his first appearance on the national scene as a member of the Civil Service Commission in 1889, thanks to his friendship with Congressman Henry Cabot Lodge of Massachusetts. Appointed police commissioner of New York City, he at once became chairman and began cleaning out corruption in the force. His reform activities upset so many people and institutions in Manhattan that Platt got him the Washington appointment from good Republican McKinley.

The President named Roosevelt to the Navy Department with great reluctance. The young police commissioner's reputation as a firebrand had preceded him, and McKinley was having enough trouble with the hawks and doves in Congress without anyone else interfering with his efforts to keep peace in his administration and in the world. He was heartened by the news from Madrid: Spanish Liberal Sagasta had acceded to power on the assassination of Premier Cánovas, and had immediately recalled General Weyler from Cuba. There was a good chance, the President believed, to achieve a peaceful settlement in Cuba—unless someone upset the applecart.

To sound out the new Assistant Secretary, McKinley invited him to the White House for dinner, and a few days later took him for a drive in

Rock Creek Park to hear more. He heard plenty, for young Roosevelt—he was still in his thirties—was not only articulate but voluble. He had written not only a four-volume history of *The Winning of the West,* but *The Naval War of 1812* as well. He was fascinated by Captain (later Admiral) Alfred T. Mahan's philosophy of sea power and its influence on history, and he had his own belligerent theories on how to establish and protect American preeminence in the world. He favored taking the initiative in a preventive war with Spain (it would be over in six weeks), not only to free Cuba, but to seize Spanish possessions in the Pacific as bases to checkmate potential Japanese intentions.

McKinley must have been startled, but he apparently remained calm and noncommittal, for he made an unfavorable impression on Roosevelt. The Assistant Secretary afterward alluded to the President as "white livered" and as having "no more backbone than a chocolate eclair."

Roosevelt went ahead with his own plans without consulting Secretary of the Navy John D. Long. He got Senator Proctor of Vermont to use his influence to have Commodore George Dewey, a Vermont friend of the Assistant Secretary's, named commander of the Asiatic Squadron. Then Fate took a hand.

On February 9, 1898, Mr. Hearst's New York *Journal* published the text of a private letter written by Dupuy de Lôme, Spanish minister to Washington, obviously stolen from the mails in Havana by rebel agents. The letter called President McKinley a spineless peanut politician, a demagogue "who tries to keep the door behind him open, while catering to the jingoes of his party." Dupuy de Lôme of course immediately resigned.

On February 15 the United States battleship *Maine* was blown up while on a friendly visit to Havana harbor, killing 260 Americans. A month later a naval court of inquiry found that the explosion was external but failed to place the blame. The assumption was that the explosive charge could have been placed by an agent provocateur of the insurgents as well as by a Spanish terrorist. In the meantime, however, martial spirit ran high, the eagle screamed, and Assistant Secretary Roosevelt made his preparations.

On February 25 the strain was beginning to tell on Secretary of the Navy Long, and he decided to take the afternoon off to get a little rest. His assistant, in collaboration with Senator Henry Cabot Lodge, immediately drafted peremptory orders reassigning ships, distributing ammunition, ordering guns for ships not yet commissioned, and sending messages to Congress asking legislation authorizing recruitment of added personnel. A "secret and confidential" cable was dispatched to Commodore Dewey at Nagasaki, ordering him to coal all ships, proceed to Hong Kong, keep vigil on the Spanish Asiatic Squadron, and "in the event of a declaration of war" to carry out "offensive operations in the Philippine Islands."

When Secretary Long came across a copy of the cable next morning, he sent Roosevelt a plaintive memo: "Do not take any such step . . . without consulting the President or me. I am not away from town and my intention was to have you look after the routine of the office while I got a quiet day off. . . . I am anxious to have no occasion for a sensation in the papers."

Madrid was bending over backward to avoid war. At the end of May the Spanish government abolished Cuban concentration camps and offered to arbitrate the *Maine* affair, to grant an armistice to the insurgents, and to convene a Cuban parliament to arrange pacification.

Still torn between the doves and the hawks, President McKinley decided to pass the buck to Congress. His April 11 message, however, asked for authority to use armed force if necessary to pacify Cuba. A week later a joint congressional resolution authorized the use of armed force unless Spain withdrew from Cuba. An amendment by Senator Teller of Colorado softened the blow to the doves by denying any intention of annexation, and promising "to leave the government and control of the island to its people."

President McKinley signed the joint resolution on April 20, the ultimatum was sent, and the war with Spain was on.

On May 1 Commodore Dewey destroyed the Spanish squadron in Manila Bay without losing a man. Roosevelt felt that he could now leave the Navy safely in the hands of Secretary Long without waiting for Sampson and Schley to destroy Cervera's fleet at Santiago. On May 6 Assistant Secretary of the Navy Theodore Roosevelt resigned his civilian post to become Lieutenant Colonel Roosevelt of the First Cavalry Volunteers.

The First Volunteers were first nicknamed by the press "Teddy's Terrors." They became the "Rocky Mountain Rustlers" before the name "Roosevelt's Rough Riders" stuck. Actually Roosevelt was only second in command. Colonel Leonard Wood, a professional medical corps officer who had fought against Geronimo, was the commanding officer. The Rough Riders were an astonishing collection of cowboys, Harvard cronies, polo players, and other college athletes. They went into training (if that is the word) at San Antonio on May 16, and a month later sailed from Tampa with General Shafter, sixteen thousand other troops, and eighty-nine newspaper correspondents, leaving behind a number of volunteer regiments, some without blankets, uniforms, or even arms. By June 24 they were already in action at Las Guásimas, the first land battle of the war. A week later the Rough Riders edged aside an infantry brigade and charged pell-mell up San Juan Hill, with Lieutenant Colonel Roosevelt in the van and Richard Harding Davis not far behind.

The road to Santiago had been opened. The American casualties in two days of fighting exceeded fifteen hundred. And Teddy Roosevelt, a hero, was promoted to full colonel.

On July 26 Spain sued for peace, and on August 8, the Fifth Corps, including the Rough Riders, left Cuba for a quarantine camp at Montauk Point, Long Island, to avoid being wiped out by yellow fever and malaria.

The War Department had vetoed Roosevelt's plan to lead a parade of his Rough Riders up New York's Fifth Avenue, but the hero was available to reporters at Montauk Point. The mantle of military glory was so resplendent that New York State Republican boss Tom Platt, much as he distrusted Roosevelt, decided to make use of it for the good of the party. He proposed that the colonel run for governor, and the colonel was delighted.

The 1898 elections cut the Republican majority in Congress, but the Rough Rider was elected governor of New York by over seventeen thousand votes. Once safely seated in Albany, however, he again began to worry Platt. As was his wont, Roosevelt took over completely. He refused to knuckle under to Platt, and when he alienated big business with proposed legislation to control corporations, Platt began plotting to get rid of him.

The chance came in 1899 with the death of Vice-President Hobart—the sixth United States Vice-President to die in office. The renomination of President McKinley was a foregone conclusion. Why not shelve Wild Man Roosevelt in the vice-presidency? Even his tremendous energy and his genius for tumult and turbulence could do little harm when constitutionally limited to one function: presiding over the Senate.

There were three drawbacks to Platt's little scheme. First, President McKinley didn't want Governor Roosevelt as a running mate: he favored Senator William B. Allison of Iowa. Second, Senator Mark Hanna, the Republican national chairman, was horrified by the idea of Roosevelt as second choice: he wanted Secretary of the Interior Cornelius N. Bliss. Third, Roosevelt himself rejected the idea. Four months before the 1900 Republican convention he declared: "Under no circumstance could I or would I accept the nomination for the vice-presidency."

However, much could happen in four months, and much of it did. Both Bliss and Allison declined the empty honor of being second choice. Commodore Dewey, now an admiral, returned triumphant from Manila Bay and let it be known that he would be available for the presidency; nobody was listening. McKinley, more indecisive than ever, could not make up his mind about who he wanted as a running mate. Platt, still determined that Roosevelt should not have a second term as governor, joined forces with Matt Quay, Pennsylvania Republican leader, to promote the Rough Rider for second choice.

When the convention opened in Philadelphia in June, McKinley had still not expressed a preference. Hanna was desperate. He telephoned Washington and pleaded with the President to do something that would prevent "that damned cowboy" from being nominated. McKinley insisted on an open convention. When Roosevelt arose to second McKinley's nomination, the hero's ovation that greeted him left no doubt as to the delegates' wishes.

McKinley and Roosevelt were nominated in short order. Mark Hanna telephoned McKinley to say: "We did our best but they nominated that madman. Now it's up to you to live."

The Democrats convened in Kansas City on the Fourth of July and renominated William Jennings Bryan. Adlai Stevenson, Vice-President in the second Grover Cleveland administration, and grandfather of the late United States ambassador to the United Nations, was their second choice.

With the free-coinage issue dead except for a few silver-mining states, with a prosperous nation not looking for a change, and with the foreign-policy issue strangled by his own incomprehensible actions, Bryan had little to excite the voters except his sensational hairdo and his unquestioned eloquence. He had lobbied in the Senate to secure the ratification of the Paris Treaty ending the Spanish-American War because, he said, he wanted to keep the imperialist issue alive for the 1900 election. Actually, once the Senate had given consent to the annexation of Puerto Rico, the Philippines, and Guam by the United States—acquisitions which seemed far removed from the Spanish War aims of Cuban freedom—the *fait accompli* was no longer a question for useful debate.

During the campaign Mark Hanna showed himself an astute politician sensitive to social trends. Two months before the 1900 election, the United Mine Workers struck the anthracite mines of Pennsylvania for higher wages. When the coal owners refused to deal with the union, Hanna, an old coal-and-iron baron himself, hurried to the anthracite fields to talk to his fellow capitalists. The Republican image of prosperity and the full dinner pail, he argued, must not be damaged at this stage by the spectre of undernourished miners' families in overpriced company towns. The operators reluctantly granted a ten per cent raise—the first in twenty years—and the Republicans came through as the friends of labor.

McKinley and Roosevelt won the election by almost a million popular votes and by 292 to 155 electors' votes.

In September McKinley traveled to Buffalo to speak at the Pan-American Exposition. On September 6 he held a public reception, and thousands lined up to shake his hand. One young man in the queue had a bandaged right hand, and the President reached to shake his left. As he did so, the young man fired two shots from a pistol concealed under the bandages, and McKinley fell, mortally wounded in the stomach.

The young man was Leon Czolgosz, an avowed anarchist, who said he thought shooting the President would be good for the country. He was later executed.

President McKinley rallied at first, but died at two on the morning of September 14, murmuring his acquiescence to God's will, and trying to sing "Nearer My God to Thee."

Theodore Roosevelt came to Buffalo to be sworn in as twenty-sixth President of the United States at three o'clock that afternoon. He was forty-two—our youngest President.

The new President asked the McKinley Cabinet to continue serving, and he assured the country that he would continue "absolutely unbroken the policies of President McKinley." Few in high places believed him completely. The Rough Rider was congenitally unable to play the part of a cautious, indecisive McKinley. He had come by his contrary, assertive nature honestly. A frail boy with weak eyes, he was constantly being picked on by other youngsters—and beaten. So he learned to box, and got a badly damaged eye for his pains. Determined to build up his underdeveloped physique, he spent summers on his ranch in North Dakota, learned to ride, loved to camp and hunt, and took exercises when kept indoors. Though he was born to the purple, his sympathies were with the underdog. A millionaire by inheritance, he was regarded as a traitor to his class by his fellows. Although Mark Hanna cautioned him to go slow with any reforms, it was not long before he opened fire on what he called "the malefactors of great wealth."

Roosevelt had been in office just two months when J. P. Morgan, J. J. Hill, and E. H. Harriman organized a New Jersey holding company called Northern Securities, designed to unite the great railways they controlled—Northern Pacific, Great Northern and Chicago, Burlington and Quincy. The President ordered Attorney General Philander Knox to begin dissolution proceedings under the antitrust laws. A surprised Morgan hurried to Washington and called at the White House in person. "If there's anything wrong," he told the President, "just send Knox to see my people and they'll fix it up."

Roosevelt replied that there was nothing to be fixed; he merely wanted the Sherman Antitrust Act observed.

The government won its case. The railways appealed, and it was not until March 1904 that the Supreme Court, by a five-four decision, declared Northern Securities in violation of the antitrust act.

Roosevelt repeated his trustbusting attacks on Standard Oil, the meat packers, and the tobacco trust. The government won all suits.

When one hundred and forty thousand anthracite miners struck in May 1902, the coal operators refused arbitration and would not recognize the union. The interests of the miners, declared the spokesman for the operators, would be cared for "not by labor agitators but by the Christian men to whom God in His infinite wisdom has given control of the property interests of this country." As this was not a presidential year, the operators expected no government intervention. They got it anyhow. As the strike dragged on for months, the President called the principals to Washington. The operators, however, refused to sit down with the union leaders. Roosevelt then made preparations to have the Army run the mines. Meanwhile Secretary of War Elihu Root went to J. P. Morgan, who financed the mine owners, and worked out a compromise settlement whereby the miners got a ten per cent raise and better working conditions—but had to forego union recognition.

Theodore Roosevelt's foreign policy did not quite match his oft-quoted motto, "Speak softly and carry a big stick." His voice was often loud and shrill in the international field, and the big stick was frequently brandished aloft in pursuit of what Roosevelt considered the rightful—if newly acquired—place of the United States as a world power. He foresaw the expansionist aims of Japan, and began building a navy second only to Britain and Germany in order to be able to insist on an "open door" in China, and to prevent the hegemony of any one nation in the Pacific. He was not happy with Kaiser Wilhelm II's early moves to assure a place in the sun for the new Germany. Bismarck had already staked out a German claim in New Guinea and the Solomons, and the German Asiatic Squadron was hovering like a vulture over the Pacific islands of vanquished Spain, just as the Japanese would do while Germany was losing World War I.

When Germany in 1902 sent warships to the Caribbean, ostensibly to collect debts owed by Venezuela, Roosevelt told the German ambassador that, unless the Kaiser agreed to arbitration within ten days, Admiral Dewey would proceed to Venezuelan waters with a suitable naval force to support the Monroe Doctrine. The Germans agreed to arbitration.

A few weeks later Argentina proposed the Drago Doctrine as a corollary to the Monroe Doctrine: European armed intervention or occupation of territory could not be justified by public debt delinquency. Roosevelt acted under this "corollary" to prevent another Venezuela crisis when he concluded an informal arrangement with the government of Santo Domingo to allow American supervision of customs on behalf of European creditors. The Senate refused consent, but Roosevelt went ahead anyhow, insisting that the informal arrangement was not a treaty and did not require Senate ratification.

Roosevelt applied the same activist policy to building the Panama Canal. The Senate had ratified a treaty with Colombia, settling details for a canal across the isthmus of Panama. The Colombian senate rejected the treaty, viewing the terms as niggardly. Roosevelt, determined that the matter should be settled before Congress reconvened, sent the U.S.S. *Nashville* to Colón, just in case there should be a revolution in Panama. The revolt took place on schedule, November 3, 1903. United States Marines from the *Nashville* landed to bar the way to Colombian troops. The revolutionists declared the independence of Panama on November 4. The de facto government of Panama was recognized by the United States on November 6, and a treaty authorizing the canal, on the same terms as that rejected by Colombia, was signed with the new republic on November 18.

Roosevelt later explained his failure to follow tradition and submit a state paper of two hundred pages to Congress, where "the debate would be going on yet. But I took the Canal Zone and let Congress debate, and while the debate goes on the canal does also."

The Rough Rider President was equally precipitate in his action in Africa, where American interests were more tenuous. When Raizuli, a Moroccan bandit, kidnapped an American citizen named Perdicaris, Roosevelt's Secretary of State John Hay (a McKinley appointee) cabled the sultan: "We want Perdicaris alive, or Raizuli dead." The American was released. Two years later Roosevelt was largely responsible for convening an international conference at Algeciras to do something about chaotic conditions in Morocco, and to put the brakes on German expansion in North Africa at the expense of France. His instructions to Ambassador Henry White were to keep on good terms with all nations, but to "help France get what she ought to have."

Theodore Roosevelt settled the Russo-Japanese War by bringing the belligerents to the conference table—in Portsmouth, New Hampshire—and became the first American President to win the Nobel Peace Prize.

In the final year of his presidency he sent "The Great White Fleet," sixteen gleaming battleships under the command of Admiral Robley D. Evans, on a round-the-world goodwill tour that was to last fifteen months. Officially the trip was a gesture of friendship, but there is no doubt that Roosevelt intended it as a display of America's new sea power, and as a warning to Japan. Admiral Evans had orders to prepare for a possible attack in the Pacific.

Roosevelt was well satisfied with his first term as accidental President, but he knew that big business was not, and that consequently the big party bosses were unhappy about his administration. He felt that, regardless of his accomplishments, his place in history would be dimmed unless he was elected President in his own right. He feared 1904. The financiers, uneasy over his antitrust actions, were talking about replacing him with their friend Mark Hanna, and TR believed that their influence with the convention would prevent his renomination.

Hanna would have indeed liked to be President, but he knew that his age was against him (he would be sixty-six in 1904) and that his health was failing. He thought, however, that the powerful support of his fellow tycoons would give him a bargaining position from which he could maneuver Roosevelt into being obligated. He reckoned without another resourceful enemy: Senator Joseph Foraker of Ohio.

Foraker for years had known the ins and outs of Ohio politics. He had been governor of the state, had his own organization in the Cincinnati region, and was a power in the Republican party. He was eager to supplant Mark Hanna as national chairman. In May 1903, he called a press conference at which he declared that Teddy Roosevelt was not only a good President but the most popular man in the country. He therefore proposed that the Ohio Republican convention in June should declare for Roosevelt's renomination. The only possible opposition to his proposal, he added, would come from Mark Hanna, and even then only if Hanna himself had presidential aspirations.

Furious, Hanna made one of his rare political mistakes. He replied immediately that he was not and would not be a candidate for the presidential nomination. In the same breath he gave the press numerous reasons why Ohio Republicans should not be committed to any candidate a year before the national convention.

On second thought, Hanna began to worry about the President's reaction. He wired TR that the issue of an Ohio endorsement of the Roosevelt candidacy had been "forced upon me . . . in a way which makes it necessary to oppose such a resolution. When you know all the facts, I am sure you will approve. . . ."

Roosevelt realized that he now had the advantage and replied at once with a telegram which he released to the press:

> I have not asked any man for his support. I have had nothing whatever to do with raising the issue. Inasmuch as it has now been raised, of course those who favor my administration and nomination will favor endorsing them, and those who do not will oppose.

Outmaneuvered, Hanna gave up. He sent a final wire: "In view of the sentiment expressed, I shall not oppose the endorsement of your administration."

The whole matter became academic when Hanna died before the Republican convention opened.

Roosevelt became the unanimous choice of the 994 delegates at Chicago. Charles Warren Fairbanks, a conservative senator from Indiana, was their second choice.

The Democrats, cognizant of the displeasure of businessmen with Roosevelt, hoped to lure conservative votes by shelving their own radicals, such as Bryan. They nominated Judge Alton B. Parker of New York, a safe and sane candidate for President, and Henry G. Davis, a West Virginia millionaire, as Vice-President, perhaps hoping that their second choice might replenish their depleted treasury. Their strategy was a failure. Judge Parker declared for the gold standard, but the Wall Street bankers declared for their archenemy Teddy Roosevelt. The New York *Sun,* mouthpiece for big business, told the story in a five-word editorial: "Theodore, with all thy faults."

The campaign got off to a slow, apathetic start, but warmed up briskly when Joseph Pulitzer began asking the President a series of questions:

*Why is the Bureau of Corporations doing nothing?
*Is it because big business is pouring money into your campaign chests, assuming that they are buying protection?
*Why was the head of the Bureau of Corporations, George Cortelyou, named to succeed Mark Hanna as national chairman upon Hanna's death?
*How much has the beef trust contributed to your campaign?
*How much has the paper trust contributed?
*The coal trust?
*The sugar trust?

Roosevelt ignored the challenge for a month, until Judge Parker charged that the trusts named had paid blackmail to keep the Bureau of Corporations from revealing damaging facts.

Roosevelt finally replied: "That contributions have been made is not the question at issue. The assertion that there has been any blackmail, direct or indirect, by Mr. Cortelyou or by me, is a falsehood."

The President was reelected by two million five hundred thousand popular votes. He carried every state north of the Mason-Dixon Line.

Once he was President in his own right, Roosevelt began four exciting and productive years. If Cortelyou had made commitments to TR's "malefactors of great wealth," his influence did not reach as far as the White House, for the President carried on his dramatic war against the trusts and influence of corporate evil with even greater intensity. The Theodore Roosevelt years marked a turning point in the relationship between government and business in the United States. Not for another quarter century, until the presidency of his cousin Franklin Roosevelt, would the country see the passage of so much social legislation. True, the mood of the nation was ready, even anxious for change, but it is doubtful that change would have taken place if the cautious, indecisive McKinley had lived out his term. It took the dynamism of his Vice-President to conceive and enact the program for which historians have ranked Theodore Roosevelt as "near great" (McKinley rates only "average").

In addition to the accomplishments previously described, the following constructive legislation emerged during the Theodore Roosevelt years:

*Regulation of railroad rates. The railways had been getting around freight rates set by the Interstate Commerce Commission by giving rebates to certain favored firms. The Elkins Act (1903) made the shipper equally responsible with the railways in maintaining the ICC schedule, and the Administration successfully prosecuted Standard Oil and several Chicago meat packers for violations. The Hepburn Act (1906) extended ICC rate control to pipelines, Pullman cars, express companies, and storage and terminal facilities.

*The Meat Inspection Act and the Pure Food and Drugs Act were both passed in 1907 following the exposé of unsanitary conditions in the Chicago packing houses by Upton Sinclair in *The Jungle,* and proof of adulteration and dangerous components in drugs and patent medicines by Dr. Harvey Wiley, Department of Agriculture chemist.

*As he pointed out in his first message to Congress, Roosevelt considered the conservation of natural resources the country's most vital domestic problem. He created a national reserve of some one hundred and fifty million acres of forest, withdrew from public entry nearly another one hundred thousand acres of land in the Northwest and Alaska. In 1908 he set up a National Conservation Commission, with dynamic Gifford Pinchot as chairman, to put the brakes on deforestation and the erosion of the country's topsoil.

*The Reclamation Act (1902), which the President imposed on a reluctant Fifty-seventh Congress, gave him the authority for important federal irrigation projects in the arid Southwest, including the building of dams at government expense in Arizona, New Mexico, and Idaho—the forerunner of Boulder Dam, TVA, Grand Coulee, and other controversial projects which would advance the argument of using national resources for public power rather than for private profit.

*Roosevelt created a new Cabinet post—Secretary of Commerce and Labor—in 1903, as a result of his experience with the striking miners and coal operators in the anthracite fields of Pennsylvania. He saw the need for government influence to bring about harmony between the emerging unions and reactionary management and ownership. It was not until 1913 that the two branches of the new department became autonomous.

On the international scene, despite his sometimes frightening tactics, Theodore Roosevelt successfully launched the United States as a world power with a balance of big stick and soft talk. Despite the panic he caused in Latin America by his cynical creation of an independent Panama in order to build his canal, and his use of Marines to collect customs and keep European powers out of the hemisphere, he sent Secretary of State Elihu Root to the Pan-American Conference in Rio de Janeiro in 1906 to proclaim a "good-neighbor policy"—a phrase borrowed by his Democratic cousin Franklin thirty years later—and deny any territorial designs by the United States. It was Cousin Theodore who in 1905 proposed the second peace conference at The Hague. His intervention in Morocco averted—or at least postponed—war between France and Germany. His bringing to the conference table the belligerents of the Russo-Japanese War certainly secured more lenient terms for the Russians than the victorious Japanese would otherwise have granted, but the concessions demanded by (and given) the Japanese, such as a free hand in Korea, did much to encourage continuation of the expansionist policy that led to the attack on Pearl Harbor. No one can deny that the emergence of the United States as a first-class power became apparent during the administration of Roosevelt I.

Teddy Roosevelt's popularity was undiminished as his second term—actually his first elected term—approached its end. There is little doubt that he would have been renominated and reelected, if he had not in a misguided moment of modesty made a written statement refusing in advance to run for another term.

Speculation as to his possible successor increased as the date for the 1908 Republican convention approached. Most frequently mentioned were Secretary of State Elihu Root, New York's Governor Charles Evans Hughes, Vice-President Fairbanks, Speaker of the House Joe Cannon, and Wisconsin's Senator Bob La Follette. The Rough Rider President, however, chose to ignore them all and pass the torch to his portly, jovial Secretary of War, a former circuit judge, dean of the Cincinnati Law School, and first civilian governor of the Philippines, William Howard Taft.

The friendship of Harvard man Roosevelt and Yale man Taft dated back to Roosevelt's tour of duty with the Civil Service Commission. Taft at the time was United States Solicitor General. Taft's infectious laugh, his dedication to public service, and his willingness to undertake any important dirty job that other men were turning down, endeared him to TR, who once called him "the most lovable personality I have ever come in contact with."

President Roosevelt brought Taft back from the Philippines in 1904 to be Secretary of War, a post his father, Alphonso Taft, had held in President Grant's Cabinet. Several times Roosevelt offered to make Taft a justice of the Supreme Court, but after much thought—more than three months of it in 1906—and considerable kibitzing by his wife and brother Charley, he decided to bide his time and wait for his chance at the presidency, a job that his father Alphonso never quite made.

Roosevelt had once considered suggesting Elihu Root as his successor, but Root's past record as a corporation lawyer did not fit the Rough Rider tradition. When the Republicans convened at Chicago in June 1908, he had decided on Taft.

On opening day, the delegates cheered Teddy Roosevelt for forty-nine minutes. Had TR recanted his former statement of refusal, he would have been renominated by acclamation. Mrs. Taft, who almost died of anxiety during the demonstration, told friends she hoped the cheering for her husband when he was nominated would last longer, to compensate for her suffering. Taft was nominated on the first ballot—but the ovation lasted only twenty-nine minutes.

James S. Sherman, a colorless congressman from upstate New York, was second choice of the Republicans.

The Democrats fell back again on their hardy perennial, William Jennings Bryan. John W. Kern of Indiana was his running mate.

The President stumped for Taft, and Taft was elected by 321 electoral votes to 162.

Washington was swept by snow and sleet as William Howard Taft was inaugurated as twenty-seventh President of the United States, and the retiring President remarked that he knew there would be a blizzard on the day he left the White House. Shortly afterward Roosevelt left for Africa to hunt big game.

The ex-President was out of the country for more than a year. When his African safari was over, and the animals he had shot were all mounted and crated for shipment to American museums, he toured

Europe, meeting kings and statesmen, representing the United States at King Edward VII's funeral, and picking up his Nobel Peace Prize en route. When he got home in June 1910, he found the Republican party in a state of disintegration.

President Taft lacked either the skill or the will to pursue the progressive policies of his predecessor, probably the former. At first Roosevelt was convinced that he had "conscientiously tried to work for the objects I had in view, as far as he could approve them." Taft's administration saw the initiation of two constitutional amendments—one authorizing a federal income tax, the other providing for the direct election of United States senators. He also favored strengthening the Interstate Commerce Commission, and continuation of antitrust prosecutions. However, Taft himself was depending more and more on the extreme right wing of his party, and two of his actions—the passage of the Payne-Aldrich tariff bill, with its stiffly protective rates and his firing of forestry chief Pinchot as a result of his conservation policy dispute with the Secretary of the Interior—angered both Roosevelt and the country. As a result the Democrats won control of the House in 1910.

The progressive Republicans besieged the Rough Rider in his Oyster Bay home on Long Island. Pinchot, Bob La Follette, and a score of others came to press upon him the political realities of the United States while he was still recording the memories of his triumphs among the wild beasts of Africa and the crowned heads of Europe. Seven Republican governors wrote him a letter urging that he save the party from the ultraconservatives.

"My hat is in the ring," Roosevelt answered the governors. "I will accept the nomination for President if it is tendered to me."

And the fight between the former friends was on in earnest, no holds barred. TR accused Taft of knuckling under "to the great privileged interests." Taft called Roosevelt and his backers "political emotionalists . . . seeking to pull down the pillars of the temple of freedom. . . ."

As soon as the Republican national convention opened in Chicago in June 1912, it was evident that the galleries were for Roosevelt and the delegates were under control of the conservatives. The choice of Elihu Root as permanent chairman (by a margin of 57 votes) doomed the Roosevelt forces to defeat. They did not take part in the balloting that renominated Taft and Sherman, but left the Coliseum for Orchestra Hall, formed the Progressive Party, and nominated Theodore Roosevelt.

When sufficient financing was secured to assure a campaign, the Progressives reconvened, confirmed the Roosevelt nomination, and made Hiram Johnson of California their second choice.

At the height of the campaign, while speaking in Milwaukee, Roosevelt was shot by a psychotic named Schrank, who said he was acting at the behest of the late President McKinley. McKinley had appeared in a dream, he said, and told him it was his duty to get rid of a third-termer. Roosevelt insisted on finishing his speech before being taken to the hospital, where it was found that his wound was not serious.

The split in the Republican party of course insured the election of the Democratic candidate, Woodrow Wilson, governor of New Jersey. Roosevelt led Taft by 4,119,538 to 3,484,980, but the Wilson-Marshall ticket polled 6,293,454 and an overwhelming 435 electoral votes.

Roosevelt consoled himself by taking off for Brazil to explore the River of Doubt (today Rio Roosevelt). The Progressive Party was finished. A party like it, he said, could not be held together, because "there are no loaves and fishes." He was a Republican again.

When the United States entered World War I, the former Rough Rider sought permission to recruit and lead his own division in France, but President Wilson declined. The days of San Juan Hill were over. However, he would serve, in a vicarious sense, in two more wars. Of his five children, three died in the service of their country. Quentin, an aviator, was killed in France in the First World War. Major Kermit died on active service in Alaska in World War II. Brigadier General Theodore, Jr., was killed in Normandy in July 1944.

Uncharacteristically, the former President died in his sleep and in bed, at home in Oyster Bay, one night in January 1919, while his friends were talking about nominating him for President again in 1920. After all, he was only sixty.

8

NORMALCY AND MEDIOCRITY

WARREN GAMALIEL HARDING, MARCH 4, 1921–AUGUST 2, 1923.
CALVIN COOLIDGE, AUGUST 3, 1923–MARCH 4, 1929.

Beginning with Ulysses S. Grant, six of the nine men elected President of the United States were from Ohio. Whoever won the 1920 election was bound to be the seventh, for both major-party candidates were Ohio newspaper publishers.

Democratic nominee James M. Cox was by far the abler man. He had served three terms as governor of Ohio, was an excellent administrator, had a social awareness and an international outlook. Moreover, he had an attractive running mate in Franklin D. Roosevelt, who had been emulating his Republican cousin Theodore as Assistant Secretary of the Navy. The country, however, was tired of the war, disillusioned by the peace, bored by President Wilson's idealism, eager for a spree of materialism, and more than ready for a change.

Any reasonably competent Republican could have won in 1920, and the party had an impressive supply of talent available. That the nominee should have been an amiable third-rater like Warren Gamaliel Harding probably surprised no one more than Harding himself. In fact, before the 1920 Republican national convention opened in Chicago, it is doubtful that anyone considered Harding a serious possibility except Mrs. Harding, Senator Boies Penrose, the Pennsylvania Republican boss, and Harry M. Daugherty, lawyer, lobbyist, and political hanger-on in the corridors of the Ohio statehouse.

Daugherty, who had run for almost everything and never been elected to anything, picked Harding as a Man of Destiny as early as 1900 because he *looked* like a President. Harding had just been elected to the Ohio state senate. He was a big, well-built man of thirty-five whose thick dark hair had not yet begun to silver, erect, bronzed, with a warm, resonant voice. Daugherty turned to Jess Smith, his closest friend, who was doomed to follow him to Washington and tragedy, and said: "Gee, what a President he'd make!"

Harding, the son of a country doctor, was a dropout from tiny Ohio Central College. He went to work as printer and reporter on the struggling Marion *Star,* and, by moonlighting as insurance salesman and tuba player, managed to buy the newspaper with a down payment of three hundred dollars. He married Florence Kling, five years his senior and daughter of the richest man in Marion. She was a forceful woman who took over the management of the *Star* and Warren Harding's career. As the population of Marion grew from four thousand to some thirty thousand, the *Star* prospered, and Harding's political star also rose. Despite the superficial character of the *Star*'s editorials, or perhaps because of it, Harding was elected lieutenant governor of Ohio, failed in his try at the governorship, but won a seat in the United States Senate in 1914.

Harding was happy in the Senate. He liked the camaraderie, the poker games, the golf, and the senatorial whisky drinking (which did not prevent him from voting to pass the Prohibition Amendment over President Wilson's veto). He was not a very conscientious senator. His absentee record passed fifty per cent. Of the bills he introduced, 103 were "private measures"—for pensions or the relief of some Ohio business institution. The other nineteen were for such world-shaking purposes as the sale of surplus rifles to the sons of veterans, the loan of Army tents to relieve housing shortages, and an act to encourage the teaching of Spanish. However, he had an imposing presence, he offended nobody, and people rather liked him, perhaps for the very reason that he was not (and never would be) a great senator. As columnist Walter Lippmann wrote, in analyzing the mood of the period: "The people are tired of greatness."

A *Literary Digest* poll showed Harding running a poor sixth. General Leonard Wood, once commander of Roosevelt's Rough Riders, was one of the front runners. As military governor of Cuba he had presided over the antimalaria campaign and the discovery of the cause of yellow fever by the Walter Reed Commission. Later, as chief of staff of the Army, he had instituted a training program that gave the United States at least a cadre of officers for the American Expeditionary Force in 1917.

Senator Hiram Johnson was another favorite. The former California governor had a double appeal: He was a Theodore Roosevelt Progressive, and he was also a rabid isolationist, violently opposed to Wilson's League of Nations.

Governor Frank Lowden of Illinois was the third popular candidate. Millionaire Lowden had converted the evil-smelling political mess he had inherited into a clean, smooth-running state administration. He was a middle-of-the-roader.

Harding made a poor showing in the primaries, winning his own state by a bare fifteen thousand votes over General Wood, and thus sending a split Ohio delegation to the convention. Without the entreaties of his wife and Daugherty, Harding would have dropped out of the race.

As the convention opened, Daugherty told reporters that there would be no nomination in early balloting. After the other candidates had failed, he said, the worn-out leaders would "get together in some hotel at about 2:11 in the morning. Some fifteen men, bleary-eyed . . . and perspiring profusely, will sit down around the big table. I will be with them and present the name of Senator Harding."

The first part of the prediction was accurate. For ballot after ballot the lead hovered over the top three, shifting only slightly with each succeeding ballot, with no candidate gaining enough strength for nomination. Then the second part of Daugherty's prediction came true—except for his presence at "the big table." After his having indiscreetly given his forecast to the press, he could hardly have expected an invitation.

Harding himself had given up along about the third ballot. He had sent a friend of his back to Columbus just before the deadline to file his candidacy for reelection to the Senate. At two o'clock in the morning of the fourth day of the convention, however, he was summarily called to the Blackstone Hotel suite where the senatorial cabal, determined to nominate a straw man who would do the Senate's bidding, had been meeting since dinner with state leaders seeking a way to break the deadlock. Was there anything in his past or present life, the senators wanted to know, which, if brought to light, could embarrass the Republican party or destroy his value as a candidate?

The freshman senator from Ohio went into executive session with himself for ten minutes. When he reappeared before his inquisitors, he swore before God and his conscience that he knew of nothing detrimental to his candidacy. That was enough for the cabal. The word was passed, and fourteen hours later on the tenth ballot the delegates nominated Warren G. Harding for President.

Word was also passed on the vice-presidential nomination. It had been offered to Hiram Johnson, who guffawed at the very idea that he could be considered as second choice to a windbag like Harding. The senators then decided that Senator Irvine Lenroot of Wisconsin would be their man.

After sitting a fourth day in the steaming tropical heat of the Chicago Coliseum, the delegates were running out of clean shirts and of patience. Much as they were anxious to escape from the Lake Michigan weather and mounting hotel bills, they were also soured on the sleight-of-hand by the senatorial cabal. As they sat listlessly mopping their faces during the dull seconding speeches after Lenroot's name had been placed in nomination, some of them were already starting for the exits. The convention was suddenly electrified by a booming voice rising above the anticlimactic confusion of departing delegates. Before the surprised chairman could call him out of order, Judge Wallace McCamant of Oregon had nominated Governor Calvin Coolidge of Massachusetts for Vice-President. The remaining delegates, only too eager for a chance to revolt against senatorial dictation, joyously made Coolidge their candidate on the first roll call, 674½ votes to 146 for Lenroot. (Six years later the senators took their revenge. When Coolidge, as President, named Judge McCamant to the federal bench, the Senate vindictively refused confirmation.)

The nomination of Calvin Coolidge, although unexpected, was not quite as spontaneous as it appeared. Considerable patient groundwork stretching back at least five years lay behind his victory at Chicago. Born in the back room of his father's country store in the tiny crossroads hamlet of Plymouth, Vermont, Calvin spent the usual circumscribed youth of a farm boy. Coaxing a living out of the grudging, stony soil of New England taught him thrift and industry. His father used to say that Calvin could get more sap out of a maple tree than anyone his size in the Green Mountains.

Young Coolidge studied law in the neighboring state to the south. He was graduated from Amherst in 1895, read law for two years in nearby Northampton, was admitted to the Massachusetts bar in 1897, and began his slow climb up the political ladder almost immediately. He negotiated the lowest rung—election to the Northampton city council—in 1899. He moved up through court clerk and city solicitor to the Massachusetts state legislature in 1907, mayor of Northampton in 1910, state senate in 1912, lieutenant governor in 1916, and governor of Massachusetts in 1919.

While he was in the state senate Coolidge attracted the attention of Frank W. Stearns, a prosperous Boston businessman. Stearns was no Harry Daugherty—politics was for him just an avocation—but he liked and admired his fellow Amherst alumnus. He apparently saw things in the unprepossessing little redhead that Coolidge himself did not see. The typically New England traits that had made Coolidge a sure vote getter in Massachusetts—frugality, caution, unimpeachable honesty, tight-lipped taciturnity—did not seem at first glance to be of great nationwide appeal. Yet Stearns, judging him presidential timber when he was still unknown outside of Massachusetts, devoted time, money, and effort to furthering his potential.

The big break came in September 1919. The Boston police force, recently unionized by the American Federation of Labor, struck for more pay and shorter hours. The Boston police commissioner ordered his men back to work, and fired those who stayed out. Governor Coolidge backed his commissioner, told him to recruit a new force, and called out the militia to keep order in Boston. When AFL president Samuel Gompers asked Coolidge to reinstate the striking cops, the governor wired back: "There is no right to strike against the public safety by anybody, anywhere, any time." The news services picked up the concise message, which found widespread approval throughout the country, and the Coolidge potentiality became a real commodity for the first time. Stearns made sure the delegates to the Republican national convention remembered the telegram eight months later.

The Harding-Coolidge campaign was unexciting. Harding stayed home in Marion. The fact that the two previous Ohioans who had conducted front-porch campaigns had died by violence while in office did not seem to bother him. Nothing seemed to bother him—certainly not the Democratic party, which seemed as sick as President Wilson and his League of Nations. True, the Versailles Treaty with its Wilsonian

League had received a majority vote in the Senate, but not the two-thirds the Constitution requires for ratification. Even with the Lodge reservations the vote was only 51 to 41. No, the country was merely anxious to get back to a full-time peace basis, to have fun and make money. The Gary strike against United States Steel to force recognition of the union was called off. The Supreme Court had decided that United States Steel was not an illegal monopoly. Attorney General Palmer had deported nearly three hundred Russians, and the anarchists Sacco and Vanzetti had been convicted of murdering a paymaster in Massachusetts. Acting under his wartime powers, Palmer had also secured an injunction against John L. Lewis and the United Mine Workers, and the bituminous-coal miners' strike had collapsed.

The senatorial bosses had ordered the front-porch campaign for Harding because they were afraid he would not follow the texts of speeches provided by the high strategists. He had a tendency to stumble over the big words. Although Harding's record in the Senate typed him as pro-business, anti-labor, and isolationist, they wanted him to straddle—gracefully, if possible—the League of Nations issue. He must offend neither the rabid isolationists, like senators Johnson, Lodge, and Borah, nor the internationalist Republican bigwigs like Hoover, Root, Taft, and Charles Evans Hughes. Both prohibition and women's suffrage were no longer issues, so Harding could just sit on his front porch and talk about getting back to normalcy.

The party strategists had planned to let second choice Calvin Coolidge do most of the speech making. Although as a personality the New England sphinx was of another breed than folksy, poker-playing, whisky-drinking Warren Harding, in political philosophy they were both good conservative mid-nineteenth-century champions of laissez-faire. The strategists started the Coolidge speaking tour in Milwaukee. However, the nasal Yankee twang and the dry, monosyllabic delivery of the vice-presidential candidate chilled and puzzled the Middle West audience. So Coolidge was shifted to the Solid South circuit, which was going to vote Democratic anyhow.

The Democratic campaign was just as dull and listless. The Democrats had less money to spend—some million and one-half, against the Republicans' more than five million—and no real issue. Cox and Franklin Roosevelt were faithful to their promise to Wilson to carry on the fight for the League of Nations, but the defeat of the League in the

Senate was a *fait accompli*, and only such Republicans as Borah and Johnson tried to keep the issue alive. There were insidious whispering campaigns, such as the allegation that Harding was of Negro ancestry, but they had no effect on the election.

The Harding-Coolidge ticket won by seven million popular votes and 404 electoral votes to 127, but more than half of the registered voters apparently went fishing.

From his front porch, Harding had promised to make use of "the best minds available," conservative minds, of course, and his Cabinet did indeed contain some well-known and able men. There were also rich men, such as Andrew Mellon, Secretary of the Treasury, whose aluminum interests were of infinitely more value than his economic advice, and Herbert Hoover, the millionaire mining engineer, in Commerce. Charles E. Hughes made a dignified Secretary of State. That Will Hays, Republican national committee chairman, should become Postmaster General was no surprise. The appointment of Harry Daugherty as Attorney General caused some raised eyebrows, even before his true character became known, but it was a foregone conclusion that the President's campaign manager would get a reward of some sort. The infelicitous (and scandalous, as it later turned out) appointment of Senator Albert Fall of New Mexico as Secretary of the Interior was confirmed by the Senate without a murmur. The fact that he was a violent anticonservationist was unimportant, as long as he was a senator. Labor Secretary "Puddler Jim" Davis held a union card, but he was generally regarded in organized labor circles as a banker at heart. Agriculture Secretary Henry C. Wallace, the father of Roosevelt's Secretary of Agriculture, Henry A. Wallace, was an Iowan and certainly a man of the soil, but he was probably more useful as a golf partner of the President's than as a friend of the farmer. What little farm-relief legislation emerged from the Harding administration was the result of bipartisan farm-bloc pressure on Congress.

One of Harding's troubles was that he depended too much on Congress; and Congress, split by factions, lacked leadership. Senator Boies Penrose was dead, and Senator Lodge was showing his age (he was past seventy). As for the House, Cannon had retired and Speaker Champ Clark was not reelected. Harding himself, incapable of providing the leadership for which he had been elected, let things slide while he devoted himself to the pleasanter things of life. While the nation was coping with bathtub gin, fulminating home brew, synthetic Scotch, and other horrors of the newly enacted Prohibition experiment, there was never a scarcity of good bonded whisky to serve at the big-money poker games in the White House.

What little semblance of a program Harding presented—adherence to the World Court, subsidies to American shipping, creation of a Department of Welfare—was rejected by Congress, and the President made no effort to revive it. He signed the Fordney-McCumber Tariff Act, raising import duties to record highs, but vetoed the Veterans' Bonus Bill. He signed the bill decreasing corporate and income taxes, but did not interfere when the newly formed Railroad Labor Board cut wages twelve per cent in 1921 and thirteen per cent in 1922. The strike of four hundred thousand shop men in protest was broken after four months. Some five hundred thousand coal miners also went out on strike for four months and were coaxed back to work with picayune concessions—without arousing any interest in the White House. The only serious labor gains during this period were the result of nongovernmental initiative: Henry Ford adopted the forty-hour week, and United States Steel cut its twelve-hour day to eight.

Action in the foreign field was instigated by Secretary Hughes rather than the White House: the formal ending of the war by separate treaties with Germany and Austria; and a Washington Conference for the limitation of armaments which resulted in the Nine-Power Treaty guaranteeing the sovereignty and independence of China, along with the Naval-Holiday Pact fixing a five-five-three ratio for capital ships among the United States, Britain, and Japan. Japan violated the first by invading Manchuria ten years later, and tried to correct the naval ratio by attacking the United States Pacific Fleet at Pearl Harbor twenty years later.

Warren Harding's catastrophic troubles actually began long before he reached the White House. His great geniality, his overwhelming desire to be loved by everybody, and his uncritical loyalty to old friends made him a deplorable judge of human nature. His naive trust in Daugherty and other of his appointees began to bear bitter fruit early in 1923.

A year previously the President had signed an executive order transferring government-held oil lands in Wyoming and California from the Navy Department to Secretary Fall's Department of the Interior. The sudden affluence which seemed to have come upon the former senator from New Mexico excited the curiosity of Senator Bob La Follette of Wisconsin and Senator Thomas J. Walsh of Montana. A Senate investigation was begun, which was also to look into rumored skulduggery in the Veterans' Bureau.

In February 1923 Charles R. Forbes, an old friend of Harding's and his appointee as head of the Veterans' Bureau, under attack for "mismanagement," submitted his resignation.

In March Forbes' general counsel, Charles F. Cramer, killed himself.

Also in March Secretary of the Interior Albert F. Fall resigned, for reasons which were not disclosed until much later.

A few weeks later Jess Smith, the close friend to whom Harry Daugherty first confided his plans to make Harding President of the United States, shot himself in the Attorney General's apartment. His suicide was also shrouded in mystery.

The smoke of suspicion which Washington had been sniffing for months was about to yield to the blazing facts of corruption. People were beginning to refer to the President's cronies as "the Ohio Gang." As the preliminary results of investigation reached the White House, Harding suffered physically. At first he could not believe that his friends had betrayed him, but the evidence of two suicides, two resignations, and what his former colleagues in the Senate were digging up was not to be denied. Harding lost weight. The gay old charmer turned somber. His doctor urged him to follow Daugherty's suggestion and take a western trip to mend fences and do a little spade work for renomination in 1924. Anything to get him out of Washington.

The President left Washington in June. He toured the Pacific Coast to Seattle, where he embarked for Alaska. He could not escape the spectre that was haunting him, however. Code messages from the capital followed him everywhere. Whenever he read one, he looked older and more haggard. The magnitude of his friends' betrayal was evidently becoming apparent.

In San Francisco he had a heart attack, and was ordered to bed for a few days. On August 2 he died in his hotel room while his wife was reading to him.

Vice-President Calvin Coolidge was spending his summer vacation at his ancestral home in Vermont. He had been doing chores and working in the fields, providing good rustic human-interest copy for the newspapers. On the day before President Harding's death, the Vice-President was "surprised" by press photographers doing a little emergency tree surgery on an arthritic maple.

That night, as on every night he spent in Plymouth, Calvin Coolidge went to bed at his customary hour of nine. He was fast asleep when President Harding died—early evening in San Francisco, but after midnight in Vermont. Getting word to the Vice-President was no simple matter, as the Coolidge homestead possessed no such newfangled inventions as electric glints and the telephone. The nearest modern device linking Plymouth and the rest of the world was a telephone at Bridgewater, a dozen winding mountain miles away on the Rutland-Woodstock road. Shortly after one o'clock a courier from Bridgewater woke up the elder Coolidge to inform him that his son Calvin was now thirtieth President of the United States.

Father John Coolidge roused his son, lit the kerosene lamps, shaved, and on instructions relayed from Washington proceeded, as justice of the peace and notary public, to administer the oath of office to his son. That homely scene in the lamp-lit Vermont parlor, with hooked rugs on the floor and framed samplers on the walls, of the bespectacled country notary swearing in his son Calvin on the family Bible, practically assured Coolidge's nomination for President in 1924. As a friend of his remarked, "A kerosene lamp is as good as a log cabin any time."

The legendary Coolidge luck was very much on the job that night. Had President Harding died a day or so later, the news would have found Coolidge a guest in the very plush home of a well-known lobbyist friend, quite a different background than that of the homespun swearing-in scene of father and son. In fact, Coolidge's visit to the lobbyist at the very moment he was to become President of the United States, with the shock troops of the press converging on him from all directions, could very well have (though it would have been unfair) brought him closer to the rather sullied image of the Harding administration.

The transfer of power to the second choice was not as drastic a change as the country had previously seen. Although Harding and Coolidge were a world apart in personality and temperament, their political philosophy was almost identical. The big, handsome, gregarious Ohioan and the slight, dour, monosyllabic Yankee were both ultraconservatives. Both were provincial. Before his nomination for the vice-presidency, Coolidge had never traveled in a sleeping car, had never ventured as far from home as Washington, D.C. Although his forebears had come to

America in 1630, no Coolidge had ever left New England to join the great westward migration. Both Coolidge and his predecessor were characters straight from the pages of Sinclair Lewis, whose novel *Babbitt* was a best seller the year of Harding's death.

Coolidge knew his way around his new job. Harding had invited him to all Cabinet meetings, and he had attended faithfully—in silence. He made no immediate Cabinet changes. The corrupt circus of "the Ohio Gang" must have deeply offended his puritanical soul and his sense of personal honesty, but he knew that his own hands were clean, and, with a political eye shrewdly cocked on the 1924 Republican national convention, he moved slowly and cautiously, on the theory that everything would blow over in time.

The winds of justice started blowing early in 1924. The government started proceedings to cancel the leases to the Teapot Dome and Elk Hills naval oil reserves which Secretary Fall had transferred to oil millionaires Harry Sinclair and Edward L. Doheny for one hundred thousand dollars in war bonds. Fall was ultimately convicted and jailed, but Sinclair and Doheny went free of charges of bribery. Sinclair was subsequently sentenced to nine months for jury tampering.

The Veterans' Bureau scandal involved some two hundred and fifty million dollars of fraudulent contracts, and Charles Forbes was sentenced to two years. The reason for the suicides of Cramer and Jess Smith became apparent. Later the conviction of alien property custodian Thomas W. Miller on charge of taking bribes to release certain German assets—deals in which the late Jess Smith profited—resulted in an indictment of Attorney General Harry Daugherty.

A joint congressional resolution asked the President to dismiss Daugherty, because his office had approved the transfer of the Teapot Dome leases. Coolidge, with his New England stubbornness, and perhaps recalling President Andrew Johnson's defiance of congressional interference in his Cabinet dismissals, turned a deaf ear. Secretary of the Navy Denby, who had innocently honored President Harding's order to turn the oil leases over to the Interior Department, took the blame on his shoulders and resigned. Attorney General Daugherty did not, despite the advice of Supreme Court Chief Justice William Howard Taft (a Harding appointee). Still Coolidge bided his time.

When, however, Daugherty refused to release Justice Department documents to the Senate investigating committee, and certain records in

Daugherty's brother's bank in Ohio mysteriously disappeared, Coolidge cut his last tie with Harding and the Ohio Gang. He finally fired Daugherty.

A few months before the Republican convention, Coolidge once more showed his stubborn courage, if not his wisdom, by again vetoing a bill for soldiers' bonuses, to be granted in paid-up insurance (Congress passed it over his veto), and in signing an Immigration Act establishing a quota based on national origins. He was spared the immediate chore of vetoing the McNary-Haugen Farm Relief Bill (which he would do later) because it was rejected by Congress.

Coolidge was renominated for President on the first ballot in Cleveland. Charles G. ("Hell and Maria") Dawes, who had been Illinois campaign manager for McKinley, controller of the currency, Chicago banker, brigadier general (procurement) in World War I, and Harding's director of the budget, was the vice-presidential nominee. Lowden had been first choice for second choice but had declined.

The Democrats took 103 ballots to nominate John W. Davis, a Wall Street lawyer from West Virginia, for the presidency. Governor Charles Bryan of Nebraska, brother of William Jennings Bryan, was his running mate.

The Democrats were handicapped at the start because the nation, through the medium of the newfangled radio, had been able to eavesdrop on their boring marathon convention. They campaigned on the issue of corruption in government, not particularly pertinent, since Coolidge was never associated with the swindlers of the Harding years. Their attacks on the high tariff and the Republicans' friendship with big business were equally ineffective, because of the country's prosperity.

The radio was favorable to the Coolidge campaign. The President's flat Vermont voice seemed made to order for the superheterodyne sets of the period, and millions got his message. The "Keep Cool with Coolidge" slogan meant no more than that the mixture would be as before. "The business of America," said the President, "is business." And he meant to get on with it.

General Dawes, with his upside-down pipe and his Hell-and-Maria bluntness, campaigned more aggressively. He attacked the Ku Klux Klan, which was becoming a political power in the Midwest, and he was not modest about the authorship of the plan for collecting German reparations which bore his name.

A third party, the Conference for Progressive Political Action, complicated the campaign by nominating senators Robert La Follette of Wisconsin and Burton K. Wheeler of Montana, but it drew most of its surprising strength from the Democrats.

The Coolidge-Dawes ticket won with nearly sixteen million popular votes to eight million for Davis and Bryan. The electoral vote was 382 to 136. The Progressives polled 4,822,856 popular votes, but only 13 electoral votes.

The President retained four Harding appointees in his Cabinet: Mellon (Treasury), Hoover (Commerce), Davis (Labor), and Hubert Work, who had taken over Interior after Albert Fall's resignation. The President replaced Secretary of State Hughes with Frank B. Kellogg. When he elevated Attorney General Harlan Stone to the Supreme Court, he sent the name of Charles Warren to the Senate for confirmation as a successor. Liberal Republicans joined the Democrats in opposing the nomination on the grounds that Warren had been snuggling up too close to the sugar monopolists—an incomprehensible reason to a man who believed big business could do no wrong. On the day when the debate promised to go on forever, Vice-President Dawes abandoned his gavel and left Capitol Hill for the Willard Hotel to take his usual afternoon nap. While he slept, the debate came to an abrupt close, and the roll call began. When it was evident that the vote would end in a tie, Dawes' secretary phoned the Willard and told the Vice-President to get dressed quickly and hurry to the Senate chamber.

The roll call ended with 40 votes favoring the Warren appointment, and 40 against. The Vice-President's vote was needed to break the tie, so the regular party-line Republicans dug up every possible parliamentary trick they could think of to delay proceedings.

When Dawes rushed puffing into the Capitol, however, he was too late. One Democratic senator had changed his "aye" vote to "nay," and there was no more tie to break.

The Senate action did nothing to increase the cordiality between the President and a majority of the senators, already at a low ebb.

Neither did it further endear Vice-President Dawes to President Coolidge. There was already a certain coolness between the two men as a result of Dawes' assuming that he would be given the same privilege that Harding had extended to Coolidge, and announcing that he would under no circumstances attend Cabinet meetings, although he had not yet so much as been invited. Dawes declared that it was bad policy to let a Vice-President in on policy decisions, because in case of a difference of opinion the President could fire a Cabinet secretary whereas he was stuck permanently with the Vice-President.

Coolidge in fact had few close friends and no confidants except his old sponsor Frank Stearns. He had heeded the advice of Andrew Mellon because a hundred million dollars, he was convinced, could do no wrong. He also had listened closely to Chief Justice Taft, another good conservative.

He did not share his thoughts or problems in matters of state with his wife, Grace Goodhue Coolidge, to whom he was indebted for saving the social life of the White House from complete disaster. Although she was Vermont born herself, she had a warm charm and graciousness that compensated at formal functions for the President's unsocial aloofness and curious fear of strangers. Even after the death of their younger son Calvin, Jr., in 1924 at the age of sixteen, Grace Coolidge kept life in the White House from reaching the level between austerity and melancholy to which the President's nature would have allowed it to sink.

She would laughingly explain some of her husband's idiosyncrasies, such as his reluctance to take off his hat. Apparently the President had an unruly lock of sandy-red hair which would fall across his forehead in the most undignified manner at the slightest provocation, and he tried to control it by keeping it under his hat. The first time she ever saw her future husband, Mrs. Coolidge used to say, he was standing by an open window, shaving, wearing only shorts and shirt—and his hat!

However stern and abstemious the life in the White House, the rest of the country was on one great spree with no thought of the morning after. The Coolidge years were characterized by Westbrook Pegler, the sports writer turned pamphleteer, as "The Era of Wonderful Nonsense." The nation, except for the farmer and the workingman, was making plenty of money and spending it freely. Detroit had never made nor sold so many automobiles (a Model T Ford cost less than five hundred dollars). Billions of dollars a year were spent for bootleg liquor (the 1926 estimate was 3.6 billion dollars). Billions more were poured into the stock market. Business got whatever business wanted, and all without a hint of bribery. Coolidge was merely expressing his faith in capitalism—he refused to penalize thrift and industry by taxes and government controls. He and Secretary Mellon ordered the Federal Reserve Board to reduce reserve requirements. Surtaxes were abolished and excess-profits and estate taxes were cut drastically to stimulate the pumping of more money into the economy. Actually the result was an increase in installment buying and speculation in land and the stock market, especially the latter.

In 1928 Congress passed Nebraska senator George Norris' bill authorizing government operation of the Muscle Shoals hydroelectric project on the Tennessee River. The dams had been built to provide power for nitrate plants during World War I, and the final disposition of the facilities had been debated ever since. Coolidge vetoed the bill because he did not believe that the government should compete with private industry. The creation of the Tennessee Valley Authority would have to await the first months of Franklin Roosevelt's administration.

Coolidge twice vetoed the McNary-Haughton agricultural relief bills, because he did not believe the farmer should be aided at the expense of the general taxpayer. Consequently farm income during the Harding, Coolidge, and Hoover administrations dropped from fifteen billion and five hundred million dollars to five billion and five hundred million dollars. By the end of the Coolidge administration forty per cent of the farms of the nation were worked by tenants, and the mortgage indebtedness on farm lands had climbed to nine billion dollars. The President apparently was not aware of what was happening.

Neither did he seem to be aware of the change that had taken place in the country's position in the world markets. Within a few years, the United States, once a debtor nation, had become a creditor nation. Our allies in the First World War all owed us money, and Coolidge was determined to make them pay. His comment, "They hired the money, didn't they?" is classic. Yet both he and Harding had raised the tariff wall higher and higher to keep out the goods the debtors would have to sell in order to earn the dollars for repayment of the loans and for buying the American wares that Secretary Hoover was making such an effort to sell abroad.

Many things happened during the Gay Twenties over which the President had no control. With Al Jolson in *The Jazz Singer,* the motion picture began to talk. New York spoke with London for the first time by radio telephone. Captain Charles Lindbergh flew solo and nonstop from

New York to Paris for the first time. Coast-to-coast air mail was established, and commercial passenger-carrying flights were begun with the Ford trimotor "Tin Goose." Admiral Byrd and Floyd Bennett flew over the North Pole. The first public demonstration of television was held in 1926, although the first public telecast would have to wait twelve more years.

In the field of foreign affairs perhaps the most spectacular accomplishment of the Coolidge administration was the Pact of Paris, popularly known as the Kellogg-Briand Pact, having originated with Secretary of State Frank B. Kellogg and French foreign minister Aristide Briand, which outlawed war as an instrument of national policy. Fifteen nations signed the treaty in Paris in August 1928, and the United States Senate ratified the pact in January 1929. Sixty-two nations ultimately signed. The treaty won the Nobel Peace Prize for Secretary Kellogg, but it did not wear well. Within ten years, Mussolini had invaded Albania and Ethiopia, Japan was making herself at home in China, and Hitler had invaded Czechoslovakia as a curtain raiser to World War II.

Coolidge finally got the Senate to vote adherence to the World Court, but with five sweeping reservations by Senator Lodge. The reservations may have been in retaliation for the President's having removed most of Massachusetts federal patronage from the senator's office, but the signatories to the Court pact accepted four of them and part of the fifth, and suggested a supplementary agreement to cover the difference. The Senate considered the action as rejection of the United States offer of adherence to the Court.

The Clark Memorandum, promulgated by the State Department in the last months of the Coolidge administration, renounced any United States claim to intervene as "international policeman" in Latin America. This abrogated the Drago Doctrine and Theodore Roosevelt's "Corollary" to the Monroe Doctrine.

The country was so bedazzled by the iridescence of the ever-expanding bubble called "Coolidge prosperity" that there is little doubt that Calvin Coolidge could have been renominated and reelected President in 1928. When, therefore, while vacationing in the Black Hills of South Dakota with a large retinue which included a company of Marines, a numerous staff, and a carload of newspaper reporters and photographers, he announced, "I do not choose to run for President in 1928," the country was incredulous and the Republican party leaders were shocked.

Getting out just before the beautiful bubble burst was sheer Coolidge luck. There is no basis for the belief in some quarters that his retirement was a shrewd, deliberate move to shift blame for the collapse of his mythical El Dorado to his successor. The panic of 1929 and the following depression must have been just as great a surprise to Coolidge as it was to Wall Street, for he had not the slightest awareness of the unsound structure he was building, nor the reasons for its disintegration.

The crisis of 1929 illuminated the unbalance in our system of distribution. The prosperity of the nineteen twenties was limited to the upper forty per cent of the population. American industry was turning out more goods than the upper forty per cent could buy, and the surplus went into savings, investment, and speculation. Not enough of the wealth seeped down to the farmer, the workingman, or the white-collar class. The Harding-Coolidge policy on war debts and protective tariffs eliminated the foreign market as a place to dispose of surplus manufactures. The growing agricultural depression reduced the farmer's buying power. The expansion of credit and easy money brought on wild speculation and unrestrained time buying.

Herbert Hoover, the Republican nominee in 1928, coasted to an easy 444–87 victory over Al Smith, largely on the basis of a continuing Coolidge prosperity, although religious bias and Governor Smith's anti-Prohibition stand no doubt hurt him in the less broad-minded areas. However, despite Hoover's slogan of "Two cars in every garage"—an extravagant paraphrase of Henri IV's promise of a chicken in the pot for every French workingman every Sunday—the nation ended up a year later with bread lines, bank failures, and Wall Street suicides.

When he left the White House, Calvin Coolidge retired to Northampton, Massachusetts, spending summers in his native Plymouth. He wrote his autobiography, and for a year turned out a syndicated newspaper column of two hundred words daily, for a sum rumored to be two hundred thousand dollars—quite a cozy amount for a frugal soul who had saved money on his Vice-President's salary. However, even two hundred words a day was apparently too arduous a task for Silent Cal, for he refused to renew the contract for a second year.

The coming of Franklin D. Roosevelt and the New Deal was a traumatic shock to the Coolidge nature, and to his social and political philosophy. It was, he said, "an era to which I do not belong." He was not with it long. On January 5, 1933, he dropped dead in his Northampton home at the age of sixty-one.

Coolidge is buried on a steep Vermont hillside not far from his birthplace. His grave is marked by a simple slab of Vermont granite bearing only the presidential seal, his name, and the dates of his birth and death.

9

THE ARISTOCRAT AND THE HABERDASHER

FRANKLIN DELANO ROOSEVELT, MARCH 4, 1933–APRIL 12, 1945.
HARRY S TRUMAN, APRIL 12, 1945–53.

But for the grace of God and the faulty marksmanship of one Giuseppe Zangara, John Nance Garner and not Franklin Delano Roosevelt would have been inaugurated as President of the United States in 1933 to preside over a nation that was standing in bread lines, besieging closed banks, selling apples on street corners, and coping with dark doubts about the efficacy of a laissez-faire economy.

The Constitution was so vague on the question of the presidential succession until 1933 that, if the assassination attempt at Miami had been made ten days earlier, and Zangara's bullets had killed President-elect Roosevelt instead of Chicago's Mayor Anton Cermak, who was riding in the same car, obstructionists and hairsplitters could well have left the country without a President. Article II, Section 1, provided that the Vice-President succeed to "the powers and duties" of the office in case of the President's death, but it made no provision for the death of a President-elect before his inauguration. The Twentieth Amendment, which made such provision, in addition to moving up Inauguration Day from March 4 to January 20, was proclaimed in effect on February 6, 1933—just nine days before the shooting at Miami. On that date thirty-nine of the forty-eight states had ratified the amendment. By October ratification was unanimous.

While it has been my contention that no Vice-President has shown his true potentialities until or unless he has succeeded to the presidency, it does not appear from the record that Garner would have been strong enough or imaginative enough to have led the nation through the critical years of the nineteen thirties. A small-town Texas lawyer of limited formal education, he had been elected to Congress for fifteen consecutive terms. In his thirty years of service, he had introduced only four pieces of legislation, and had seldom taken the floor to praise or damn. He was a congressman's congressman—gregarious, convivial, well liked, useful because of his penchant for compromise. Little known outside the capital, he achieved congressional status and stature by sheer seniority—he was minority leader in the Seventy-first Congress and finally, at the age of sixty-three, Speaker of the House in the Seventy-second Congress, succeeding veteran Republican Nicholas Longworth.

As Speaker of the House he was a natural candidate for the Democratic nomination for the presidency. He did not seek the nomination, and had little hope of attaining it, but his colleagues, notably Sam Rayburn, who was to succeed to the speakership eight years later, convinced him that it was his duty. Noblesse oblige.

Fellow Texan Rayburn became Garner's campaign manager. As chairman of the Texas delegation to the 1932 convention he had no difficulty in securing the Texas votes as a nucleus. With the help of the Hearst papers—William Randolph Hearst had finally given up his own presidential ambitions and settled for the role of President-maker—he entered Garner in the California primary and defeated both Roosevelt and Al Smith. On the convention floor at Chicago, however, Garner could not muster enough strength to break the Smith-Roosevelt deadlock. Roosevelt had a majority but lacked the two-thirds then required for nomination. After the third ballot had produced no result, Rayburn made a deal with Jim Farley and Louis McHenry Howe, Roosevelt's chief strategists, whereby Garner would release the Texas delegation to Roosevelt in return for Roosevelt's endorsement of Garner for the vice-presidency. The California delegation still balked—until Farley threatened to swing the Roosevelt vote to Newton Baker, former Secretary of War, a Wilsonian Democrat and William Randloph Hearst's *bête noire*. Rather than risk having a champion of the League of Nations in the White House, Hearst agreed to the Roosevelt-Garner ticket. And when William Gibbs McAdoo, chairman of the California delegation (also Woodrow Wilson's first Secretary of the Treasury and, incidentally, the ex-President's son-in-law) declared that California would cast its 44 votes for Franklin D. Roosevelt, there was no more contest.

When Roosevelt flew to Chicago to accept the nomination in person, he shattered the first of the many traditions that he was to break during his terms of office. In addition to being tradition breaking, the trip was intended to forestall the obvious Republican campaign gimmick: The Democratic candidate was a cripple; a vote for a hopeless invalid was a vote to make a half-baked Texas roughneck President of the United States at a crucial moment in American history. Roosevelt had had twelve years to adjust to the handicap left by an attack of polio, which had occurred shortly after his unsuccessful campaign for Vice-President on the Democratic ticket with James M. Cox of Ohio in 1920. He was still paralyzed from the waist down, and was unable to stand alone or climb stairs. Yet he was otherwise in vigorous good health, as he had demonstrated by two terms as governor of New York, and as he wanted further to demonstrate to the country by his personal appearance at the convention.

His acceptance speech rang with phrases that were to carry him to victory over Herbert Hoover (by a seven million majority of popular votes, an electoral vote of 472 to 59) and were to find a possible place in history: " . . . the forgotten man," " . . . a new deal for the American people," " . . . a crusade to restore America to its own people." The tone of his inaugural address ("We have nothing to fear except fear itself.") was reassuring. And the whirlwind action that followed left the country breathless. It also left Vice-President Garner doing what came most naturally—helping to push through Congress the President's program: the repeal of Prohibition, stabilization of farm prices, mortgage relief for the farmer, insurance of bank deposits, controls for the stock market (the Securities and Exchange Commission), unemployment relief, help for small businesses.

Although Garner tried to keep up with his old contacts and old habits—swapping yarns with his cronies and putting out bourbon and branch water in his office for the boys from the congressional press galleries, Roosevelt did his best to make him an integral part of the Administration. He brought him into Cabinet meetings. He sent him to Manila to represent the President at the inauguration of Manuel Quezon as first President of the Philippine Commonwealth. He called on him constantly to carry the word to Capitol Hill on New Deal measures that had priority.

Garner was an experienced manipulator of votes in the Congress and a loyal Democrat. He held his nose with one hand and with the other beat the drum for measures which his Texas brand of political philosophy—he might have been called a fundamentalist Southern Democrat—found revolting. He approved many of the New Deal bills, even though he did not like to dilute the word "Democrat" with qualifying adjectives—and during the first Roosevelt administration he found that he could be a loyal member of the team. He did believe that the dizzy pace of the Roosevelt program toward a welfare state was too strenuous for an old party dating back to Jefferson. He said as much, too—and learned what all his predecessors had learned before him: a Vice-President's role in policy making varies between zero and a "thanks but" from the President.

Among the priority projects that Garner was asked to shepherd through Congress during the hectic first months of the Roosevelt administration were:

*Creation of the Tennessee Valley Authority from the abandoned wreckage of the World War I power-and-nitrate project at Muscle Shoals, Alabama. New aims: developing the Tennessee River for navigation, flood control, and electric-power production, and creating improved chemical fertilizers for agriculture.
*Abandonment of the gold standard and devaluation of the dollar to about sixty cents.
*Consolidation of rural credit agencies under the Farm Credit Act.
*Legalization of 3.2 per cent beer (theoretically nonintoxicating) pending the ratification of the Twenty-first Amendment (enough states had ratified when Utah, the thirty-sixth, acted in December 1933).
*Creation of an Agricultural Adjustment Administration (AAA) within the Department of Agriculture.
*Passing of the National Industrial Recovery Act creating the NRA (Hugh Johnson, administrator), to provide codes for fair competition and collective bargaining, and the Public Works Administration (under Harold Ickes), to attack the unemployment problem.
*Recognition of the Soviet Union as the legal government of Russia. Foreign minister Maxim Litvinov came to the White House to formalize the resumption of diplomatic relations.

*Withdrawal of United States Marines from Haiti, and the release of Cuba from the terms of the Platt Amendment of 1903, which gave the United States the right to intervene in case Cuban independence were threatened; relinquishing of the United States protectorate over Panama.

*Incorporation of the Export-Import Bank with a capital of eleven million dollars.

*Passing of the Crop Loans Act.

*Establishment of the Rural Electrification Administration.

*Passing of the Social Security Act.

*Passing of the Frazier-Lemke Farm Bankruptcy Act, postponing foreclosure of farm mortgages for up to five years in some cases.

*Adoption of other recovery measures budgeted at more than ten billion dollars.

*Passing of the Wagner Act, guaranteeing collective bargaining and setting up the National Labor Relations Board.

The first years of the Roosevelt program had the conservatives gritting their teeth and muttering about "that Man in the White House," whose radical ideas were taking the country down the road to bankruptcy and socialism—not creeping but galloping socialism. The American Liberty League was organized in 1934 to combat Roosevelt and the New Deal; but, while it furnished an outlet for many angry men, it did not deter the Democratic national convention from renominating Roosevelt and Garner at Philadelphia in 1936. And the electorate gave its resounding endorsement to the New Deal in November when the Roosevelt-Garner ticket defeated the Republican Landon-Knox combination by the most decisive vote in the history of United States presidential elections. The popular vote was twenty-seven million to sixteen million, the electoral vote 523 to 8. Wags revised the old political saw, "As Maine goes, so goes the nation," to read "As Maine goes, so goes Vermont."

The flags and bunting of the second inauguration had scarcely disappeared from the streets of Washington before the sour notes in the sweet Roosevelt-Garner harmony developed into crashing discords. The great differential between the importance and the impotence of the office of Vice-President was finally made unmistakably clear to Cactus Jack Garner, and he did not like what he saw. His break with the President came in four progressive stages.

The cause of the first stage was John L. Lewis, whose bushy black eyebrows were even more magnificent than Garner's own tufted white ones. Lewis, finding his leadership of the United Mine Workers too confining for his talents, had broken with the craft-union pattern of the American Federation of Labor to form a Congress of Industrial Organizations—a vertical rather than horizontal arrangement that would accept all workers within the same industry, regardless of craft—and for which he was later tossed out of the AFL. Lewis was aiming at the unionization of the previously union-proof auto and steel industries. As a first step he had formed the United Auto Workers, which had promptly called a sit-down strike against General Motors for recognition.

The sit-down strike was something new. Called on December 30, 1936, it continued for six weeks until General Motors agreed to recognize the UAW as a bargaining agent. Garner was furious. He told the President that he was abdicating his powers to Lewis, and Roosevelt told him that he was not going to interfere at the risk of causing bloodshed. Garner's normally pink complexion went through all the intermediate shades between red and purple.

The sit-down strike became a not-too-secret weapon of labor for the rest of 1937. Of the more than four thousand strikes recorded for that year, an astonishing percentage were sit-downs. And John L. Lewis's CIO succeeded in unionizing Big Steel.

The second, and perhaps the bitterest, point of disagreement was what was euphemistically called (in Roosevelt's special message to Congress) a Bill to Reorganize the Federal Judiciary. The provisions of the bill, as carefully drawn by the White House, would empower the President to name "additional judges . . . in all Federal courts . . . where incumbent judges of retirement age do not choose to retire or resign." This would have given the President the right to appoint up to six justices, as there were that many in the Supreme Court who were past seventy and still clung to their prestigious gowns.

The thinly disguised attempt to circumvent a Supreme Court not overly friendly to the New Deal was not worthy of so astute a politician as Franklin Roosevelt. The landslide of the past November must have made him inordinately overconfident—and careless. Although "the Nine Old Men," as he called the court, had struck down more than a half-dozen of his pet New Deal measures, notably the Agricultural Adjustment Administration, the NRA and several other provisions of the NIRA, the Farm Bankruptcy Act, and the Bituminous Coal Act, Congress was deeply devoted to the constitutional principle of the separation of powers. Members of both Houses were resentful of any intrusion upon the legislative prerogatives by the White House, and they were shocked by the President's attempt to remodel the judiciary branch to his taste. Vice-President Garner was spokesman for the outraged legislators rather than for the Administration.

Roosevelt tried to make support of the "Court-packing Bill" (as his opponents called it) a matter of party loyalty. The Senate Judiciary Committee responded by withholding approval of the bill. Rather than help push the bill through the Upper House over the committee's disapproval, Garner went fishing, and ignored Roosevelt's attempts to bring him back to Washington. When Senate majority leader Joseph T. Robison dropped dead of a heart attack while trying to force the bill to the floor in the dampest, limpest, hottest part of a Washington July, the bill died, too. But not the President's antagonism against those who had opposed it.

In the 1938 congressional elections, he took to the hustings to speak in favor of opponents of those legislators who had fought against the court-packing bill. The electorate responded to the President's attempt to purge the dissenters by sending eighty-three more Republican representatives to a still-Democratic House.

The last straw for Garner was Roosevelt's decision to seek a third term, a move that so deeply offended the Texan's sense of orthodoxy that he resolved to enter the race for the 1940 Democratic nomination himself. He of course found Roosevelt too firmly entrenched.

Roosevelt's choice as a running mate to replace Garner was his Secretary of Agriculture for eight years—Henry Agard Wallace, the very antithesis of Cactus Jack. Wallace was an intellectual and a practical farmer, an idealistic visionary and a money-making editor-publisher, a pseudo-mystic and a militant crusading liberal. The son of a former Secretary of Agriculture in the Harding and Coolidge Cabinets, Henry C. Wallace, and a grandson of the Henry who founded *Wallace's Farmer and Dairyman*, the *Wall Street Journal* of the rural Midwest, Henry A. Wallace had developed a hybrid corn which revolutionized the economics of the corn-fed hog.

When word reached Chicago, site of the 1940 Democratic convention, that Roosevelt wanted Wallace, consternation struck the party professionals like a withering blast. Postmaster General Jim Farley, ranked high among Roosevelt's strategists, thought it would be "a terrible thing" if that "wild-eyed fellow" should become President of the United States. The big-city bosses could not imagine such an execrable speaker carrying on a successful campaign. The old-line politicos, who did not understand Wallace, could not see how the voters or even the delegates could understand this dreamy theorist who dabbled in Tibetan mysticism and Jewish metaphysics. When Secretary of State Cordell Hull stood firm in his determination not to accept the vice-presidential nomination, the pros tried to rally support for Senator John Bankhead, Governor Paul McNutt of Indiana—anybody but Wallace.

News of the near-rebellion of the delegates was telephoned to the White House by the President's alter ego, Harry Hopkins. Roosevelt fumed. He saw the anti-Wallace uprising as a repudiation of the New Deal and an effort by the conservative wing of the party to set the clock back. He drafted a letter declining the nomination—to be used in case Wallace were not nominated—in order to give the convention a clear choice between "social progress and liberalism, and . . . the forces of conservatism, reaction and appeasement. . . ."

The delegates got the message, swallowed hard, and nominated Wallace. The Roosevelt-Wallace ticket defeated the Willkie-McNary ticket by nearly five million popular votes. The electoral vote was 449 to 82.

When Henry Wallace became Vice-President, he refused to have the responsibilities of his office restricted to the Senate chamber: he expanded his duties to include the entire world. He made speeches about "the century of the common man." He liked to quote from his book *New Frontiers* (published in 1934, when John F. Kennedy was still in his teens), in which he described a land of scientific, artistic, and spiritual wealth to be conquered by "continuous social inventions." He wanted to share American food surpluses with the hungry everywhere and said so—a radical idea which did not seem quite so radical when it was later expressed in the Point Four program announced by Truman in his 1949 inaugural address, or in the Food for Peace and other foreign-aid programs which were to follow. Vice-President Wallace's enemies, however, derided him for wanting to give a quart of American milk to every Hottentot.

A generally controversial character, Wallace puzzled friend and foe alike by the reverse development of his ideological pattern. Most professional liberals were sympathetic to the communist experiment in Russia during its first decades, only to become disillusioned later. Wallace, however, was violently opposed to Roosevelt's recognition of the Soviet Union because of the brutal means by which Russian peasants were forced to adopt collective farming. However, when the Nazis attacked the Soviet Union in 1941, Wallace did a complete flip-flop and began a passionate love affair with the Russian people, complete with all the blind spots usually associated with a great infatuation. His appearance as speaker in New York's Madison Square Garden at a meeting of the American-Soviet Friendship Society was not out of harmony with the Administration policy. Roosevelt had already exempted Russia from the embargoes of the Neutrality Act, and had offered a billion dollars of lend-lease aid to Moscow.

Foreseeing that the United States would inevitably be drawn into Hitler's war in Europe, Roosevelt was hurrying preparations beyond the limit of theoretical neutrality. We would become the arsenal of democracy. Lend-Lease was enacted, and seven billion dollars authorized to help friendly nations. Britain was given fifty overage destroyers in exchange for the right to build American bases in British possessions. United States Marines landed in Iceland, and United States naval vessels escorted convoys as far as Icelandic waters. Shipments of oil and scrap iron to Japan were halted. More than sixteen million men were registered for the first peacetime draft in United States history. German and Italian consulates in the United States were ordered closed; and Axis funds in this country were frozen. American forces occupied Dutch Guiana, with permission of the Netherlands government in exile, to protect the aluminum-ore deposits. Roosevelt met Winston Churchill on a battleship in the North Atlantic to promulgate the Atlantic Charter, an eight-point statement of postwar aims of a country that was not actually at war.

Even before the Japanese attack on Pearl Harbor, "the day that will live in infamy," President Roosevelt, now a confirmed tradition breaker, again attempted the impossible. He tried to make of Henry Wallace something that neither tradition, nor the Constitution, nor the practical machinery of American government intended a Vice-President to be: an intrinsic cog in the executive branch. On June 30, 1941, he created an Economic Defense Board, with Henry Wallace as chairman, to coordinate all trade policies in the interests of national defense.

Wallace was given authority and power, and lost no time in using both. Once the Japanese had crippled our Pacific Fleet, and then given us a breathing spell by failing to take advantage of our wide-open Pacific Coast, the Economic Defense Board became the Board of Economic Warfare. Its function of buying strategic materials abroad overlapped previous assignments given to the Reconstruction Finance Corporation, and brought Wallace into nose-to-nose confrontation with Secretary of Commerce Jesse Jones, with whom he did not see eye to eye. And when Wallace got the President's authority to move in on the economics of Lend-Lease agreements—usually to make sure that the goods involved were not produced under substandard labor conditions—he made another enemy, Secretary of State Cordell Hull. Together with a surprising aggressiveness, for an outwardly shy person, Wallace possessed an almost incredible lack of tact. He unceremoniously trampled underfoot so many dedicated and sincere men on Capitol Hill and in the agencies that the President had to move in and establish peace by making a fresh start. He reduced Wallace to the vice-presidency again. He abolished the Board of Economic Warfare (and Wallace's job with it), and created an Office of Economic Warfare in its place. He also removed the disputed foreign procurement functions from Jesse Jones' control, but named Jones' friend Leo T. Crowley head of the new OEW.

July 15, 1943, the date of the executive order reshuffling the economic warfare agencies, marked the end of Henry Wallace's chance to become President of the United States. Despite his having become a controversial character, he was still Roosevelt's first choice for the vice-presidential nomination, should FDR decide to run for a fourth term—and there was not much doubt that he would. However, the President was either too tired, too ill, or too engrossed in plotting the last stages of a victorious war—perhaps all three—to fight for his choice. He could see for himself that Wallace was a hot potato, and the chief Democratic party wire-pullers had little difficulty in convincing him that to insist on Wallace as his running mate would split the party. Even should Wallace succeed in getting the nomination, his presence on the ticket would do irreparable harm.

I first became aware that there was a movement under way to dump Wallace some months before the 1944 Democratic convention when Eugene Casey, one of FDR's White House secretaries, came to Toledo to make a speech. Casey told me that Henry Wallace was one of the most Christlike men he had ever met, but also one of the most naive.

Unfortunately, his being Christlike was greatly outweighed by his naive approach to the political facts of life, thus limiting his usefulness to a Democratic ticket. At the time I was puzzled by Casey's meaning. It was not until several years later, when Casey was indicted in Baltimore for income-tax manipulation, tried, convicted, and sent to a federal penitentiary, that I finally understood what he meant by "naive."

Roosevelt did not cold-bloodedly dump Wallace. Instead he sent him on a mission to China which would keep him out of the country until the eve of the national convention, which was to convene in Chicago on July 19, 1944. He still felt he had a commitment to Henry Wallace, and he dictated a letter to be read to the convention by the permanent chairman, Senator Sam Jackson of Indiana. It contained these phrases:

> . . . I have been associated with Henry Wallace during his past four years as Vice President, for eight years earlier while he was Secretary of Agriculture, and well before that. I like him and I respect him and he is my personal friend. For these reasons I would vote for his renomination if I were a delegate to the convention. At the same time, I do not wish to appear in any way as dictating to the convention. . . .

Meanwhile the stop-Wallace boys were losing no time. Bob Hannegan, national committee chairman, mobilized the conservatives of all stripes—hard-shell professional Southerners, economic royalists and other Roosevelt-haters, premature McCarthyite types, and just orthodox politicos who resented the intrusion of such amateurs as Wallace into what they regarded as bread-and-butter politics. He also formed an inner circle of blue-ribbon Democrats who had a direct line to FDR's ear: Mayor Ed Kelly of Chicago, stage manager par excellence of national conventions; Ed Flynn, the erudite manitou of the Bronx, New York; Dave Lawrence of Pennsylvania, then serving his apprenticeship as kingmaker; Ed Pauley, the oil millionaire who held the purse strings of the Democratic national committee; and George Allen, secretary of the Democratic national committee.

On the other hand, Wallace had two powerful champions in Philip Murray, who had succeeded John L. Lewis as head of the CIO, and Sidney Hillman, Russian-born boss of the clothing workers' union, member of the War Production Board until a heart attack in 1942 knocked him out of government, and in 1944 chairman of the newly formed Political Action Committee of the CIO with three-quarters of a million dollars to bet on a winning—pro-labor—ticket. Murray and Hillman were for Roosevelt a fourth time, of course, but they were going to bet on Wallace until presented with an equally attractive candidate.

Hannegan et al. paraded a series of alternatives to Wallace before Roosevelt: James Byrnes, William O. Douglas, Sam Rayburn, Harry Truman, Paul McNutt, Scott Lucas, Alben Barkley, John G. Winant.

The President was drawn to Byrnes, who had spent more than half his life in government as congressman, senator, Supreme Court justice, director of the Office of War Mobilization. Unfortunately he was from South Carolina, too far south to pass muster as a liberal Democrat. Murray and Hillman stamped him as unacceptable to labor. Furthermore, Roosevelt was convinced that the fact that Byrnes, born a Catholic, had left the church in his adult years would lose Catholic votes for the ticket. Byrnes had no idea that he would be passed over.

Alben Barkley, a perennial vice-presidential possibility, got secondary mention because of his age (he was sixty-seven, five years older than Roosevelt). His loyalty to Roosevelt was questioned by some because of a blistering attack he had delivered from the Senate floor on Roosevelt's veto of a revenue bill, followed by his resignation as majority leader. However, he later withdrew his resignation, apparently believing all had been forgiven, that he was still in the running as a candidate for second place.

Sam Rayburn, who became Speaker of the House at the death of William Bankhead shortly after the 1940 convention, had for months been considered a serious contender for second choice. However, a pre-convention rift had developed in the Texas delegation. Roosevelt's "a plague on both your houses" declaration in the settlement of the Wallace-Jones feud had made Jesse Jones the rallying point for anti-Wallace conservatives who considered themselves anti-Administration. With two Texas delegations clamoring to be seated in Chicago, Rayburn withdrew his name.

Hannegan, Ed Pauley, and the others of the anti-Wallace cabal had brought the name of Harry Truman prominently and frequently to Roosevelt's attention over a period of months. It was favorably received. The President was impressed by the accomplishments of the Truman Committee, and found Truman progressive enough in his political and sociological thinking to be acceptable as a running mate. He did not, however, receive the unqualified blessing of the White House. Roosevelt declared that he would also be happy to run with Mr. Justice William O. Douglas of the Supreme Court, who was not only a known liberal in the New Deal tradition, but was fourteen years younger than Harry Truman.

So the delegates to the 1944 Democratic national convention arrived in Chicago under the mistaken impression that the choice of a vice-presidential candidate was to be an open race.

My own impression of the 1944 convention is among the most vivid of my career. Not only was it my first national convention—I was a member of the Ohio delegation—but it was probably one of the most memorable conventions in history for many reasons, some of them rather surprising. As a comparative tyro in national politics, I was fascinated by the backstage mechanics involved in the functioning of a major political party as a country-wide organism. I marveled at the twenty-four-hour spectacle of confusion and indecision, of pressure groups working at violent cross-purposes, of transparent power plays and puerile propaganda tricks, of expert intrigue and tragic personal disappointments, of overnight shifts in loyalty and passionate devotion to a principle. I was particularly impressed by the skill of the old pros, who, by their single-minded determination and sometimes dubious tactics, brought order out of chaos to achieve an end result that was in the best interests not only of the party but of the nation.

As a member of the Resolutions Committee, Harry Truman had come to Chicago some days before the convention opened. He had driven from Washington by way of Independence, Missouri, in order to pick up his wife and daughter Margaret. He had been loading suitcases into his car in Independence when his phone rang. It was Jimmy Byrnes calling from Washington to announce that the White House had given him the green light for the vice-presidency.

"Will you nominate me, Harry?" he asked.

Truman said he would be most happy to oblige.

He had hardly hung up before another long-distance call came through from Alben Barkley. He was also a candidate for the vice-presidency, and he, too, wanted Truman to place his name in nomination. Truman told him he was already committed to Byrnes.

When he arrived in Chicago, Truman not only was not a candidate himself, but he was working hard for Byrnes. On July 16 he had Sunday breakfast with Sidney Hillman and tried to sell him Byrnes. Politely, in the herring-and-sour-cream accent that had survived nearly forty years in America, Hillman said no, the Political Action Committee was still backing Wallace. Truman then wondered, if Wallace couldn't make the grade, who was PAC's second choice for second choice?

"You," said Hillman.

"I'm not running," said Truman. "I'm for Byrnes."

Truman's Monday breakfast was with Philip Murray of CIO; Tuesday he was with William Green of AFL. Both repeated the same message: if not Wallace, organized labor would support Truman. Top men of the railroad brotherhoods told him the same thing.

Harry Truman loyally reported all this to Byrnes, who seemed not at all concerned. The director of War Mobilization had arrived in Chicago fully convinced that he would be second choice. He jauntily commandeered the spacious, expensive Blackstone Hotel suite recently vacated by Tom Dewey after the Republican convention had nominated him for the presidency (and which Ed Pauley thought he had reserved for himself). Apparently Roosevelt, not wishing to wound old friends, had smilingly avoided outright rejection of both Byrnes and Barkley, and had done so with such good humor that each believed he had the President's backing. At any rate, Jimmy Byrnes was so confident that even Bob Hannegan thought Roosevelt must have changed signals.

The President was on his way to California to board a cruiser for Hawaii. The itinerary of his private train was kept secret for security reasons, but Hannegan knew it was due to pass through Chicago on the morning of July 19, the day the convention was to open. He and Pauley went to the railway yards to bring the Chief up to date on convention prospects. They told him that neither Byrnes nor Barkley was willing to withdraw, that Wallace had no chance, and that all would be total chaos unless he gave the national chairman a note—which they had previously discussed—to be used in case of emergency, expressing the presidential preference.

Roosevelt produced a few lines on White House stationery, addressed to Hannegan as follows:

> Dear Bob:
> You have written me about Bill Douglas and Harry Truman. I should, of course, be very glad to run with either of them and believe that either of them would bring real strength to the ticket.

Hannegan and Pauley were disturbed by the President's insistence on including Justice Douglas's name. In fact, they made use of FDR's endorsement of Truman for several days before releasing the text of the note, and then only after it had been amended. Hannegan talked the President into having Secretary Grace Tully retype the note so that Truman's name would appear before Douglas's.

At this point, Truman was still refusing to run, Douglas was indifferent and without an organization working for him, and Wallace was gaining strength, despite what Hannegan had told the President.

The convention was called to order later on that Wednesday, July 19. When Truman proved still adamant, Hannegan showed him the Roosevelt memo. Truman immediately went to Byrnes's palatial suite and laid the cards on the table.

Jimmy Byrnes, the little Irishman from South Carolina, was shocked He was incredulous that his decades in the service of his party and his country should end suddenly against a blank wall. He picked up the phone and placed a long-distance call to the President.

Roosevelt would not talk to him.

Byrnes understood at last. He released Truman from his promise to place his name in nomination for Vice-President, checked out of the VIP suite, and became a spectator for the rest of the convention.

By the time the preliminary formalities of the convention were over, Hannegan had overcome Truman's reluctance by telephoning Roosevelt in San Diego—the President did not refuse to talk to the national chairman—and allowing Truman to overhear FDR's booming voice declare that "if that stubborn Missouri mule wants to split the Democratic party in wartime, that's his responsibility." Truman was a candidate.

But so—very much so, in fact—was Henry Wallace. Even before a bitter Alben Barkley made his listless, unenthusiastic speech to place Roosevelt's name in nomination for President, it was obvious that organized labor was making its first big bid to exert political influence on a national scale. CIO's Political Action Committee especially had done a pretty fair job of placing delegates on the floor, and a magnificent job of packing the galleries. After Barkley's speech nominating Roosevelt, the sound and fury lasted for half an hour, but the demonstration was about as spontaneous as the nomination was surprising. However, when Wallace strode to the microphone to make an unscheduled and unexpected seconding speech (which was in effect a plea to the party not to abandon the liberal principles of the New Deal), the response from the floor and the galleries was deafening.

Roosevelt won on the first ballot, 1086 to 89 for Senator Harry Byrd of Virginia.

The evening session of Thursday, July 20, saw the convention come within a split hair of capture by pandemonium and the CIO. The President's acceptance speech was to be delivered by remote control from San Diego. Hannegan and Pauley, who were running the convention, hoped to get to the vice-presidential nominations immediately afterward. They had to abandon their plans.

Someone in the Wallace camp had printed thousands of counterfeit tickets of admission to the galleries, which were jammed to the aisles with banner-waving Wallace-ites as soon as the doors were opened. More thousands bowled over a guard and stormed another entrance to overrun the floor, usurp seats belonging to the delegations, and block the aisles. There were probably close to thirty thousand persons crowded into space intended for twenty thousand. An organist, who had been handed a program and a timetable, was somehow induced to begin playing an hour ahead of schedule, and the public-address system boomed out "Iowa, That's Where the Tall Corn Grows," the Wallace battle hymn, until the party kingpins were tearing their hair.

It was obvious that an organized plan to stampede the convention for Wallace was under way. The nomination of Truman would have been impossible during this night of pandemonium, even with Roosevelt backing, and it was my definite impression that Roosevelt would have been perfectly willing to run with Wallace. At that point in history, the President was so involved with the problems of war and peace, the atomic bomb, and the future of the Grand Alliance that the question of his running mate was really of minor importance. He did have definite ideas of men with whom he would *not* run, and the party kingpins knew the names. However, I really believe that Roosevelt would have run not only with Wallace or Truman, but with Rayburn, Kerr, Lucas, Douglas, or any of several others. The real champions of Harry Truman were Bob Hannegan and Ed Pauley, and their strength lay in the fact that the big delegations recognized their relationship with the White House: if they were not actually speaking for Roosevelt, at least they were not acting against his wishes.

As soon as the too-brief period of applause following the Roosevelt acceptance speech had died away, the stampede was on. Cries of "We want Wallace!" became a chorus. The interlopers shrieked in the galleries, paraded on the floor, snake danced in the aisles, and flaunted their Wallace banners everywhere. The organist pulled out all stops as "Iowa, That's Where the Tall Corn Grows" thundered from the loudspeakers. The situation was rapidly getting out of hand.

The convention stage managers—who also happened to be the Truman high command—decided that it was time to fight fire with fire. Pauley sent a man with an axe to the organ console with orders to disconnect the organ from the public-address system unless the organist left the Iowa cornfields immediately. Hannegan ordered the outer doors opened to the overflow crowd, hoping that the unorganized influx would choke off the demonstration by the organized interlopers. He was successful. Women screamed and fainted, men grunted, ribs cracked, marchers stumbled over upset chairs, the rhythm of the rebellion was broken. Mayor Ed Kelly told Hannegan that he would authorize the adjournment of the session because the overcrowding violated Chicago fire laws. Pauley found a delegate who would move for adjournment because the delegates were unable to reach their seats.

What the delegate said and what permanent chairman Jackson said were lost in the din and confusion. A few shouts of "No, no!" arose from the crowd as Hannegan crossed the platform to whisper something in Jackson's ear. The chairman immediately banged down his gavel and declared the session adjourned.

Hannegan had headed off the Wallace stampede, but he was still a long way from making Harry Truman the second choice. He called his staff into emergency nocturnal session, to agree on strategy. It was indeed a solemn gathering: the frail, handsome, anemic-looking Hannegan (he had not many more years to live), who was convinced that the 1944 convention was about to nominate a President of the United States, not merely a Vice-President; Ed Pauley, outwardly calm but inwardly just as violently determined to sidetrack a man he did not believe fit to become President; George Allen, the rotund, jocund jester who for once was without a quip; Ed Flynn, whose Broadway-style clothes were more appropriate to a character out of Damon Runyon than to the thoughtful, Bronx savant he was reputed to be. Ironically, it was these same men, four years earlier, who had induced a hostile convention reluctantly to accept Henry Wallace as second choice because the President wanted him, and who now were determined to persuade another convention inclined toward the same Wallace that Harry Truman was the better man—also because the President wanted him.

The key to defeating Wallace, Hannegan was convinced, lay with the dozen favorite-son candidates. If he could convince the favorite sons that they should release their pledged delegates to Truman, the nomination would be in the bag. The task, however, was not an easy one. With the two leading candidates sharing almost equal strength, a deadlock could well develop, and the nomination might fall to a compromise candidate. Every favorite son thus considered himself a possible dark horse. Hannegan put his men to work to convince them otherwise.

The persuaders worked hard through the night and during the morning session, while nominating speeches were being made. On Pauley's list of favorite sons was Senator John Bankhead of Alabama. As Alabama was first on the alphabetical roll call by states, a switch of votes from Bankhead to Truman at the outset could very well start the bandwagon rolling. Senator Bankhead, however, was stubborn. He thought he wanted to ride along for at least one ballot before releasing his delegates, but promised to think it over.

There was a steady parade of governors, senators, and state chairmen through Hannegan's and Pauley's offices underneath the stage while the nominating speeches were being made overhead. Senator Bennett Clark's nomination of Truman stirred no tumultuous excitement except for the Missouri delegation. The demonstration for Iowa's Judge Richard Mitchell's nomination of Henry Wallace evoked more enthusiasm from the galleries than on the floor. The seconding speeches that followed were of the same tenor as the violent attack on the enemies of progress and the party dictators in their smoke-filled rooms by Dick Frankensteen, a United Auto Workers official and a member of the Michigan delegation. I remember that Frankensteen's speech lambasting the political bosses for trying to unseat Wallace got a tremendous ovation from the galleries but did little to help Wallace's cause among the delegates.

A dozen favorite-son candidates were nominated, notably Bankhead of Alabama, Barkley of Kentucky, Scott Lucas of Illinois, Paul McNutt of Indiana, and Robert Kerr of Oklahoma. And they were all staying hopefully through the first ballot.

Just as the voting was about to begin, Senator Bankhead came to Ed

Pauley's subterranean headquarters to announce that he had decided to release his delegates to Truman. Pauley rushed to the platform to ask Chairman Jackson to delay the roll call, but Alabama had just been called, and, before he could reach the rostrum, Alabama had voted for Bankhead.

The Alice-in-Wonderland atmosphere of the convention prevailed through the first ballot. The Ohio delegation had caucused before the voting session opened, and a majority of the delegates were still supporting Wallace. Yet when the roll call reached Ohio, Ray Miller, who was acting as chairman of the delegation, stepped to the microphone and cast Ohio's entire vote for Truman. Immediately Jack Kroll, a delegate who was more important in national labor affairs than in Ohio politics, leaped up and tried to grab the microphone. As Miller pushed him off and the two men tussled, Ohio had been recorded as voting for Truman, and the roll call proceeded down the alphabet.

The first ballot gave Wallace a plurality over Truman of 429½ to 319½, but no majority. The favorite sons, with nearly four hundred delegates voting for them, held the balance of power. Most of them clung to it, too, through the first roll call of the second ballot. Even Mayor Kelly of Chicago, who was committed to vote Illinois for Truman, was still backing Scott Lucas on the second ballot. The break came with Maryland. Then Oklahoma's Kerr, who had been hopefully hoarding the popularity accruing from his keynote speech, with obvious regret released his delegates to Truman, making, with Maryland, 40 more votes for the Missourian. Next Paul McNutt withdrew and Indiana gave Truman 22, Wallace 2. The swing was on. The bandwagon was moving so fast that state delegations fell over each other in the rush to caucus and jump aboard before they were crushed in the stampede. New York, a Wallace state, 93 for Truman. . . . Massachusetts, 34 for Truman. . . .

I shall never forget the expression on Jimmy Byrnes's face when the 16 Kansas votes definitely gave to the man who had promised to sponsor him the prize he had coveted. Byrnes had been in and out of the box where he sat with impassive dignity beside Bess and Margaret Truman, but, as the critical moment approached, he had rejoined the South Carolina delegation on the floor. He was sitting not far from the Ohio delegation, so I had a close look at his face when the Kansas vote was announced. He suddenly appeared smaller than ever, and for a fleeting instant his features seemed contorted in a classic mask of frustration.

Had a photographer caught him in that unguarded moment, the picture could have served as an all-time portrait of a politician watching a lifetime ambition snuffed out in one tragic second.

The final count gave Truman 1,031 votes. Only 105 delegates remained loyal to Wallace until the end.

Hannegan and his pros had done their work well—better, I suspect, than most of them realized. Their prime purpose was to eliminate Henry Wallace as a possible President of the United States. Not many, without FDR's instinct and insight, would have picked the little man from Missouri, with his bespectacled, double-breasted, bourgeois façade, to be the true protector of the Rooseveltian faith. Yet out of all the confusion and fumbling of the democratic process, the convention had picked the best man for second choice. Even Sidney Hillman, who had very nearly engineered the nomination of Henry Wallace as the Democratic candidate for Vice-President, admitted to Jonathan Daniels a year later that Wallace was really an ineffective leader.

For Franklin Roosevelt's historic fourth assault on the bastion of the United States presidency, he was thus yoked to as unlikely a running mate as he had been in his first crusade. The country squire of Hyde Park, the Hudson Valley aristocrat with a dozen forebears among the *Mayflower* passengers, was to the manor born. Educated by tutors and European travel until he entered Groton and Harvard (Phi Beta Kappa, editor of *The Crimson*), he had an impressive political career. He had been a state senator in New York, Wilson's Assistant Secretary of the Navy during the First World War, unsuccessful Democratic candidate for Vice-President in 1920, governor of New York (1928–32), and three times President of the United States.

On the other hand, Harry S Truman (the S was not an abbreviation, but a compromise between the names of both grandfathers—Shippe and Solomon) was, so to speak, to the farm born. He made his entry into the world on his parents' farm near Lamar, Missouri, and grew up with a pitchfork in one hand and a milking stool in the other. After attending public school, he tried his hand at odd jobs in Kansas City—a year on the Kansas City *Star*, another as a railway timekeeper, and a whirl as a helper in a bank. At the age of twenty-two he returned home to run the family farm for eleven years. Meanwhile he had joined the National Guard—bad eyes since the age of nine kept him out of West Point—and when the Guard was federalized with the entry of the United States into

World War I in 1917, Truman went overseas as a captain with the 129th Field Artillery. He saw combat in France, and won the reputation among his battery mates as the fastest calculator of trajectories (there were no computers doing the work then) in the American Expeditionary Force. He was discharged with the rank of major.

A civilian again at the age of thirty-five, Harry Truman made two important decisions: He married his grade-school sweetheart at a modest church wedding in Independence, Missouri (at Franklin Roosevelt's wedding, the bride was given away by the President of the United States, her uncle, Teddy Roosevelt); and he went into business with a sergeant from his battery. The Truman-Jacobson haberdashery in Kansas City failed, but Truman refused to go into bankruptcy. Instead he paid off all his debts over a period of years.

Truman's rural background led him into rural politics. He became a Jackson county commissioner, with the title of "judge," and handled millions of dollars building highways and a new courthouse. His record of handling public funds without the slightest smudge of sticky fingers attracted the attention of Tom Pendergast, notorious boss of the malodorous Kansas City Democratic machine. In 1934 Pendergast was warding off attacks of a hostile press that had been digging up stories of graft, corruption, and election frauds and laying them at The Boss's door. At the same time he was trying to extend his influence, and he was in dire need of an untarnished Democratic candidate for a seat in the United States Senate, someone whose honesty was unimpeachable, untainted by contact with the city machine. Harry Truman was just the man.

At fifty, Truman was still paying off the debts of his ill-fated haberdashery. Since his mother had lost the family farm to foreclosure, he and his wife had been living with his mother-in-law in Independence. He jumped at the chance for a senator's salary and won. After an undistinguished first term, he ran for reelection in 1940.

The second race was a squeaker. Boss Pendergast was in jail on an income-tax charge. His machine had stripped its gears and blown a gasket. Some of his chief mechanics were in jail or under indictment. A reform governor had cut the spurious electoral lists down to size. Two reform candidates were running against Truman. Yet with the help of Bob Hannegan, who was to bludgeon him into accepting the vice-presidential nomination four years later, Truman was reelected.

His 1940 campaign gave him a chance to examine some of the results of defense spending in his own state. He was appalled by what he found in Pulaski County. The waste, duplication, graft, and confusion that went into the construction of Fort Leonard Wood were reminiscent of the situation he had uncovered years before in Jackson County road building. As a member of the Senate Appropriations Committee he had previously made an automobile tour of military camps from New Jersey and Pennsylvania to South Carolina and Georgia, and found similar inefficiency.

On February 10, 1941, the day the House had voted to raise the national debt limit to sixty-five billion dollars, Truman arose in the Senate to propose a Special Committee to Investigate the National Defense Program. His suggestion was adopted, he was made chairman, and the committee given the munificent budget of fifteen thousand dollars. However, the watchdog committee turned in such impressive reports as the nation's industry swung over to a total war footing that the second budget was one hundred thousand dollars. The Truman Committee, as it came to be known, won the respect and admiration of business and government agencies alike. Furthermore, it was a perfect example of bipartisanship in action: all of its forty reports were unanimous. And for a total of three hundred and sixty thousand dollars expended, the committee saved the taxpayers fifteen billion dollars.

The record of the Truman Committee made a useful pendant to a history that was meager except for its reputation of integrity—a bare minimum, it would seem, for a man seeking the second highest office in the land. Truman campaigned alone, with Democratic national committee secretary George Allen at his elbow to prompt him on the technique of coast-to-coast electioneering. He drew small crowds, but he felt perfectly at home with them because he identified with them. In fact, the unprepossessing, unassuming little man, the farmer turned unsuccessful businessman, the county judge who spoke of commonplace things in a flat, midwestern voice had a great appeal to the voter whom Roosevelt called "the forgotten man."

There is little doubt, however, that it was the Roosevelt magic that defeated governors Tom Dewey of New York and John Bricker of Ohio. The millionaire champion of the ill-fed, ill-clad, ill-housed third of the nation had a built-in charm that neither his opponents nor his running mate could equal. In twelve years the electorate had grown so used to his person, tall and imposing despite his useless legs; the jaunty angle of his cigarette holder, the boxing-glove chin, the warm, resonant voice with the Harvard accent that could persuade anyone except perhaps the "economic royalists," that even if there had been no question of changing commanders in mid-war it is doubtful that Roosevelt could have been defeated in 1944. As it was, the Roosevelt-Truman ticket triumphed over the Republicans by three million and six hundred thousand popular votes and an electoral vote of 432 to 99.

When Harry Truman took the oath of office on January 20, 1945, at the White House, just below what would later become known as "the Truman balcony," he was less than three months away from becoming President of the United States at one of the most critical moments in world history. The ceremony was held at the White House instead of on the Capitol steps because (officially) the grim spirit of wartime required stark simplicity, but probably (unofficially) to spare the President's ebbing strength. In any case, Truman approached the overwhelming responsibility with less equipment, training, and awareness than had any American Vice-President before him.

It has always been my contention that the presidency is an office needing tremendous capabilities which not all elected Presidents have been able to fill; and that the vice-presidency is an office requiring no capabilities whatever, regardless of what potential the Vice-President may possess. Many Vice-Presidents have had great capacity, unrealized in the vice-presidency, which may expand to its full possibilities when or if these men are given the power of the chief executive. In my opinion, Harry Truman is the living proof of this premise.

Roosevelt allowed Truman to sit in on Cabinet meetings, but they were few and far between. The Vice-President had only a few private meetings with his chief, and most of them concerned chores which the presiding officer of the Senate was to discharge on Capitol Hill. One of these was to ease confirmation of Henry Wallace as Secretary of Commerce through a resentful Senate. Wallace had campaigned loyally for the Roosevelt-Truman ticket and as a reward was offered a Cabinet job. When he chose to be Secretary of Commerce, thus replacing his erstwhile enemy Jesse Jones, a chorus of screams arose from the anti-Wallace senators. It took all of Truman's skill to quiet the rebellion.

When Roosevelt took off for Yalta on a month-long trip to confer with Churchill and Stalin, the Vice-President was aware of his agenda only in the most general terms. The three world leaders were to plan the final stages of the European war, now approaching an Allied victory; arrange for the control and occupation of Germany, and for the entry of the Soviet Union into the Pacific war; set a date for the organization of the United Nations; and make other postwar agreements which Stalin was later blithely to repudiate.

When the President returned to Washington, Truman must have felt a chill of apprehension. Intimates were shocked at Roosevelt's gaunt appearance. Even those who did not see him but listened to the radio broadcast of his report to Congress—the speech in which he apologized for remaining seated and for the first and only time referred to his iron braces—could not help remarking the utter weariness in the once-golden voice, and the occasional slurring of syllables as by someone drunk, exhausted, or in the first phases of a cerebral "accident."

In his *The Man from Independence,* Jonathan Daniels indicates that Truman, even before he became Vice-President, was aware that Roosevelt would probably not live to finish his term. Edward McKim, Truman's old Battery D sergeant, who had become an Omaha insurance executive, had come to Washington to make plans for accompanying the vice-presidential candidate on his coast-to-coast campaign tour. Truman took McKim to a White House reception, and as they left, the ex-sergeant stopped on the sidewalk and said to the ex-battery commander:

"Hey, bud, turn around and take a look. You're going to be living in that house before long."

Truman looked back at the classic columns of the stately façade.

"Eddie, I'm afraid I am," he said. And later he added, "And it scares the hell out of me."

The massive cerebral hemorrhage that killed the President struck late in the afternoon of April 12, 1945, at Warm Springs, Georgia, where he had gone to work on his Jefferson Day address. The Senate had just adjourned for the day when Harry Truman was summoned to the White House for what he expected to be another routine Capitol Hill assignment. When Mrs. Roosevelt informed him that since four thirty-five in the afternoon he had been President of the United States, he was stunned. Although he had not been unaware of Roosevelt's decline, he was aghast at the magnitude of the duties and responsibilities—many of them unknown to him previously—which had suddenly been thrust upon him. The much-quoted request he made of the White

House correspondents next day summed up his first reactions: "Boys, if you ever pray, pray for me."

President Truman took the oath of office that evening in the White House. It was administered by Harlan F. Stone, Chief Justice of the Supreme Court. As he swore to uphold the Constitution of the United States and defend it against all enemies, domestic or foreign, Harry Truman's self-doubts, shock, and stage fright were not only genuine but warranted. He had inherited the job of winding up a global war of which he, as Vice-President, was shockingly ignorant, both as to details of strategy and as to postwar plans. He knew of course that the American forces had crossed the Rhine, that the United States First and Ninth armies had encircled more than three hundred thousand Germans in the Ruhr, and that the trap was about to be closed. He knew that the United States Tenth Army, with heavy Navy support, was committed to secure Okinawa at heavy cost as a base for the final assault on Japan's main islands. But he knew nothing of the Manhattan Project, the experiments at Alamogordo, New Mexico, or the existence of the atomic bomb, which he would have to decide to use—or not use—in the Pacific, since the European war was apparently won. He had to learn all that a President of the United States should know about a war in progress from such subordinates to the commander in chief as Secretary of War Stimson and chief of staff George Marshall. He was told about the atomic bomb and how the first tests would be made, probably within three months. For the inside story of the Pacific war he was stymied by the reluctance of some freewheeling theater commanders to keep Washington abreast of events. He found that General Douglas MacArthur had sent a special courier with advance recordings of his "I have returned!" speech, which he would deliver on his Leyte landings in the Philippines, to the Voice of America studios in New York—at the very time Washington was frantically trying to contact the general. He cross-examined Secretary of State Edward Stettinius on postwar commitments and problems and discovered what everybody knew: that President Roosevelt had been his own Secretary of State.

On the domestic side Truman felt more at home, for as a senator he had participated in eight years of the Franklin Roosevelt Revolution, the greatest socioeconomic upheaval since the days of Theodore Roosevelt. He not only knew and sympathized with FDR's program, but was ready and willing to carry it forward.

Overawed though he was, Harry Truman lost no time in coming to grips with his new job. He had been President barely two weeks when he played host (by radio) to the representatives of forty-six countries meeting in San Francisco to organize the United Nations. The murder of Mussolini, the suicide of Hitler, and the surrender of Nazi Germany all followed each other before the end of his first month in the White House. At three months he crossed the Atlantic to confer with Churchill and Stalin at Potsdam on the problem of postwar Germany. A British general election midway through the conference retired Churchill in favor of a Labor government, and Clement Attlee returned to Potsdam to represent Britain. Twenty years later the problem of Germany is still unsolved, but Potsdam was extremely useful to Harry Truman. It was his first experience in power politics and foreign affairs, and it gave him a chance to size up Stalin and the Russians at first hand.

Sitting across the table from the vodka-drinking Stalin left President Truman, an old bourbon man himself, with a feeling of uneasiness. To the Missourian doubter, the Soviet dictator, likable though he was, was not a man to be trusted. This instinctive opinion was to determine two decisions that would affect the history of the world: the dropping of the atomic bomb, and the formulation of the pattern of Soviet containment as the foreign policy of the United States.

By this time, of course, Truman had been made fully aware of the progress, potential, and purpose of the atomic bomb. The first test of the bomb had been made at Los Alamos, New Mexico, the day before the Potsdam conference opened on July 17, 1945. It had been successful, a fact that Truman decided not to share with the Russians. The conference, however, did issue a joint declaration on July 26, calling upon Japan to surrender unconditionally or face complete destruction from the air. The Japanese text of the ultimatum was printed on leaflets and dropped over Japanese cities next day by B-29s, although no mention was made of the terrible new weapon which was to achieve the "complete destruction."

The ethical question of whether or not the atomic bomb should have been dropped at Hiroshima is still being debated by academic second-guessers twenty years after the fact. Harry Truman, faced with an immediate decision, undoubtedly weighed the military and political factors first, before considering the ethics of using a new weapon hitherto unknown to man. The siege of Okinawa, which lasted from April 1, before he became President, until June 21, when the last Japanese resistance there ceased, certainly gave weight to the military estimate that a final triphibian assault on the main islands of Japan would cost anywhere from five hundred thousand to one million American casualties. Okinawa, with heavy naval and air support for the United States 10th Army, was won at the cost of nearly eighty thousand American casualties. The immediate factors to be considered were whether shortening the war and saving a half-million American lives would not counterbalance X thousand Japanese casualties. For an American President, there could not be two answers. The question of responsibility for breaking open the gates to the Atomic Age was not to be considered at this point, inasmuch as German scientists had long been working on the problem of nuclear fission, and were quite possibly continuing their work in Russian custody.

Having met Stalin, Truman was ready to use any device that would bring about Japanese surrender before the Russians could enter the Pacific war.

The B-29 *Enola Gay* dropped the first atomic bomb on Hiroshima, a city of war industries, at eight-thirty on the morning of August 6, 1945. An estimated sixty thousand persons died.

On August 7 the Soviet Union declared war upon Japan.

More leaflets were dropped from American planes on Japanese cities, warning of further destruction. As Tokyo apparently still failed to get the message, another bomb was dropped on Nagasaki on August 9, with the same appalling result.

On August 10 Tokyo sued for peace. On August 14 President Truman announced the Japanese surrender. The formal capitulation was not signed until September 2 aboard the U.S.S. *Missouri* in Tokyo Bay.

President Truman has been criticized for the haste with which he dismantled the most magnificent fighting organization history has ever known—more than fifteen million men armed with the best equipment the world's leading industrial power could turn out. However, Truman was under terrific pressure from members of Congress, who in turn were under pressure from fifteen million mothers who wanted their boys home the day before yesterday, to say nothing of the hundred million civilians who wanted new cars, steaks without rationing, and the general reconversion of the economy to peacetime purposes.

Still, Truman himself was already thinking in terms of a peaceful world. The day after the announcement of Japanese surrender, the OPA ended the rationing of gas and oil. And on September 6 the President sent to Congress his twenty-one-point domestic program, which was in effect an extension of Franklin Roosevelt's New Deal.

Early in 1946 he announced that, because of the increase in the cost of living since the prewar norm of 1941, labor was entitled to a thirty-three per cent increase of wages. The declaration set off an outcry in expected quarters, and a series of strikes which the President did not welcome. During 1946 there were one hundred sixteen million man-days lost because of work stoppages. The Missouri mulishness of Harry Truman insisted on making it clear to labor leaders like John L. Lewis that his declaration was not giving them carte blanche to take over the economy of the United States. When Lewis pulled out four hundred thousand bituminous-coal miners in May of 1946, Truman took over the soft-coal mines. The strike was settled a week later on Truman's terms. When the railway brotherhoods threatened to strike—and did after he had ordered the railways seized by the government—he set the wage increase he thought was fair and gave the brotherhoods until five o'clock of the afternoon of May 24 to decide on it. The brotherhoods settled.

Despite his political preoccupation with domestic issues, Truman was not unaware of his responsibility for the Pandora's box he had opened when he unleashed atomic energy for the first time. On January 7, 1946, he created a Committee on Atomic Energy in the State Department, with Dean Acheson as chairman. Two weeks later an Atomic Energy Commission was created in the United Nations (Bernard Baruch was named United States representative) for the purpose of limiting the use of atomic energy to peaceful purposes. The Soviet Union (working on its own atomic research, and expecting to break the American monopoly with the help of American communists) sabotaged the Baruch plan.

We shall never know how Franklin Roosevelt would have handled the Russian acrobatic evasion of the Yalta agreements had he lived. Despite the charges by his enemies that Roosevelt was mentally incompetent at the time of Yalta and was completely taken in by Stalin, Averell Harriman, who had undertaken several Roosevelt missions to Moscow and who was present in the Crimea, has declared that he warned FDR of the Russian intentions and that the President was quite aware of the situation. How he would have reacted is of course anybody's guess.

The Truman reaction, however, was one that nobody would have expected from a President-by-accident whose previous contact with foreign affairs consisted largely in commanding Battery D, 129th Field Artillery, 35th Division of the AEF, to lob shells into the German lines in the Vosges, the Meuse-Argonne sector, and the St. Mihiel salient in 1917–18. When it became apparent that Stalin was creating a *cordon sanitaire* between the Soviet Union and Western and Central Europe and the Near East, Truman decreed that our national security required that we set up our own cordon to contain the further expansion of the Soviet cordon.

He kicked Secretary of State Stettinius upstairs to head the United States delegation to the United Nations and made his friend Jimmy Byrnes (whom he had always believed should have been the rightful heir to the presidency) Secretary of State. He tried to keep the reins of foreign policy in his own hands, however. When Secretary of Commerce Henry Wallace in a New York speech criticized the Administration's foreign policy, as exemplified by Byrnes's "tough" line with Russia, Truman asked for and received Wallace's resignation from the Cabinet. And when Byrnes himself seemed to be freewheeling in his dealings with Moscow, Truman replaced him with General George Marshall.

United States–Soviet relations continued to deteriorate. When the expansionist policy of the new Russian imperialism showed itself in northern Iran and in Greece, Truman wasted no time in making counter moves. He asked Congress (which at war's end had discontinued Voice of America broadcasts to Greece and Turkey to save some hundred thousand dollars) for four hundred million dollars in aid to Greece and Turkey, and he sent American military advisers to help put down the Greek communist uprising. When the Russians stymied efforts to write peace treaties with Italy, Hungary, Finland, and the Balkan nations allied to the Axis, he put into effect the Marshall Plan to speed recovery of the Western European nations. And when Soviet diplomacy wrecked efforts to write a German peace treaty and the Red Army refused the Allies all land access to Berlin in an effort to force abandonment of the former German capital, Truman ordered the Berlin airlift into operation until the blockade was discontinued.

On the home front Truman was not doing as well. Rising prices, widespread labor trouble, and housing shortages had cut the President's popularity, according to the Gallup poll, to one-half of the high point, reached shortly after Roosevelt's death. The feeling was reflected in the 1946 congressional elections, which gave the Republicans a majority of eight seats in the Senate and fifty-eight in the House.

The new Congress (the Eightieth) joyously kicked to death some of President Truman's pet projects, took no action on others, and repassed over his veto such measures as the Taft-Hartley labor relations bill, with its odious (to labor) clause limiting the union shop. As the 1948 presidential year approached, the pollsters, the political pundits, and even the dejected party professionals predicted a Democratic disaster. President Truman, titular head of the party, could not be denied the presidential nomination if he wanted it, and apparently he did. But he was a President by accident; he would never have been considered of presidential timber in 1944 had not Roosevelt still been alive and in the running. Was there any reason why he should be of presidential timber now, four years later? There certainly was, but the pros had been strangely blind to the qualifications he had demonstrated in his nearly four years as accidental President.

When the gloomy delegates, who had been reading the papers, met in Philadelphia in July 1948 to go through the motions of nominating, cheering, and parading, they were unexpectedly electrified by the little guy from Missouri, the artillery captain whom nobody knew and whom nobody had really wanted except the chairman of the national committee, and, by osmosis, President Roosevelt. The nomination for the vice-presidency of old Senator Alben Barkley (he was past seventy) did nothing to raise party enthusiasm, despite his long-term popularity.

The early tedium of the convention was broken only by minor incidents. The Ohio delegation was supporting favorite son William Julian. The convention was noisy and turbulent. The late Ray T. Miller, delegation chairman, had been selected to place Julian's name in nomination. At the conclusion of his well-delivered speech, replete with the traditional "the man who," he had worked himself up to a tub-thumping climax to announce the name of this great American, when his mind went blank. He forgot the name of the man he was nominating. Despite helpful shouts of "Julian" from his delegation, the name finally came to him only after what seemed an eternity.

But when Harry Truman took the podium past midnight, to make an acceptance speech after the one-man show by Barkley—who had made a stirring keynote speech, was the convention chairman as well as vice-presidential nominee—he startled the convention into spontaneous enthusiasm by declaring that he and Barkley would win—and why.

The Republican party, he said, had always been a party of privilege and for the privileged, and the Eightieth Congress, the Republican "Do-nothing" Congress, had proved it. The Republican Congress, he declared, had failed the common man by ignoring the consumer in favor of the profit-making producer and middleman; by not passing the Taft-Ellender-Wagner housing bill to substitute decent dwellings for urban slums; by passing the Taft-Hartley bill instead of "moderate legislation to promote labor-management relations"; by leaving untouched the minimum wage and proposals to improve social security; and by doing nothing about the all-important civil-rights bill or providing proper medical care for the elderly. (President Lyndon Johnson nearly twenty years later paid tribute to Truman's pioneering by flying to Independence, Missouri, in July 1965, to sign the Medicare Bill in the Truman Library in the presence of the eighty-one-year-old ex-President.)

Truman ended his acceptance speech by announcing that he would call "that worst Eightieth Congress" into special session—to put the Republican party on the record.

At the height of the Truman demonstration that followed, Secretary of the Treasury John Snyder was occupying a box near the Ohio delegation. When the din was at its loudest, I saw the dignified Cabinet member standing on a chair in his box, vigorously tinkling a very tiny dinner bell. The resulting tinkle could hardly have been heard by Snyder himself above the general uproar.

The Democratic convention, however, ended on a note of discord. At the insistence of Minneapolis mayor Hubert Humphrey the delegates inserted a stronger civil-rights plank in the platform, praised Truman's courageous stand, and called on the Congress to carry out the President's program to abolish the poll tax and segregation. The Mississippi delegation and half of Alabama stalked off the floor to form the Dixiecrat party and nominate South Carolina governor J. Strom Thurmond for President as a champion of states' rights and white supremacy.

Henry Wallace also formed a new "Progressive Party," which promptly nominated him for the presidency on a program of pro-labor, antimonopoly, "human rights above property rights," pro-United Nations and pro-peaceful understanding with the U.S.S.R. He was applauded in Moscow and adopted by the United States Communist party as its own presidential candidate. In his political naïveté, Wallace sincerely believed that as an independent he could carry with him his not-inconsiderable liberal backing. Before the polls opened, however, he realized that his campaign had been captured by the Communists, and, although he polled more than a million popular votes, he disappeared from the political scene.

The Republican ticket of New York governor Tom Dewey and former California governor (later chief justice) Earl Warren made the mistake of believing the pollsters, who gave them an odds-on victory, and the political pundits, who predicted a Republican landslide. They coasted along on a sort of back-to-normalcy theme, Democratic incompetence to cope with inflation and communism, and the superiority of private enterprise over government initiative and such radical concepts as public power.

Truman's whistle-stop campaign gave the Republicans no quarter. He tore into the "Do-nothing" Eightieth Congress, which had laid itself wide open by reluctantly reconvening for eleven sweltering Washington summer days; listening listlessly to Truman's plea to do something about housing, the farm program, universal military training, medicare, and the St. Lawrence Seaway; and going home again, having still done nothing.

The enfranchised farmers and small-towners who crowded around the rear platform of the Truman special train when it stopped at the most unlikely places cheered the Truman approach. They loved to hear him lash out at both the Republicans and the voters who, by staying away from the polls in 1946, were responsible for the Republican majority in the Eightieth Congress. Unless they wanted another four years of Republican inertia, he told them, they had better get the hell out to the polls in November and vote Democratic. The crowds would yell back, "Give 'em hell, Harry."

The pollsters and the pundits stuck by their computers to the last. On election eve Gallup made it Dewey, 49.5%; Truman, 45.5%. Elmo Roper was even more emphatic: Dewey, 52.2%; Truman, 37.1%. The New York *Mirror* predicted "a possible electoral vote landslide" for Dewey. Walter Lippmann hoped that Truman would be cooperative in the three months before Dewey's inauguration. The polls had hardly closed in the West before the Chicago *Tribune* headlined, DEWEY DEFEATS TRUMAN. As election night wore on, and Truman's popular-vote lead passed the million mark, the late Hans V. Kaltenborn, the veteran broadcaster, explained that the inevitable Dewey lead would become apparent when the returns from rural precincts began coming in—a prediction that Truman later loved to mimic, copying Kaltenborn's precise, prim pronunciation.

The final score: Truman, with a popular plurality of two million votes, won 303 electoral votes to Dewey's 189. J. Strom Thurmond on the Dixiecrat ticket got 39 electoral votes. Henry Wallace got none.

Crow was featured on the November menus of restaurants patronized by the political experts of press and electronic journalism. They ate it with more or less grace, although some pretended they were savoring breast of pheasant under glass. The widely read and respected Walter Lippmann called the Truman victory one of Franklin Roosevelt's "most impressive . . . electoral triumphs." The New York *Post*'s I. F. Stone saw it as an achievement for Henry Wallace, because Truman campaigned for social reform and peace. They all seemed reluctant to assess the election results as the crown of laurels placed by the people of the United States upon the brow of a little man who had been nominated for the insignificant vice-presidency to forestall the nomination of a controversial Wallace, an unknown compromise character who achieved the presidency by the accident of death, but who had on his own and by his own record, been elected to the presidency in his own right by a safe popular and electoral majority. The vice-presidential worm had turned again.

At his inauguration, Harry Truman made a point of his "Point Four" program "for making the benefits of our scientific advances and industrial progress available for the improvement and growth of underprivileged areas" in order to promote the cause of peace and freedom. He was not entirely successful in achieving his aims, but even in his failures he reinforced his record for decisiveness and courage that led the seventy-five historians taking part in *The New York Times*–Schlesinger symposium to rank him with the six "near-great" Presidents.

On the home front he finally secured his Housing Act, providing federal aid to slum clearance and low-rent public-housing projects. He secured an increase in the minimum wage from forty to seventy-five cents an hour by amending the Fair Labor Standards Act of 1938. He appointed a commission to secure enforcement of the antidiscrimination clauses in government contracts, increased benefits under social security, and named another commission to bring in a report on a national health program—although this project did not materialize until fifteen years later under Lyndon Johnson's administration.

Truman's second term—the first and only term for which he felt he had a personal mandate—saw the signing by twelve nations of the North Atlantic Treaty, a pact of collective security; its implementation by an appropriation of 1.3 billion dollars by Congress for military aid; the admission of Greece and Turkey to the alliance although they are neither Atlantic nor northern nations; and the appointment of General Dwight Eisenhower as first commander of the multination NATO armed forces.

Also during this period the United States, Britain, and France, fed up with Russian intransigence, officially ended the war with Germany and pledged the defense of West Germany against attack. A peace treaty with Japan was also signed, restoring Japanese sovereignty and containing a mutual-defense clause.

Truman himself announced the end of a United States monopoly on the atomic bomb. In September 1949, he said there was evidence "that an atomic explosion had occurred in the U.S.S.R." The following January he ordered the Atomic Energy Commission to proceed with developing the hydrogen bomb. Less than two years later Julius and Ethel Rosenberg were found guilty of stealing United States atomic secrets and passing them on to the Soviet Union, but they were not executed until 1953.

Perhaps Truman's most grievous mistake was to sanction withdrawal of the last contingent of American combat troops from South Korea in June 1949. (The demarcation line between American-controlled South Korea and the Soviet-controlled North had been fixed at the Thirty-eighth Parallel in 1946.) A year later, almost to the day, Communist North Korean forces invaded the South.

Truman reacted with alacrity, boldness, and decision. An emergency session of the United Nations Security Council passed a United States resolution calling upon member states to use force to meet the aggression. (The Russians were absent.) Truman ordered first the Navy and Air Force to the aid of the Republic of Korea, then sent ground forces into action a week after the first attack. A month later United States Far Eastern Commander General Douglas MacArthur was made chief of a unified United Nations command.

MacArthur's brilliant landing behind enemy lines at Inchon and his sweep through North Korea to the Yalu River were followed by two egregious miscalculations: he disregarded intelligence reports of Chinese troops massing beyond the Yalu, and he split his forces in the north, leaving a gap to the southwest of the XX Corps. As a result, some two hundred thousand Chinese "volunteers" poured through the United Nations lines, forcing the disastrous winter retreat, the evacuation through Hungnam, and the loss of all North Korea. The Chinese penetrated seventy miles beyond the Thirty-eighth Parallel before they were thrown back to the line of demarcation and the situation more or less stabilized.

MacArthur blamed the rout on Washington's policy of fighting a limited war. Truman, on advice of his Joint Chiefs of Staff, was determined to keep the action localized in Korea and prevent the conflict from expanding into a general war. MacArthur wanted to bomb Chinese bases in Manchuria, cross the Yalu in pursuit when the occasion demanded, and openly wage war on China despite China's pretense of noninvolvement. He had made several pronouncements to that effect, and Truman had met him in mid-Pacific to remind him that the President was still commander in chief, and that all declarations pertaining to policy must first be cleared with the White House.

MacArthur was just as stubborn as the man from Missouri. When in March 1951 the lines were stabilized in the general vicinity of the Thirty-eighth Parallel and there was a lull in the fighting, Truman advised MacArthur that he was preparing a statement pointing out that, inasmuch as South Korea had been cleared of invaders, the time had come to discuss a settlement. Before the Truman declaration could be released, MacArthur issued what was practically an ultimatum, calling upon communist China to agree to a truce or face air and naval attacks. President Truman forthwith relieved General MacArthur of his command and ordered him home.

It took political courage to fire a man like Douglas MacArthur, with his hero image, his great popularity, and his powerful friends in high places. Truman, however, had no alternative if he were to preserve the prestige and power of the presidency and the principle of civilian control of the military.

General Matthew Ridgway replaced MacArthur. The Chinese poured a half-million men into two offensives in April and May. Ridgway threw them back, inflicted two hundred thousand casualties, then counterattacked, driving as far as forty miles north of the Thirty-eighth Parallel in places. The war then settled down to minor ground actions and major air activity. Truce talks were begun at Kaesong in July 1951, dragged on for a year, and bogged down on the question of prisoner exchange. Then the Korean War became a domestic political issue.

General Dwight Eisenhower, campaigning as Republican candidate for the presidency of the United States, told his audiences in 1952 that he was not sure further United Nations involvement was necessary in Korea. How many million wives and mothers voted for Eisenhower because he promised that, if elected, he would make a personal trip to Korea can only be estimated. There were more than enough, in any event, to defeat Adlai Stevenson.

Eisenhower kept his pledge, flew to Korea, a month after election, looked around for a few days, and came home to announce what he must have known before his departure: there was no simple solution to the problem of Korea.

An armistic agreement of sorts was finally signed at Panmunjom on July 27, 1953—three years and 157,830 American casualties after the original unprovoked communist attack. A dozen years later there was still no peace treaty. There were still fifty thousand American troops helping patrol the armistice line to keep the North Korean communists honest—and out of South Korea. South Korea itself was a free, viable republic, thanks to the guts and sacrifice of the hundreds of thousands of South Koreans who fought and died for their own cause (two hundred and sixty thousand casualties), to the Americans, Turks, British, Australians, New Zealanders, French, Dutch, Thais, Filipinos, and other nationalities who made up the United Nations forces.

Although the Korean War is generally regarded as having ended in a stalemate, the word "checkmate" is more accurate. From it the communists learned, at a cost of some one million, five hundred thousand casualties, that the United States would not hesitate to spend its blood and treasure ten thousand miles from home to block the cynical takeover by force of a free and peaceful nation by international bullies, in violation of solemn agreements and common decency. And the unhesitating decision to stop the aggression was made by a bespectacled little man named Truman who was pushed into a job he didn't want, who was not remotely considered to be of presidential timber, and who became the President of the United States to usher in the Atomic Age only by an act of God and the determination of Democratic national chairman Bob Hannegan to keep Henry Wallace out of the White House.

10
THE MAKING OF A VICE-PRESIDENT

James K. Polk is the only man in United States history who went to a national convention an avowed candidate for the vice-presidency, and walked out a more or less reluctant nominee for President—which he subsequently became. Many an avowed candidate for President, however, particularly since the turn of the century, after the early ballots have shown his cause to be hopeless, has been not only resigned but eager to become the second choice.

It has been my privilege, since the early years of the first Truman administration, to occupy a ringside seat while the younger generation of aspiring politicos fought their way through the ranks of fading elder statesmen to the upper echelons of party leadership. These promising Democrats served their apprenticeship—some of them in the sweet uses of adversity—during the eight Eisenhower years. Most of them were senators—John Kennedy of Massachusetts, Kefauver of Tennessee, Sparkman of Alabama, Johnson of Texas, Jackson of Washington, Fulbright of Arkansas, Symington of Missouri—but there were governors, too—Stevenson of Illinois, Brown of California, Harriman of New York, Clement of Tennessee—and there was Mayor Wagner of New York City. All of them had a respect for the vice-presidency which did not exist fifty years ago. Perhaps the mortality rate among chief executives, the realization that Truman was the third Vice-President since the turn of the century to inherit the White House had given the office more prestige.

I knew all of the rising generation, of course, and was closely involved in the political careers of some. I first met John F. Kennedy when he was a freshman congressman from Massachusetts. We had both been Democratic candidates for the House in 1946, the year that produced the Eightieth Congress and the first Republican majority in both Houses in fourteen years. Kennedy successfully bucked the tide, while I was defeated in the Ninth District of Ohio by 300 votes.

I had more frequent contacts with Jack Kennedy when I came to Washington four years later. President Truman appointed me Price Stabilizer in 1950, and the young congressman from Massachusetts, extremely alert in fielding requests by his constituents, had reason to call at my office on many occasions. I was impressed by his youth—he was only thirty-three at the time, and he looked boyish even for that age. And I was even more impressed by his extreme shyness, a great contrast to most of the aggressive political figures who called at the Office of Price Stabilization. It would have been difficult not to admire him.

One day in 1951 Senator Estes Kefauver of Tennessee telephoned me for an appointment. As the senator was still years away from his bitter crusade against the high cost of pharmaceuticals, I wondered what price problems he was coming to discuss. At that time Kefauver was chairman of a Senate committee investigating crime and racketeering, and the televised hearings, with underworld characters in co-starring roles, ran up Crosley ratings that popped the eyes of television executives and made the senator a familiar figure in every living room with a TV set. Knowing this, as well as his enviable record in the Senate on behalf of people and party, I should have guessed at least half of his mission, although I confess that I was surprised by both halves.

First, the senator had decided to announce his candidacy for the presidency of the United States.

Second, he wanted me to manage his campaign.

I was flattered—and embarrassed. I told him that, while I admired his record as a senator and his service to the party, my own loyalty was first to President Truman. I appreciated the senator's confidence, but, until the President announced his intentions, I could make no commitments. I also pointed out that my job was time consuming and would not allow me to devote myself to an honest effort necessary for a successful result in the early New Hampshire primaries. Senator Kefauver was completely understanding.

Soon afterward he announced his decision to enter the New Hampshire primaries as a candidate for the Democratic nomination for the presidency, a tactical error as far as the senator's friendship with the titular head of the Democratic party was concerned.

At the top of Harry Truman's list of virtues was loyalty. When Tom Pendergast, the Kansas City boss, went to jail for an income-tax irregularity, Truman refused to denounce the man who had engineered his first election to the United States Senate. "Tom Pendergast never asked me to do anything dishonest," he said. And for Truman loyalty was a two-way street. He expected not only personal loyalty from the persons to whom he had been loyal, but party loyalty as well. Truman loved the Democratic party only slightly less than he did his wife Bess and his daughter Margaret. And Truman was convinced that, when Estes Kefauver made a road-show production out of his rackets investigation, he was building up his own image at a possible risk of damaging the Democratic party.

The President was opinionated on many subjects, but on none was he more stringent than conformity to the social code by his associates and subordinates. And he felt that Kefauver's mores did not come up to his standards.

Shortly after Kefauver announced his candidacy, President Truman declared that he himself would enter the New Hampshire primary. Frank McKinney, chairman of the Democratic national committee, and Secretary of the Navy John Sullivan, a New Hampshire man himself, had convinced the President that he should take on the Tennessean, who had not bothered to ask the blessing of party leadership, in the interests of party discipline.

Truman went into New Hampshire with all the prestige of the presidency and the power of federal patronage behind him. He had a record of accomplishment that stood up well against one hundred and fifty years of American history. He had presided over the final defeat of the Rome-Berlin-Tokyo Axis. He had blocked the communists in Greece and the Middle East. He had begun rebuilding war-wrecked Europe with the Marshall Plan. Despite the Gallup poll and the premature headlines of the Chicago *Tribune,* he had run up an impressive plurality of 114 electoral votes over Governor Dewey in the 1948 presidential election. Important political figures stumped New Hampshire in his behalf.

Yet Kefauver was undaunted. He out-Trumaned the Truman whistle-stop technique that had won in 1948. He barnstormed the state, town by town, practically voter by voter. He shook so many hands that his fingers looked like Vienna sausages. And he won the New Hampshire primary from the President of the United States.

His victory did little to endear Estes Kefauver further to Harry Truman. Even after the President announced that he would not be a candidate for another term, and Kefauver went on to win every primary in which he had entered a slate of delegates pledged to his candidacy, high-ranking Democrats such as Senator Scott Lucas of Illinois espoused President Truman's reluctance to embrace the able and ambitious gentleman from Tennessee.

When the perspiring delegates trooped into Chicago in the summer of 1952 for the Democratic national convention in the hall back of the stockyards, Estes Kefauver had the most votes promised any one candidate, and the least chance of becoming his party's nominee for the presidency. This apparent paradox was a matter of practical politics. The Tennessean lacked two vital elements he needed to win: block support by large delegations (New Hampshire had only 4 delegates), and the approval of the President he hoped to succeed.

The use of the term "practical politics" is not intended to perpetuate the legend of party bosses in the proverbial smoke-filled room defying the popular will and the common good by making their own private choice at two in the morning between sessions of the convention. No one can deny that some of our worst Presidents have been foisted upon us by the injudicious choice of cynical men working for private ends; some of these choices have luckily been rejected by the electorate. More often than not, however, the professional politician of our day is an earnest, honest practitioner, ready and anxious to use his skills in the art and science of government for the good of the greatest number. To the amoral principles of Machiavelli he prefers the words of John Viscount Morley, the British statesman and essayist who wrote a century ago: "Those who would treat politics and morality apart will never understand the one or the other."

Practical politics, as several practitioners of the profession—notably the late Georges Clemenceau, perennial Premier of France—have said, is the art of the possible—a struggle for power in which persuasion, argument, compromise, and various forms of quid pro quo are all essential elements. It is the discovery of a common denominator—the achievement of party unity through consensus and party loyalty—rather than the secret deal, which creates the candidates for President and Vice-President.

The 1952 Democratic national convention opened without President Truman or word of his preference. Although the President was a member of the Missouri delegation, he had given his proxy to Thomas Gavin, Kansas City councilman. All eyes would be upon Gavin when the first ballot was taken, as it was assumed that his vote would go to Truman's choice. There were signs of a ground swell in the making for Governor Adlai Stevenson of Illinois, but it was common knowledge that Stevenson had been approached by both Truman and Democratic national chairman McKinney, as well as many others, and had responded with a firm no.

No candidate had the necessary majority on the first ballot. Kefauver's pledged delegates gave him a lead over Senator Richard B. Russell of Georgia, Averell Harriman of New York (whose campaign was being managed by Franklin Roosevelt, Jr.), Vice-President Alben Barkley, and a scattering of favorite-son candidates such as Fulbright and Kerr.

The much-awaited Gavin vote was cast for Vice-President Barkley, who later withdrew after a conference with several prominent labor leaders. The union officials had wondered, within the Veep's hearing, if a man of seventy-five (Barkley's age at the time) were physically qualified to assume the duties of the presidency in an emergency.

The second ballot made it quite plain that neither Kefauver nor Russell would pick up any votes beyond their original first-round strength. The uncommitted delegates were either sitting on their hands or continuing to vote for favorite sons. But the Stevenson ground swell was growing.

President Truman finally arrived in Chicago and persuaded Averell Harriman to withdraw in favor of Adlai Stevenson, if Stevenson could be persuaded to run. Stevenson's reluctance was genuine enough. He had given his word to a group of Illinois businessmen that he would serve out his term as governor, and, even at the risk of being accused of playing coy, he refused to renege on his promise. However, the pressures on him were increasing, and there were signs that some of his close advisers were weakening.

The uncommitted delegates had been tremendously impressed by Stevenson's welcoming address as host governor. So had many of the committed delegates. Here was a man who was not only articulate and eloquent, but whose words made sense. His poise and obvious sincerity had already captivated the convention. He was a leader who could appeal to both the emotions and the intellect.

While the clans had been gathering, I had received a call from Jack Kennedy. Kennedy had been nominated as Democratic candidate to oppose Henry Cabot Lodge for Lodge's Massachusetts seat in the Senate. I had won the Democratic nomination as senator from Ohio, and the rather doubtful privilege of fighting for the seat occupied by Senator John W. Bricker, incumbent, and a three-term Republican governor of Ohio. Kennedy both championed and depended upon the younger Democrats, and he thought that Stevenson, who was only fifty-two and therefore not in the elder-statesman class, might respond to an appeal from the rising generation of his party. He asked if I would join with him; Archie Alexander, the senatorial nominee from New Jersey; Walter Granger, nominee from Utah; and several others in signing an open letter to Stevenson, urging him to become a candidate for President. Although as a delegate I was committed to Ohio's favorite son, Robert Bulkley, until he released the delegation, I was more than happy to add my signature to the Kennedy letter. I was hoping that Stevenson might be swayed by the knowledge that this year's candidates of his party were supporting him.

During the balloting, except when the Ohio delegation was caucusing on the floor, I sat in a room behind the stage with a council of the pendragons of the Democratic party: Frank McKinney, national committee chairman; Dave Lawrence, the stocky national committeeman from Pennsylvania, who had served his apprenticeship as kingmaker in the earliest days of the New Deal; Colonel Jacob Arvey, national committeeman from Illinois; Jim Farley, the veteran party strategist; Carmine DeSapio, New York committeeman; Ed Pauley, former party treasurer; Francis Meyers, Democratic whip in the Senate; and a dozen other party wizards on the national, state, or big-city level who had for years been conjuring votes out of battered old derbies as well as silk hats. They were keeping score as state after state swung into line behind Adlai Stevenson—Lawrence with the cool dignity of a successful prophet, Arvey with the perspiring nervous enthusiasm of a trainer whose horse is coming up fast on the ouside at Churchill Downs.

Adlai Stevenson was nominated on that third ballot.

Immediately the hunt was on for a suitable second choice. Jake Arvey, who had been designated by Stevenson's general staff as one of the beaters of the bush, approached me for an appraisal of the situation. I was already on record in the Ohio press; as I was leaving Toledo for Chicago, two reporters from the Toledo *Blade* asked me to predict the ticket, and I had said, "Adlai Stevenson and John Sparkman."

As a matter of fact, I had made the same prediction several months earlier at a dinner party in the executive mansion in Columbus. Ohio governor Frank J. Lausche was in Washington for the Jefferson-Jackson Day dinner, and his wife Jane had asked Mrs. DiSalle and me to come down from Toledo to help entertain Senator Sparkman and his wife. The Alabama senator was in town for a speaking engagement. After dinner we joined the Washington gathering by television to listen to President Truman's address. When the President announced that he would definitely not be a candidate for renomination, I turned to Sparkman and said: "That settles it. In my opinion, Adlai Stevenson will be our candidate for President, with you as his running mate."

Jake Arvey, however, wanted more than my personal preference. He asked me for a list of all vice-presidential possibilities, with the pros and cons for each. I felt that the nominee for the vice-presidency would have to be a man from the South, because Stevenson, known as a northern liberal, had limited appeal to the conservative southern wing of the Democratic party. I reached for a scratch pad and commented on them thus:

Senator Kefauver, despite his strong showing on the first two ballots, could not be nominated. Truman's antagonism was one drawback; the other was the fact that many delegates from below the Mason-Dixon Line considered the senator's liberalism both hypocritical and a betrayal of his Old South heritage.

Senator Russell, although he had scattered support among his fellow senators, valued his senatorial status and seniority above the vice-presidency.

Senator Fulbright had shown strength during the early presidential balloting, but he faced several impossible hurdles. The fact that he had voted for the Taft-Hartley Bill alienated spokesmen for organized labor; and he had developed a special gift for raising the well-known hackles of President Truman. The scholarly senator from Arkansas first ran afoul of

White House favor in 1946, when the Republicans had captured a majority in Congress. Fulbright, who had studied at Oxford and admired the British parliamentary system, thought the election was an expression of the people's will and suggested that Truman should respond to it by resigning as President in favor of a Republican, just as the British Prime Minister resigns when he loses a majority in the House of Commons. President Truman had other ideas and expressed them with his usual picturesque directness.

Fulbright had further incurred the well-known Truman wrath by the activities of his senatorial investigating committee. The chairman's digging into operations of the Reconstruction Finance Corporation had not only involved several Truman appointees, but had stirred up headlines, Republican guffaws, and endless cartoons about pastel minks and deep-freezes. The President felt that the senator had needlessly battered the Democratic party image to no end except his own personal glory. We could cross off Senator Fulbright.

My list ended with Senator John Sparkman, who seemed to me the only Southerner capable of national acceptance. His senatorial record was excellent. The Senate Press Gallery rated him and Lister Hill as giving Alabama the best representation of any state in the union. The press at large had consistently rated him high on ability. His attitude and votes on the issues of housing and assistance to small business were impeccable. In fact, aside from the civil-rights issue on which he was forced to reflect the more narrow views of his Alabama constituents, he could be considered a true liberal.

The morning after Stevenson was nominated, he picked Sparkman as his running mate. The Kefauver backers were deeply disappointed, but they could hardly deny a presidential nominee's right to choose his own man for the Number Two spot.

Before the opening of the next day's session, while making my way backstage as a member of the committee to escort Sparkman to the rostrum to accept the vice-presidential nomination, I encountered a curiously solemn Adlai Stevenson. When I congratulated him, he said he truly did not know whether or not he should be thankful for my part in his draft, as it meant taking on an assignment that he would have preferred to avoid at that time. His reluctance was so genuine that I could only marvel at his lack of elation at winning the prize for which so many would have given an arm and a leg.

On the rostrum, I reminded Senator Sparkman of my prediction in Columbus earlier that year.

Sparkman of course went down to defeat with Stevenson in November. Eisenhower carried Ohio over the Stevenson ticket by a majority of nearly five hundred thousand, and I lost my senatorial race by three hundred and sixteen thousand votes. Jack Kennedy, however, demonstrated his growing stature by successfully bucking the Republican tide. While Eisenhower was winning Massachusetts by two hundred thousand, he was handily wresting a Senate seat from an Eisenhower favorite, Henry Cabot Lodge, the incumbent.

The blossoming of the brilliant Kennedy personality was not blighted by the eight frosty Eisenhower years ahead. His talents expanded, his charm matured, and his appeal gained substance and momentum. He was obviously headed for bigger and better things.

I was only briefly in close contact with Jack Kennedy during his freshman year in the Senate. Shortly after the 1952 election, President Truman asked me to return to Washington as administrator of the Economic Stabilization Agency. This was a lame-duck appointment to carry through the transitional period between administrations, and I was reluctant to pull up roots again in Ohio for such a short period. However, I was in debt to the President for his many past kindnesses to me, so I packed a suitcase and came to Washington.

During my short tour of duty I had official reason for meeting the man whose Senate seat would be warmed for the next eight years by John F. Kennedy. Henry Cabot Lodge did not take his loss lightly. That a scion of the two first families of New England should lose during a Republican year to the grandson of a Boston saloonkeeper left him stunned and bewildered. An able and personable young man in his own right, he received first aid from all sides to ease his hurt. He was named liaison between President-elect Eisenhower and the retiring Truman administration, and it was while he held that position that I reported to him on the status of economic stabilization in the United States, and on the turnover of responsibilities to the incoming command. His appointment as the new United States ambassador to the United Nations had also just been announced, and I congratulated him. Bitterly he declined congratulations.

"What for?" he asked. "You'll be leaving the worst job in government, but I'm giving up the best—a seat in the United States Senate."

While Jack Kennedy was bulldozing the first few miles of his road to the White House, Estes Kefauver had recovered from his disappointment and was doing a little road building of his own. During a Democratic fund-raising dinner in Chicago, the Tennessean asked me if I would attend a gathering of some of his friends who were in town for the occasion. I accepted, and there again Kefauver announced that he had decided to try again for the presidential nomination. Once more he asked me to manage his campaign, and his friends joined in the plea. I told him that I wanted time to consider the matter, and that I would give him an answer after I had made a survey of the situation.

Kefauver flew me back to Toledo after the meeting. While the senator was dozing at the back of the plane, one of his associates told me how anxious Kefauver was to have me accept the responsibility, and that the senator would certainly be extremely appreciative were he to become President. How would I like to be Attorney General? Or would I prefer an appointment to the Supreme Court to fill the first vacancy? I replied that I had great confidence in Senator Kefauver's ability, political views, and integrity, and in his fitness for the job. My willingness to lead his campaign, however, would depend not on the expectation of any reward, but on the amount of political support that could be mustered for his candidacy throughout the nation.

Back in Toledo I picked up the phone and placed long-distance calls to Democratic party leaders from coast to coast to assess their feeling toward Kefauver as a possible presidential candidate in 1956. When I had what I thought was a representative cross section, I flew to Washington to report to the senator. I told him that everyone I had spoken to had expressed appreciation for his leadership, gratitude for the hard work he had put in for the party, and indebtedness for the loyal assistance Kefauver had given Democratic candidates for governor and Congress by making speaking appearances on their behalf in practically every state. However, they all felt a super-obligation to the man who in 1952 had reluctantly assumed the role of sacrificial goat against Eisenhower, the national hero. For having taken on one difficult assignment and discharged it brilliantly, every man I approached thought Adlai Stevenson should be renominated in 1956.

I advised Senator Kefauver to stay close to Washington, immerse himself in his homework, and cultivate his growing reputation as an outstanding senator. Should Stevenson reconsider or stub his toe over some unforeseen obstacle, Kefauver could become the presidential candidate without entering a single primary. And should Stevenson respond to what seemed an almost universal sentiment of party leaders that he make a second try, Kefauver could have the vice-presidential nomination hands down.

Kefauver huddled with his advisers of the moment, and decided against the option play in favor of a heads-down charge through the center of the line. He was not interested in being second choice. It was all or nothing. Kefauver entered a number of primaries. When the Tennesseean won his first in Minnesota, his backers shook their heads sadly over the decline of my political acumen. I had obviously missed the boat.

As the time for the '56 Democratic convention approached, however, the Stevenson forces rallied and piled up an impressive number of pledged delegates. When the California primary was reached, Kefauver dropped out of the race and became himself a staunch Stevenson supporter. Once resigned to the fact that he could never clear the first hurdle in the presidential sweepstakes, he stopped acting like a candidate and became more the frank, out-and-out liberal that he really was.

Meanwhile Adlai Stevenson had managed to alienate the affections of President Truman by replacing Democratic national chairman Frank McKinney, Truman's favorite, first by his own man, Steve Mitchell, and later by Frank Butler, both of whom were persona non grata with Truman. Truman and McKinney had been quietly drumming up support for the candidacy of Averell Harriman, who had become governor of New York since the 1952 convention. Harriman was gaining headway, and there was talk of an alliance between him and Governor Frank Lausche, Ohio's favorite-son candidate. Despite the axiom that politics makes strange bedfellows, this was hard to believe. Lausche, an extreme conservative, did not see eye-to-eye with Truman or his stalking horse Harriman, who was considered a far-out liberal. However, the apparent hopeful strategy was that Lausche would get strong support from the southern states, which could be used by the Harriman forces in a stop-Stevenson movement.

Governor Lausche had asked me to place his name in nomination. I had agreed, but had not bothered to write a nominating speech, as I was sure the governor would not actually enter the lists unless he felt sure of substantial support. He knew, of course, that Stevenson was my first choice. To make sure that President Truman also knew, I visited him in his suite at the Blackstone to explain that I could not support Harriman. I said I had supported Stevenson in 1952, that I approved of the principles on which he had conducted his campaign and believed he again deserved my support. The ex-President insisted that he was not trying to influence others, but that personally he was still backing Harriman.

The 1956 Democratic convention orated, cheered, perspired, caucused, and demonstrated its way into a second sweltering day, and I had not yet written the Lausche nominating speech. The press, however, as the feeling spread that Lausche might truly develop into a dark horse, began hounding me for an advance text. I then composed a dissertation emphasizing the governor's good record in office and his great vote-getting ability in Ohio, and submitted it to Lausche and his staff. During the silence following its reception, I thought I could see frost forming on the walls. The staff members found I was not lavish enough in my praise of the governor's virtues. One of them, Ray White, "an old newspaper man himself," suggested rewriting the opening paragraph with the words: "God has blessed this nation by making available, at this point in its history, a man of Governor Lausche's unparalleled values. . . ."

In the governor's presence I told Ray that whenever I heard a speaker at a political meeting call upon God, I moved away for fear that the Almighty in His anger might send down a bolt of lightning to destroy those who called on Him for partisan ends. Besides, phrases of this sort were completely foreign to my nature. There was another long and painful silence before Lausche turned to Ray White and said he agreed that the proposed change would be in bad taste. My original speech, almost unchanged, went to be mimeographed and was given to the press in the early hours of the third day.

The roll call of states was passing through the Ms and Ns and approaching Ohio. Massachusetts had nominated Adlai Stevenson in a brilliant, witty, and wildly applauded speech by its young junior senator, John F. Kennedy. Averell Harriman's nomination was seconded by Harry Truman, a precedent-breaking move by a former President. The Truman speech was received with noisy enthusiasm, but it was obvious that the delegates' cheers were for Truman personally, rather than for his candidate. The sentiment for Stevenson was so strong that it could be felt on the floor like a rising wind. It was obvious that Stevenson would be nominated on the first ballot.

Just before Ohio was called, Governor Lausche asked that his name not be placed in nomination.

As Stevenson's success had been a foregone conclusion, the actual balloting, achievement of a majority, demonstrations, and parades were somewhat anticlimactic. The candidate's acceptance speech, with perspiration glistening on his bald head in tribute to the Chicago summer, was as stirring as was expected. But the real drama, the real suspense of the convention at this point was provided by Stevenson's choice of a running mate.

Among the delegates, Estes Kefauver was an odds-on favorite, but Stevenson was under great pressure from many angles. There was the long-standing hostility of Truman and the old-guard Democrats, in the first place. There were the unreconstructed Southerners, who still resented The Keef's liberalism. And there were of course the many influential champions of a surprising number of candidates for the long-despised and now-sought-after Number Two spot. Stevenson, foreseeing endless debate and bitter dissension on the convention floor, and wishing to avoid being a party to dividing the Democrats, declared for an open convention. The delegates themselves would have to choose the vice-presidential candidate.

Immediately the stampede was on. The post once considered by so many stalwarts of presidential stature as not worth any of a lot of rather nasty things was now up for grabs, and there were many would-be grabbers. Kefauver found himself in competition with two other Tennesseans—Senator Albert Gore and Governor Frank Clement, who had been roundly cheered for his aggressive keynote speech. Hubert Humphrey of Minnesota kicked his hat into the second ring, as did Mayor Bob Wagner of New York and Senator John F. Kennedy of Massachusetts.

Kefauver's handlers asked me to place the Tennessee senator's name in nomination for Vice-President. I personally favored Kefauver because of both friendship and his capabilities. He was passionately devoted to the Democratic party and had campaigned for Democratic candidates in almost every state in the union. He was an outstanding senator and a man of courage. Some of the opposition to his nomination was caused by his liberal positions on such fundamental questions as civil rights, the very principles for which a Democratic party nominee *should* stand nationally. And, if for no other reason, I believed Kefauver should be nominated to give the lie to malicious rumors that he would be passed over because the crooks and gangsters who had appeared before his investigating committee had influence in the upper echelons of the party. Despite all these factors, however, I told Senator Kefauver that I could not immediately agree to make his nominating speech. I could not take an action which would bind many members of the Ohio delegation without consulting them. I promised an answer by ten o'clock next morning after the Ohio delegates had caucused.

In the meantime I was besieged by backers of the other vice-presidential hopefuls seeking the support of the Ohio delegation. I told them of my personal preference, but invited them to present the cases for their candidates before Ohio caucused next morning. I had personal friends in every camp and believed that each of the aspirants would have made an able and politically acceptable candidate. Since only one could be nominated, however, I was for Kefauver.

After the supporters of the various candidates had made their pitches to the delegation, I announced that I had been asked to place Senator Kefauver's name in nomination. To do so, I explained, would substantially commit Ohio to the support of the senator, and I sought the delegation's advice. The caucus voted that I should accept the invitation, and I went at once to Kefauver's headquarters to dictate a ten-minute nominating speech.

The usual mechanics of reproduction—typing and mimeographing—consumed so much time that I had barely reached the convention hall and was making a back-door entrance when I heard Ohio being called. I dashed to the rostrum, and was still out of breath as House Speaker Sam Rayburn, who was chairing the convention, introduced me. I was just getting my second wind and was reaching the pith of my speech when Mr. Sam tapped me on the shoulder and said in a stage whisper, "Two more minutes."

I was not aware of the rules change that had cut nominating speeches from ten minutes to five. I made a quick adjustment, and Kefauver was duly nominated, seconded, and acclaimed. He was entering one of the most exciting races on record for the vice-presidential nomination. He found himself competing on an equal basis with the junior senator from Massachusetts—John F. Kennedy.

When the balloting started, it was evident that Kefauver's lead had been cut by a surprising show of strength on Kennedy's part. Then Kennedy went into the lead—but without a majority. The lead seesawed back and forth. At one point Kennedy was within a few votes of nomination. On the next ballot a shift of votes within several state delegations gave Kefauver the required majority.

Actually it was the Ohio vote that weighted the scales and gave Kefauver the nomination for Vice-President over John Kennedy. Many of the Ohio delegates personally favored Kennedy, but voted for Kefauver because Ohio had nominated him. On each roll call Ohio cast all but 6 of its 64 votes for Kefauver.

That night after the convention adjourned, Senator Kennedy and I remained on the platform after most of the delegates had left the hall to the monumental trash pile of standards, banners, placards, and other traditional debris of a national political conclave. We had a friendly discussion of the events of the day. Kennedy accepted his defeat with mixed feelings of regret and resignation. I gave him my reasons for supporting Kefauver, and tried to console him with the thought that the convention's decision was actually better for his political future. If he had been nominated as Adlai Stevenson's running mate and Stevenson should be defeated—as seemed almost certain in view of General Eisenhower's persistent hero image—Kennedy would be blamed for the defeat of the ticket because of the political postulate (later to be proved erroneous) that no Catholic could win in a national election. Now, with four to eight years running room before the big jump, he stood a good chance, as a young, vigorous, and politically promising candidate, of shattering tradition and sweeping both the convention and the country.

Jack Kennedy bore no ill will. The surprising showing he had made in the vice-presidential race made him a great favorite in speaking engagements across the country. And despite the fact that Ohio's support for Kefauver had cost him the nomination for Vice-President, he came into Ohio several times to support me in my campaign for governor.

In 1957 I went to Boston to speak at a bipartisan testimonial dinner for Senator Kennedy. I began by saying that there were two great nominating speeches made at the 1956 convention: the one by Senator Kennedy nominating Adlai Stevenson, and the one I made nominating Senator Kefauver for Vice-President. My speech had been important, I said, because it had saved Jack Kennedy from defeat and therefore kept him alive politically. When Kennedy arose to speak, he thanked me for my services as a political lifesaver.

Two years later, after I had been elected governor of Ohio, Kennedy repeated the story at a small gathering at the executive mansion in Columbus. He added that he hoped I would not make a career out of preserving his political future.

Kennedy's campaign for the presidency really began in Chicago in 1956, and he had my support even before he publicly announced his candidacy. I remember having dinner with Adlai Stevenson in New York in 1957, when the two-time loser told me he was through with politics and would never again run for public office. I tried to convince him that he should not relinquish his position of leadership this early in the game. Even if he persisted in refusing to be a candidate in 1960, he should keep his very considerable strength and following in order to influence the choice of a man who believed in his principles and would follow in his footsteps. At another time, former-Senator William Benton, a great Stevenson admirer, joined us and argued in a similar vein.

Adlai Stevenson was certainly sincere in his reluctance to become another William Jennings Bryan. His apparent indecision was undoubtedly based on an understandable desire not to offend his millions of enthusiastic followers or to compromise his own principles, for along the way he had given Kennedy his word that he would not be a candidate. I believe his refusal to make the nominating speech at Los Angeles in 1960, despite Kennedy's eloquent presentation in Chicago four years before, was not intended as a snub but was a confused attempt to remain neutral in the eyes of his devotees. After all, he did support Kennedy when the campaign got under way. Up to the time when he died suddenly in London during the summer of 1965, I am sure that Adlai Stevenson did not realize the influence that he had had on the American scene and on the Democratic party. He was, as James Reston said in *The New York Times* at the time of his death, "the right man at the wrong time."

As the 1950s raced toward the 1960 date with destiny at Los Angeles, the hopefuls began making pilgrimages to Columbus. The fact that the votes of the Ohio delegation had made Kefauver rather than Kennedy the vice-presidential candidate in 1956, and that I as governor would influence the 1960 delegation, made the Ohio state capital the Mecca for Democratic *hajjis*. Governor Robert Meyner of New Jersey was an early visitor. So were Governor G. Mennen Williams of Michigan and Senator Stuart Symington of Missouri.

Senator John F. Kennedy came to Columbus in June of 1959 and stayed at the executive mansion. He was accompanied by his brother Ted (now upholding one-half the senatorial tradition of the Kennedy clan) and John Bailey, Connecticut state chairman and one of John Kennedy's senior advisers. Kennedy was worried about what Ohio would do, and during the evening a number of prominent Ohioans dropped in to try to enlighten him. Next morning he held a news conference at the Ohio Press Club. He handled himself with the maturity, poise, wit, and intellectual depth that were later to make his televised press conferences so colorful. The assembled statehouse correspondents and local reporters were visibly and deeply impressed. When he returned to his seat beside me, I told him that he need worry no longer about what I was going to do, and that furthermore I was sure that the Ohio delegation to the 1960 convention would support him.

Between that June day and my formal announcement of support for John F. Kennedy six months later, there was considerable newspaper speculation on my position. Some of the editorial conjecture was inspired by jealous rivalries within the state organization, some by Ohioans honing private tomahawks. Kennedy was being kept constantly off balance by Ohio politicians who were telling him they could not rely on any commitment that I might make. The senator consequently made frequent trips to Ohio for reassurance, which I always gave him. He returned to Columbus again shortly before the Wisconsin primary.

During one of his visits we discussed the advisability of his coming into Ohio as a candidate for the Ohio delegation's support. The possibility encouraged talk of other entrants into the race for Ohio support, notably Ohio's senator, former governor, and popular vote-getter Frank Lausche. The next time I talked to Jack Kennedy, he told me that he had spoken to publisher Louis Seltzer of the Cleveland Press, who in turn had conferred with Senator Lausche. The senator had assured the publisher that if Kennedy entered the primary, he, Lausche, would not.

In the late fall of 1959 I met briefly with Robert Kennedy and John Bailey at the Drake Hotel in New York City to discuss the details of how and when I should make my public declaration. It was quite a stormy session. Bobby Kennedy, demonstrating his fierce, single-purposed devotion to his brother, wanted to know the mechanics and timetable of the announcement, while I was just as determined to keep the specifications to myself. After a rather sharp exchange it was agreed that I would discuss the particulars with the candidate himself. The agreement was possible as a result of the levelheaded intervention of John Bailey. Bailey, who since has been functioning as Democratic national chairman, was then helping candidate Kennedy in the basic job of making nationwide contact with political leaders. Without Bailey's all-important mediation at the Drake Hotel conference, Jack Kennedy might have felt himself engaged on three fronts—Ohio, Wisconsin, and West Virginia as well—and the required effort might have changed the outcome in at least one of those states.

From that day on, Bob Kennedy and I had frequent contact in the furtherance of Jack Kennedy's nomination and election. I never ceased to marvel at his unfailing energy and dedication, even at the risk of great physical damage to himself, to the fulfillment of his brother's ambition.

My tentative plan for declaring my support was approved by Jack Kennedy later during a very brief meeting at the Pittsburgh airport. I told him I intended to announce that I was a favorite-son candidate for the presidential nomination, committed to the Kennedy cause, and that candidates for the Ohio delegation to the convention who agreed with this basis would be similarly committed.

I was amused by the story in a weekly news magazine reporting our brief conversation as a "clandestine" meeting at the Pittsburgh airport where we had tried to preserve secrecy by registering as Mr. Smith and Mr. O'Donnell. Actually, there was a "Mr. Smith" who registered that day—Steve Smith, Senator Kennedy's brother-in-law—and Ken O'Donnell, a close Kennedy adviser. And many people recognized the future President and me as we walked through the lobby of the airport. Kennedy had come to Pittsburgh to address a bar association meeting that night. I had come from speaking to a luncheon in Steubenville and was back in Columbus before five that evening.

The schedule we had agreed upon was this: Senator Kennedy would make his formal declaration on the morning of January 2, 1960. I suggested making my announcement on January 6, which is my birthday. I felt that this was an appropriate timetable, since it would inform the electorate that the favorite-son candidate was not seeking support for some dark horse, and would give the dissidents a chance to line up delegates for other candidates.

The dissidents jumped the gun. Two days after the formal Kennedy announcement, an apparent leak in Washington sparked various distorted versions in the press of what had happened and would happen. I immediately telephoned Senator Kennedy and told him I was moving up my declaration and would make it the next day, January 5.

On the morning of the day that was to dispel all doubts and uncertainties, members of my staff and Democratic state chairman William Coleman had breakfast with me at the mansion. There was no more question about the support of Jack Kennedy than there was about the fact that we were already five days into the new year. After the last round of coffee, we all drove together to the statehouse, where the fourth estate was awaiting the word.

I don't know what the gentlemen of the Ohio press expected that morning, but they seemed genuinely surprised by my announcement that the Ohio delegates committed to favorite son DiSalle would also be committed to Senator John F. Kennedy. The questions flew as thick and fast as deerflies at an August picnic. Carl DeBloom of the Columbus *Dispatch* asked the state chairman, "Mr. Coleman, is Senator Kennedy really your choice?"

William Coleman smiled stiffly. "I am a good soldier," he said.

It was my turn to be startled. I wondered what there was about eggs, bacon, or coffee at the executive mansion that had induced the state chairman's reluctance to say now he was for Kennedy.

But there were other surprises in store. Ray T. Miller of Cleveland, county chairman of important Cuyahoga County, was in Washington when he heard of my announcement, and nearly developed apoplexy as a result. He immediately called Senator Kennedy and sputtered his protest, but was told that I would designate the Ohio delegates to the 1960 convention. Miller was furious. As Cuyahoga County contained about one-sixth the population of the state, and many of its citizens held high public office, Miller demanded twice as many delegates as had been allotted to him in what was considered a fair ratio to the rest of the state. When he was refused, he announced he would run his own slate of delegates committed to Albert Porter, and that the Porter delegates would support Kennedy at the convention. His heart was set upon a contest to see who would be for Senator Kennedy the most. Final score: the DiSalle slate, 56 delegates; the Miller-Porter slate, 8.

Despite the mounting mass of similar evidence, the poison-rumor factory of certain Ohio politicians continued to operate full blast. Senator Kennedy still received regular warnings against the perfidious Mike DiSalle, who could be trusted for only one certainty: to desert at the first shift in the wind. I had in fact received assurance from several friends in Washington that substantial financial support would be forthcoming if I should oppose Kennedy in Ohio. The rumors must have reached the ears of Senator Hubert Humphrey of Minnesota, then girding his loins for an assault on the presidential nomination. Apparently encouraged by them, he came into Ohio accompanied by James Rowe, the Washington attorney I was to meet again when he moved over to Lyndon Johnson's camp after Humphrey abandoned his campaign. They came to see me just before the Wisconsin primary, and I told them that, aside from my political, personal, and friendly attachment to Jack Kennedy, I had made a firm commitment which was irrevocable. As he said goodby, Humphrey smiled and said, "I'll be back to see you again after I beat Kennedy in Wisconsin and West Virginia."

I told him that I would welcome his return, but that, if it depended upon a successful result in those two primaries, I was afraid I would never see him again.

Another rumor had me in a deal with Senator Kennedy whereby I had given my support for the promise of a top-level federal job which I would leave the governorship to accept. In truth, I had never asked for, expected, or received any commitment of personal reward. My only expectation was that there would be consideration for the state Democratic organization.

The question of commitments came up again at the 1960 Governors' Conference held that year in Glacier National Park, Montana. Governor Robert Meyner of New Jersey took me aside one evening to say that he had talked with John Kennedy the previous week, and that, while he had been reluctant to endorse any one candidate, he had been curious about how far the senator was committed.

"I expect that by this time you have every Cabinet job promised," he said he told Kennedy.

Kennedy's statement that he had made no commitments whatever surprised the governor. Few Presidents indeed have gone through a campaign without making some commitments. The senator went on to say, according to Meyner, that there were two men who could have anything they might ask for. Neither had asked, and he had pledged nothing, but he felt a personal obligation to Mike DiSalle and Abe Ribicoff for their early and important support.

The 1960 Governors' Conference was very much preoccupied with national politics, particularly as on its opening day Harry Truman, in announcing he would not attend the 1960 Democratic convention, had bitterly attacked the candidacy of Jack Kennedy. Several Democratic governors wondered if the Truman hex was still powerful enough to hurt Kennedy's chances. John Bailey, a senior Kennedy strategist attending the conference as an observer, believed not. Connecticut governor Abe Ribicoff agreed. I went even further. I predicted that, in spite of Lyndon Johnson's picking up delegates in increasing numbers, Kennedy would be nominated on the first ballot. Ribicoff then declared that, if that were so, Kennedy would have to offer the vice-presidency to Lyndon Johnson.

Bailey scoffed at the idea. He was sure that Johnson would not accept the nomination, because he was already in a position of great power. As majority leader in the United States Senate, he was the most powerful man in the country. He enjoyed the position and would be reluctant to give it up for the more or less figurehead spot of Vice-President.

I demurred. I told John Bailey that if members of the Kennedy high command did not want Johnson as a running mate, they had better not make him the offer because he was sure to accept. I said that his role of majority leader would be much less powerful under a Democratic President, and that, while Johnson certainly enjoyed his present status, the pressures of the job had been physically trying for some years and he would welcome a move to a less strenuous and more exalted post. In addition to being a more relaxed job (an advantage not to be scorned by a man who had survived a coronary occlusion), it was an honor no man could lightly reject. And, further, if Johnson were ever to become a national figure, he would have to give up his provincial role as a Texas senator.

I also pointed out that, when Lyndon Johnson announced that he was a candidate for the Democratic presidential nomination, he had left himself an opening. When he was asked whether or not he would accept the vice-presidency, instead of comparing the office to the by-products of digestion or a fate worse than death, as many of his predecessors had done (in slightly different words), Johnson said that he had always served his country whenever he had been asked and in whatever capacity he could best serve. This struck me as a great deviation from the attitude of the usual candidate for the presidency, who traditionally denied his interest in any minor nomination.

As it turned out, the nomination for the vice-presidency provided more drama, more suspense, and more puzzles for future historians to solve than did the main event. When the Democratic delegates deplaned or detrained in Los Angeles, took their first breath of the petroleum-scented atmosphere, signed hotel registers, and took off for the convention in the Sports Arena, John Fitzgerald Kennedy was the obvious front runner. Johnson was a strong second, with scattered delegate strength from the North as well as his pledged southern delegates. Adlai Stevenson was a large question mark.

Kennedy had won his front-running position by being available to any Democratic candidate who needed help anywhere in the United States. Keynoting state conventions, speaking at fund-raising dinners, wherever help was needed, he was one of the few Washington VIPs who could be counted on to respond. He built a large, loyal party following that came enthusiastically to his support at convention time.

As the balloting began, a number of strange situations developed as a result of convention rules. Many a VIP who made resounding speeches to nominate or second the nomination of "the man who" was unable to vote for his candidate. Orville Freeman, for example, who placed John Kennedy's name in nomination, was a member of the Minnesota delegation and bound by the unit rule which requires that the votes of all the delegates be cast as the majority indicates. Minnesota's vote was cast for Hubert Humphrey. Senator Eugene McCarthy, who made the nominating speech for Adlai Stevenson, was also bound by the Minnesota rule. Senator Thomas J. Dodd of Connecticut seconded Lyndon Johnson's nomination for President, but his vote was cast for Kennedy, under the Connecticut delegation's unit rule.

Ohio was not acting under the unit rule, but the 64 Ohio votes cast for Kennedy on the first ballot represented a larger undivided bloc of delegates than did those of any other state. For a moment just before the balloting began it appeared possible that the Ohio vote might not be unanimous. Two delegates were toying with the idea of voting for Johnson. There was a heated argument on the floor. I reminded both potential apostates of their original commitments. I suggested to one of them—a congressman—that he might have difficulty explaining to his constituents why he had reneged on the conditions of his membership in the delegation. Ohio cast 64 votes for John F. Kennedy.

The enigma of Adlai Stevenson cropped up again during the balloting. When he entered the Sports Arena to take his seat with the Illinois delegation, one of the most enthusiastic and apparently spontaneous demonstrations of the whole convention burst into near-delirium. The Stevenson organization had lost none of its fanaticism, despite its eight lean years of existence. I happened to be sitting next to Mayor Dick Daley of Chicago, and I asked him what this phenomenon meant.

"Nothing," said Daley. "Ten days ago I told Adlai that if he wanted to be a candidate, Illinois would support him as a favorite son. His reply was negative. As a result, Kennedy will receive the bulk of the Illinois votes. The rest will go to Symington."

Without the basic support of Illinois, Stevenson had practically no chance to reverse the popular swing toward Kennedy. His ambiguous position, in the face of the almost religious fervor of his backers, could only be explained by the conflict between his own desires and his pledge to Kennedy, and his loyalty to those who still thought he could be nominated. To Kennedy he had said he would do nothing to seek the nomination; to his cohorts he must have said that he would do nothing to interfere with their efforts to secure the nomination for him. None of the Stevenson zealots would have considered for a moment putting forth their champion for the second choice. It would have been *infra dignitatem* for a man who had twice led the ticket to take second place to a New England upstart half his age—although his grandfather, Adlai E. Stevenson, whose namesake our own Adlai was, had been second choice to Grover Cleveland and served as Vice-President, dignified white mustache and all, during the second Cleveland administration.

Balloting began on the evening of July 13. As the roll call approached the end of the alphabet, the Kennedy tide continued to rise inexorably. Washington floated him over the seven hundred mark. West Virginia, Wisconsin, and Wyoming made the final score Kennedy, 806; Johnson, 409; Symington, 86. It was all over but the shouting—and the naming of the second choice.

After the convention adjourned that night, Bobby Kennedy asked me to come to the Biltmore at eight-thirty next morning, as his brother, the nominee, wanted region-by-region advice on the vice-presidency. Present at his hotel headquarters (Kennedy had field headquarters in a bungalow adjoining the Sports Arena and a hideaway apartment halfway to Hollywood) were Governor Pat Brown of California, Mayor Dick Daley of Chicago, Governor Dave Lawrence of Pennsylvania, Carmen DiSapio and Mike Pendergast of New York, Governor G. Mennen Williams of Michigan, Governor Abe Ribicoff, and John Bailey of Connecticut. The nominee said that he wanted to talk about the second choice, but what he wanted particularly was our reaction to the possible nomination of Lyndon Johnson.

The resulting moment of silence spelled surprise. The names that had been most often pronounced during the night were those of senators Stuart Symington of Missouri, Henry M. Jackson of Washington, and Hubert Humphrey of Minnesota, and Governor Orville Freeman of Minnesota. I knew that Jack Kennedy had given careful consideration to them all. At a meeting with me at his hideaway apartment before the convention began, Kennedy had asked me personally to sound out Symington. Although Symington had been reluctant to discuss the matter, he finally indicated that he would be amenable if no announcement were made before the presidential nomination.

Bob Kennedy himself had brought in Senator Jackson for a pre-convention discussion of the second spot. As I was present, I quickly said that, while Scoop Jackson was certainly acceptable to me personally, I felt that the decision should be left exclusively to the presidential nominee. The nominee had traveled through the whole country and could therefore judge the national political climate better than any man from one particular region. Furthermore, he would have to work with his running mate during the campaign and, hopefully, after the election, as well. There was no question in my mind not only that the nominee would pick the man best qualified to succeed him, but that he alone could judge which man could work with him in closest harmony.

The nominee had obviously made his decision during the night before the group meeting at the Biltmore. His choice—approved by his father, Joseph P. Kennedy, who was coaching from the sidelines—was Lyndon Baines Johnson. He was afraid, however, that Johnson would not be interested.

One of our group expressed similar doubts that Johnson would accept. Jack Kennedy said that he had already made overtures that morning, and he seemed actually surprised that Johnson was willing to become his running mate. As Mrs. Evelyn Lincoln, Kennedy's personal secretary, recalls in her book *My Twelve Years with John F. Kennedy* (David McKay), the nominee had left his Biltmore quarters early that morning and gone down the back stairs to Johnson's suite. He was back in twenty minutes to tell his staff that Johnson would run provided Sam Rayburn approved. What Kennedy wanted to know from us was this: Would the Johnson candidacy for Vice-President be helpful or harmful to the Democratic ticket in the states with large electoral votes?

Almost to a man we told Kennedy that, if he wanted Johnson, we were sure our delegations would support him. Only Governor Williams expressed serious misgivings. Michigan had a heavy labor vote, and the unions, particularly the United Auto Workers, did not like Johnson because he had voted for the Taft-Hartley Act.

Kennedy asked Ribicoff and me to stay when the representatives of the big-vote states filed out and were replaced by the Southerners: governors Daniel of Texas, Almond of Virginia, Vandiver of Georgia, Ellington of Tennessee, Combs of Kentucky, as well as Governor Luther Hodges of North Carolina, who was to become Kennedy's Secretary of Commerce, North Carolina's Governor-to-be Terry Sanford, and several southern senators. This second group unanimously and enthusiastically accepted the idea of Lyndon Johnson as the vice-presidential candidate.

The only bramble patch the nominee had to cross that morning should have been a four-lane throughway for a liberal Democrat such as Jack Kennedy: the labor leaders and professional liberals. As I was leaving the Kennedy headquarters after the meeting, I ran smack into Walter Reuther, the United Auto Workers boss, and Arthur Goldberg, then AFL-CIO counsel, later successively Secretary of Labor, justice of the Supreme Court, and Adlai Stevenson's successor as ambassador to the United Nations. Both were livid with indignation at the thought of Lyndon Johnson as Kennedy's running mate. They intimated that labor VIPs had been led to believe by the Kennedy camp that the second choice would be Humphrey, Symington, Freeman, or Jackson, any one of whom would be acceptable to labor. Both Reuther and Goldberg predicted there could be a liberal-labor bolt from the Democratic party if Johnson were nominated. Later Alex Rose, who spoke for both the Hatters' Union and the New York Liberal party, half-threatened to keep Kennedy's name off the Liberal party ballot and to withhold campaign funds.

Kennedy had considered these contingencies, weighing them against the advantages of Lyndon Johnson as a running mate. First, the good of the country was to be considered. Johnson was undoubtedly skilled and experienced in the art and science of government, should an emergency arise. (I was never personally aware that Jack Kennedy ever had a premonition that he might die in office.) He had once told an interviewer that he knew of no one better qualified to be President of the United States than Lyndon Johnson. Second, the party stood in need of help. Kennedy was only too aware of the handicap imposed upon him by the religious issue. He remembered how the Solid South had broken its Democratic ranks rather than vote for Governer Alfred E. Smith, a Catholic. Smith had lost Texas in 1928. Kennedy could not afford to lose Texas (and its twenty-four electoral votes) in 1960. With Lyndon Johnson, a Protestant Texan, on his ticket, he would have a better chance of an outcome based on merit rather than bias.

As for the disgruntled caliphs of Big Labor, they would somehow have to be re-gruntled. Where else could they go? They certainly were not going to rally round Dick Nixon, who seemed certain to be the Republican candidate. And as for the hints at tightened purse strings, Kennedy was not worried. He would have access to other sources of campaign funds.

When I left the Biltmore, I rejoined the Ohio delegation in caucus and reported on the morning's developments. Attorney Harvey Johnson (no kin) moved that Ohio support Lyndon Johnson, and the motion was passed without opposition. I immediately notified Jack Kennedy, who relayed the word to Senator Johnson. Later, when candidate Johnson was campaigning in Ohio, he told me that, while he was debating with himself whether or not to face the floor fight that Bobby Kennedy had predicted, it was the knowledge that Ohio had caucused and was solidly behind him that helped influence his decision to say yes.

There are a number of published versions of what went on in the madhouse that was the Biltmore later that day, notably a transcript of an informal oral statement by Johnson himself, and a memo left by the late Phil Graham, publisher of the Washington *Post*. Graham was deeply involved in the frantic, confused proceedings, and entrusted his notes to Theodore H. White, who incorporated them into his best-selling *The Making of the President—1964* (Atheneum). President Johnson, in a reminiscent mood at a birthday luncheon for senior Senator Aiken of

Vermont, added a few off-the-cuff sidelights. I was not one of the excited crowd milling in and out of Lyndon Johnson's hotel suite that hectic day, nor was I privy to his innermost thoughts. However, from what both Johnson and Jack Kennedy told me later, I believe I can outline briefly what happened.

On the night of Kennedy's nomination, House Speaker Sam Rayburn telephoned Johnson at 2 A.M. to declare indignantly: "I want you to know there's a rumor going around that you're going to be on the ticket. That would be the most idiotic thing you could do. Don't you think of leaving the majority leadership!"

"Yes sir," Johnson told the senators he replied. "But nobody has talked to me about it."

In a matter of hours practically everybody was talking about it. First of all, there was the presidential nominee himself. Lyndon Johnson was scarcely out of bed before Jack Kennedy called at his hotel suite to thank him for his telegram of congratulations and to sound him out on the vice-presidential situation. Johnson said he wanted to take counsel with his advisers, but he was obviously receptive.

In view of Speaker Rayburn's violent objections—Mr. Sam was not only a fellow Texan and an old friend, but was his campaign manager—Johnson sought opinions from as wide a spectrum as possible. Lady Bird, although expressing wifely deference to whatever decision her husband might make, was rather less than enthusiastic. A long-distance phone call to Cactus Jack Garner, an old Texan and an old Vice-President himself, evoked an even more violent, hostile, and spicy reaction. The late Senator Robert Kerr of Oklahoma, Governor Price Daniel of Texas, Texas congressman Homer Thornberry and John B. Connally, later Governor of Texas, all joined in a strongly negative chorus.

Jack Kennedy of course knew from whom Johnson would seek advice, and he sensed what that advice would be. He took immediate countermeasures. He sent his first team of persuaders, headed by former Democratic national treasurer Ed Pauley, who had been a Johnson supporter, to take Sam Rayburn to breakfast and to convince him that it was extremely important for Johnson to accept the vice-presidential nomination.

The main political arguments were two: Should Johnson refuse the vice-presidential nomination, and Kennedy fail to be elected, Johnson might be blamed for the defeat. Furthermore, if Kennedy were elected, there was a strong possibility that Johnson, having rejected the vice-presidential nomination, could very well lose his job as majority leader of the Senate as a result of his failure to cooperate.

The nominee himself also spoke to Rayburn personally, turning on all the Kennedy charm, using irrefutable logic and the appeal to party loyalty. As I have said before, I do not believe that all this pressure was necessary. Kennedy, however, knew how much Johnson relied on Rayburn's advice, and he wanted to make sure that Mr. Sam was convinced beyond the slightest doubt that Johnson should be on the ticket.

The choice of his varsity persuaders was a masterstroke of political strategy and shrewd insight into human nature. Let's look at the line-backers he sent in to support Pauley, the chief persuader: Hale Boggs, Tommy Corcoran, and Ed Foley.

Hale Boggs, at the time a Louisiana congressman, had been defeated for the Louisiana governorship largely by an anti-Catholic bloc of voters. He was close to the Kennedys, but even closer to Sam Rayburn, godfather of Johnson's bid for the presidency. Tommy Corcoran, a member of Roosevelt's original braintrust, was close to both Kennedy and Johnson, but he was also a bosom pal of Rayburn's. And Foley, while a good friend of Jack Kennedy, was an even closer friend of Lyndon Johnson.

The arguments that these men put to Rayburn were well thought out. Did Rayburn want Dick Nixon to be President of the United States (Nixon was the Speaker's *bête noire*)? This was a distinct possibility without Johnson on the ticket. Did Rayburn want the Southern Baptists to put Texas in the Republican column again? Kennedy intended to make the Vice-President an integral part of the Administration. Didn't Mr. Sam want to see his old protégé Lyndon become the first functional, non-ornamental Vice-President in history? All that talk about the powerless vice-presidency was so much eyewash. The presiding officer of the Senate had tremendous power. He could actually control debate by recognizing the right speakers, ruling on points of order and personal privilege, and keeping a tight rein on parliamentary procedure. Furthermore, Johnson would not be risking his majority leadership, since he would continue to be a candidate for the Senate from Texas. So even if he should be defeated for the vice-presidency, he would almost certainly be reelected to his Senate seat and thus go on being majority leader.

Sam Rayburn was impressed. At eleven o'clock that morning, Johnson remembers, Mr. Sam burst into the Johnson suite to report that he had been talking with the presidential nominee.

"They want you," Rayburn said. "I rather think the thing for you to do is to go on the ticket."

Johnson's forehead wrinkled into the now-familiar furrows of perplexity.

"How can you say that," was the bewildered question, "after what you said last night?"

"Because I'm a damn sight smarter man than I was last night," Rayburn replied.

The other objectors had second thoughts, too, and by early afternoon Johnson was not only willing but eager to be Kennedy's running mate. All he wanted now was a call from Kennedy headquarters, wrapping up such details as the timing of public announcements, the selection of the nominating speaker and seconders, and assurance that the presidential nominee had not changed his mind.

The afternoon crawled toward evening and still the final word had not come from the nominee. Instead brother Bobby Kennedy tried to see Johnson. He was unsuccessful. Lady Bird barred the entrance to the inner sanctum where her husband was making frantic efforts to remain calm and collected. Lyndon at this point would see no one but the nominee himself. If Bobby had anything to say, he could say it to Sam Rayburn or Phil Graham in the next room.

What Bobby had to say was as cheery as a newly dug grave. Brother Jack was having trouble with labor and the liberals, who were ready to fight to keep Johnson off the ticket in order to save the northern Negro vote and union support. If Johnson wanted to avoid the embarrassment of a floor fight, said Bobby, if he wanted to withdraw in the interests of party unity, why brother Jack would understand. Lyndon could be national committee chairman. . . .

There was general consternation in the Johnson suite. What was the meaning of Bobby Kennedy's message? Was it actually a polite request from the nominee to get lost? Or was it all Bobby's idea, cloaked in generalities and offering unpleasant alternatives? The fact that Bobby did not want Johnson on the ticket was no secret. The two men had never been exactly bosom pals (their arctic relationship reached absolute zero during the elimination rounds of Johnson's choice for a running mate in 1964, and there is some reason to believe that Bobby had assured the liberal-labor people that the second choice would be made from among Middlewesterners. While Bobby was widely believed to be the mastermind behind his brother Jack's career, it was always Jack who ran the show. He trusted Bobby completely, and relied on him because he could evaluate Bobby's reports exactly and knew what weight to give them against his own judgment. There was a very warm relationship between the two brothers, and I am certain that Bobby would have done anything to further Jack's career. But when the chips were down and all reports in, it was Jack who made the important decisions—as the afternoon's events were to prove.

Graham tried to get Jack Kennedy by phone, but it took an agonizingly long time. The Biltmore switchboards were as tightly tangled as a bucket of worms. In the corridor outside the Johnson suite, minions of the law were tripping over television cables while trying to clear out enough of the sweating newsmen to comply with fire regulations. Inside the suite Lyndon Johnson was fighting to retain his composure.

At last the phone call came through. Of course he wanted Johnson, said Jack Kennedy. He had just prepared a statement which he was going to read on television. If Graham would put Johnson on the phone, the nominee would read it to him.

A short time later Johnson was in the hall with Lady Bird, beaming into the cameras, and saying how happy he would be to become John Kennedy's running mate.

That night Lyndon Johnson's name was placed in nomination by Governor David L. Lawrence of Pennsylvania, a man who earlier in the year was not even sure that he wanted to see Kennedy head the ticket. Lawrence was afraid of the religious issue, and as late as the spring of 1960 would much rather have seen Jack Kennedy in the number two spot. He did not actually declare himself for Kennedy until he reached Los Angeles for the convention. Once exposed to the Kennedy magic, however, all misgivings evaporated. He had delivered the Pennsylvania delegation to Kennedy, and, at Kennedy's request, he was doing the same for Johnson—"a logical thing politically," as he told Edward T. Folliard, political columnist for the Washington *Post*, five years (to the day) later. At any rate, Lawrence's eloquent nomination speech, plus the general knowledge that the Texan was Kennedy's man, turned the trick. The floor fight was astutely avoided. The 1960 Democratic convention not only did the presidential nominee's bidding; it carried out the

Founding Fathers' original idea of electing the Vice-President as the second choice according to the ballots cast for President. The convention picked the man who had polled the second highest number of votes cast for President: Lyndon Johnson.

I have often wondered whether the generally accepted belief that Jack Kennedy could not have won without Johnson on the ticket is accurate. The theory was that Kennedy needed Texas and the Solid South to win, and could not have won without Johnson as second choice. Let us reexamine the score:

The Kennedy-Johnson ticket carried Texas with its 24 electoral votes, plus two other southern states: Louisiana, 10; South Carolina, 8; total, 42 electoral votes.

The Kennedy-Johnson ticket lost six states in the Far West: California, 32; Oregon, 6; Washington, 9; Colorado, 6; Idaho, 4; Alaska, 3; total, 60 electoral votes.

Would a Kennedy-Jackson ticket have done better in the Far West (Senator Jackson is from Washington State) by conceding Texas, Louisiana, and South Carolina, in return for the western states? The differential, in favor of the West, would have been 18 electoral votes. The Solid South which Johnson was supposed to secure for the Democratic ticket went almost solidly (with the exception of Texas, Louisiana, and South Carolina) Republican. Lost to the Kennedy-Johnson ticket were: Alabama, 6; Mississippi, 8; Florida, 10; Kentucky 10; Tennessee, 11; Virginia, 12; total score for the Solid South—for the Kennedy-Johnson ticket, 42 electoral votes; for the Nixon-Lodge ticket, 57 electoral votes.

It should be pointed out that the Johnson presence on the ticket may have won Georgia and North Carolina, although they were expected to remain in the Democratic column. It was the doubtful states of Louisiana, South Carolina, and Texas that might properly be credited to Johnson, as well as the five of Alabama's eleven electors who remained loyal to the party ticket while the others were casting their votes for Senator Harry Byrd.

Second thoughts, of course, are futile at this late date. On the night of July 14, 1960, the Democratic convention decreed that two curiously disparate candidates, John Fitzgerald Kennedy and Lyndon Baines Johnson, were to walk arm in arm down the road that was to carry both of them into the history books.

11

TRAGEDY AND TRANSMUTATION

JOHN FITZGERALD KENNEDY, JANUARY 20, 1961–NOVEMBER 22, 1963.
LYNDON BAINES JOHNSON, NOVEMBER 22, 1963—.

The extravagant exchanges of invective during the primary campaigns and the aftertaste of gall and wormwood following Johnson's failure to wrest the grand prize from Kennedy at Los Angeles could well have left a lasting bitterness between first- and second-choice nominees. The fact that no rancor appeared may be attributed to the Texan's great political acumen and to Kennedy's ability to forgive and forget in the interest of the broader objective.

Johnson's style of campaigning was in marked contrast to Kennedy's. His folksiness and homespun earnestness complemented the sophisticated sparkle of Kennedy's intellectual approach. And he fitted his attack to meet the point at which Kennedy needed the most help.

We in Ohio saw that Kennedy was running into trouble in the state. Early polls indicated that the religious issue was a strong anti-Kennedy factor in several key counties. Some areas reported that Kennedy's Catholicism would influence as much as fifty-eight per cent of the voters. The polls also showed that Nixon was more popular than Kennedy among the women voters. Some pundits attributed this to the success of the Republican attempt to tag the Democrats as the war party. The fact that twice within twenty-five years, with Democratic Presidents at the helm, the nation had become involved in global war may have put off wives and mothers from voting for another Democratic administration.

Most of us believed, however, that the religious issue was an equally strong factor. Women seemed to take their church affiliations much more seriously than did the men.

Kennedy's personality, charm, and quick intelligence obviously won over thousands who saw him in person or on television. The day after his first TV debate with Nixon he came into Ohio, and there was no doubt that he had answered the question raised by Republicans as to his maturity and experience. Starting at Painesville early in the morning, his trip through Cleveland, Lorain, Elyria, and Akron to an enthusiastic evening meeting in Canton was a triumph. Northern Ohio had never seen such crowds. After the Cleveland ovation, Senator Lausche, who rode in the procession, declared that the crowds were the largest and noisiest of any since General Eisenhower had returned as conquering hero from his victory in Europe. Even more impressive than the mass reaction, I thought, were the individual remarks tossed at Kennedy as the motorcade passed: "You were great on TV last night, Jack." "You sure clobbered Nixon." "We're all for you now, Jack."

It was all very warming, but it still did not overcome the bias and fear by some Ohioans that a vote for Kennedy would by remote control make Washington the voice of the Vatican. We told both Bobby Kennedy and the candidate himself of this situation. We suggested that Lyndon Johnson's appearance in the state was essential to combat this religious prejudice.

Senator Johnson answered the call. He made a short but smiling invasion of Ohio, shaking thousands of hands, handing out ball-point pens, making thousands of folksy personal contacts. He made his principal target Columbus, because the concentration of correspondents in the state capital would give him the best statewide press coverage. He spoke from the statehouse steps, hallowed because Abraham Lincoln had spoken there on his way to Washington for his first inaugural. He spoke at Ohio State University. He traveled to the southern half of the state to speak from the courthouse in Chillicothe. The crowds that greeted him were everywhere large and enthusiastically friendly.

Johnson met the religious issue head-on. He constantly referred to himself as a Protestant from Texas, proud of being the running mate of a Catholic from Boston. He called the partnership the very epitome of Americanism, and described how Senator Kennedy's brother Joe, a Catholic from Boston, was flying as copilot with a Protestant from Texas when shot down over the English Channel during World War II. Nobody asked their religion when they gave their lives for their country, he said.

Johnson's approach was extremely effective, and perhaps if he could have given more time to Ohio—obviously impossible because of the campaign demands upon him—the state returns might have been improved. As it was, Nixon won Ohio's 25 electoral votes by 2,217,611 to Kennedy's 1,944,248.

I have often wondered about the actual influence of religious bias as compared with other Republican campaign weapons. The charges of immaturity and inexperience, as I have already said, were disposed of by the Kennedy-Nixon television debates. The issue of ill health was never pushed as hard as it had been during the primary campaigns, although both Kennedy and Johnson had medical histories. Kennedy actually was never completely free of pain throughout his political career. Although his adrenal insufficiency was being corrected therapeutically, his bad back and other minor souvenirs of his ordeal in the Pacific war plagued him to the end, and he was wearing his spine-bracing corset when he was assassinated. Yet his personal appearance—his scorn of hat and topcoat in all weather—gave a convincing picture of excellent health. As for Johnson's massive coronary thrombosis in 1955, the Republicans could not very well make an issue of that since General Eisenhower's heart attack had not been considered as a bar to the presidency less than a year after he left the hospital.

Some capital was made of Kennedy's great wealth, although neither Nixon nor his running mate Lodge was exactly a pauper. Although Johnson's wealth was closely scrutinized four years later, in 1960 nobody seemed to point out that the standard-bearers of the Democratic party, champions of the common man, were both millionaires. Although Kennedy's wealth was inherited, Johnson's rise to opulence was his own doing, in the manner of a Horatio Alger hero.

As the world knows, the American electorate rejected the Republican arguments by a scant 118,000 popular votes but by an electoral-vote margin of 84. And John F. Kennedy became the youngest man elected President of the United States and the first Roman Catholic to occupy the White House.

It was my privilege to visit the new President rather frequently during his historic thousand days in office. I found him to be the same youthful, hard-hitting, quick-to-laughter intellectual he had shown himself during the campaign, despite the awareness of the awesome responsibilities that had fallen, at his own behest, upon his young shoulders. Although he was deeply concerned with the historic nature of his great office, he had not allowed his grimly serious duties to black out his sense of humor—fortunately, because he went through one of the most trying periods of his presidency less than a hundred days after his inauguration.

On the day after election, as governor of the state, I had expressed regret for our failure to deliver Ohio to the Kennedy-Johnson ticket, and had told the President-elect that I took full responsibility for having struck out. When I saw him again in Washington three months after his accession to office, and asked him how he liked his new job, he smiled wistfully, and said it was a job that nobody should complain about losing.

"You have probably noticed," he said, referring to my earlier remark, "that I have been very busy assuming massive responsibility myself."

The Bay of Pigs fiasco of the United States-supported invasion of Castro's Cuba by Cuban refugee legions was only a few days in the past. President Kennedy had publicly accepted complete responsibility for the affair, which was drawing worldwide criticism, and he seemed anxious to talk about it freely. He told me that while the project had been conceived and approved by the previous Administration,* he could of course have vetoed it on assuming office. He had grave misgivings about the adventure, he said, but hesitated to substitute his own judgment for that of the intelligence experts of the CIA, and of such professional military minds as the Joint Chiefs of Staff and his predecessor, the architect of the Allied victory in Europe. And, having accepted the previous plans, he saw no advantage to the nation in trying to shift the blame for failure. By taking the full responsibility upon his own shoulders, he said, he had hoped to put an end to speculation and rumor.

However heartbreaking the failure in human terms for the Cuban patriots, and the humiliation of deciding against retrieving "national honor" by not following through with outright armed intervention by enough American power to right the balance, the fiasco was not without valuable results for the President. It had taught him, he said, the immense importance of being able to evaluate properly the recommendations of others. For example, he said, he always knew what weight he could give to a report by brother Bob; but, at the time he was forced to

* General Eisenhower has said he approved the concept but not the final plan.

make a decision on the Cuban expedition, he could not give proper appraisal to reports from people whose capabilities, reliability, and powers of observation and judgment were not well known to him. He could understand a mistaken opinion as to the readiness of Cubans to revolt against Castro, but he found inexcusable an inaccurate report describing terrain.

President Kennedy told me that his first impulse had been to order American air and naval support to redress the situation, but that he had restrained himself because overt action in Cuba would have given the Russians an excuse to move against Turkey and other countries adjacent to the Soviet Union where the United States maintained military bases. At that time, Kennedy was anxious to avoid a confrontation with the Soviets that involved the danger of nuclear war, although he did not hesitate to assume the risk later when it was apparent that Moscow had misinterpreted caution for cowardice. When the chips were down in the Cuban missile crisis, it was the Soviet chief who threw in his hand.

There is no doubt that the world situation was constantly foremost in John Kennedy's mind. He was keenly aware that the survival or destruction of civilization could very well depend on a decision of his, and he was apt to be impatient with those who thought he was too concerned with the danger of a nuclear holocaust. He once said that it was extremely important that Nikita Khrushchev never be pushed to the point of no return. Kennedy believed that if the then Russian leader ever found himself in a corner from which he could not extricate himself without losing face, he would not hesitate to precipitate global war.

Jack Kennedy's preoccupation with foreign affairs came naturally. He had traveled and lived abroad. He had seen something of the backstage workings of diplomacy when his father was ambassador to Britain. He knew the European mind and European living at first hand. He had written a youthful but perceptive book on international affairs, *Why England Slept*.

His Vice-President, on the other hand, was comparatively parochial. Lyndon Johnson's travels had been limited largely to trips between Texas and Washington. Kennedy decided to broaden his geographical education by sending him on missions abroad. Most of the trips were of ceremonial character or goodwill gestures, but a few, like the trip of reassurance to Berlin, while perhaps not as spectacular as Kennedy's later *"Ich bin ein Berliner"* speech, had definite overtones of international politics. He went to Senegal to celebrate the independence of that former French colony. He swept through Southeast Asia from Formosa via the Philippines, Vietnam, and Thailand to India and Pakistan. He was in Rome to see Pope John and later to attend his funeral. He visited Scandinavia and the Low Countries. As Vice-President of the United States, he was required by protocol to meet world figures, but he was much more at home in the streets, shaking hands just as if he were campaigning back in Johnson City, Texas. He passed out ball-point pens and souvenirs, asked questions through an interpreter, and through interpreters assured the startled natives that the United States was their friend and would help them fight poverty and disease.

The natives of India and Thailand and Italy were puzzled but friendly. After all, he bore enough resemblance to the Hollywood Texan they had seen in the movie Westerns to be vaguely familiar. Nowhere did he encounter the rudeness and hostility that he had met in his own Texas where a crowd in a Dallas hotel lobby pushed, shoved, and spat at him and his wife during the 1960 campaign. The climax of his home-folks diplomacy, of course, was his accosting of the Pakistani camel driver on the road from the Karachi airport and inviting him to come down to the ranch some time. Through the intermediary of several agencies which might profit by the attendant publicity, Ahmed Bashir did visit the United States. He captivated Washington by his simple charm and the untutored poetry of his observations. What might have been either a ridiculous or disastrous stunt became a triumph of international good will.

Johnson was not happy as Vice-President. He was restless, despite Kennedy's efforts to keep him busy with important chairmanships, such as those of the Peace Corps Advisory Council, the Aeronautics and Space Council, the Committee on Equal Employment Opportunity. As head of the latter he spoke at Gettysburg one hundred years after the battle that marked the turning point in the Civil War. The speech, in my opinion, marked the turning point in Lyndon Johnson's coming of age as a national political figure. With it, he burned his southern bridges behind him. It was no longer a Texas senator but a Vice-President of the United States who declared:

> The Negro says "Now." Others say "Never." The voice of responsible Americans—the voice of those who died here and the great man who spoke here—their voices say, "Together." There is no other way.

Although he chafed under the constitutional shackles of the vice-presidency, Johnson was still a good team player. He found presiding over the Senate dull business compared to the infighting and arm twisting he had loved while majority leader. He didn't really enjoy trying to implement a younger man's program, yet there was never any public difference between the two men. The Vice-President always cleared his speeches with the White House. And if he thought the President was inept in his approach to domestic politics, he kept his own counsel.

Actually, Jack Kennedy was anything but inept. His interest in domestic politics was easily matched by his skill in, and knowledge of, the field. There has been a tendency to compare him unfavorably with Johnson in his handling of Congress, but two men using different methods can achieve identical results in the same situation, depending upon timing and propitious circumstances. Kennedy spent much time on the phone with senators and made many personal contacts with congressmen.

In 1962 President Kennedy traveled the country extensively, speaking on behalf of the election of new candidates for Congress and the reelection of incumbents. He was in demand everywhere but in the southeastern part of the country. There was no reluctance on the part of congressmen and senators to be associated with a popular young President who, they knew, would draw much larger crowds than would come to hear the candidates alone. Kennedy's taking the road in support of congressional candidates was part of his basic strategy to insure the successful legislative session of 1963. His political traveling was halted in October 1963 by the Cuban crisis. However, his deft handling of the confrontation with Khrushchev could only be considered a plus for every Democratic candidate for the House and Senate.

Earlier he had reason to gnash his teeth when news media criticized him for lack of leadership, for he spent long hours with legislators on behalf of his program, seeking their support on the basis of logic, the common good, and personal friendship. He was annoyed to find so many of them more concerned with local and personal interests than with national issues.

"What do they expect me to do?" he complained once, when editorial carping was playing hob with his blood pressure. "Even if I wanted to buy them off with favors for their constituents, there aren't enough military bases, air fields, and shipyards to go around."

He was enough of a political realist, of course, to understand the necessity of a legislator's publicly protecting his rear even while privately approving a progressive forward-looking program. The political facts of life demand that a friendly senator or congressman be reelected in order to be useful.

Yet President Kennedy himself was vitally interested in domestic politics, campaign strategy, and the techniques of vote getting. One night at a White House gathering following a dinner for the President of India, he took me aside and asked what we were going to do to improve the political climate in Ohio. He was concerned about the situation there, he said, and wanted to discuss it at length; but, as he was going to Cape Cod for a few days, he suggested I call his personal secretary, Evelyn Lincoln, and make an appointment for the following week. When I phoned Mrs. Lincoln, she inquired as to the nature of my business, and I replied that I wanted to talk about something in which the President had little interest: Ohio politics. She laughed and said that, as the President was at that moment flying back from Hyannis Port, he probably would not want to see me until he got off the plane.

When I kept my appointment at the White House, before we got down to the business of discussing the variations in direction, force, and pressure of the political winds of my state, President Kennedy presented me with a photograph taken the night of the dinner for the Indian President, already framed and autographed by both the President and Mrs. Kennedy.

The last time I saw Jack Kennedy we were both attending the funeral of Attorney James McInerney, a mutual friend, in the fall of 1963. We talked by telephone several times after that, chiefly about a subject that fascinated us both: automation. He suggested that I write him a rough agenda for a possible White House conference on the problems of automation and that I come to Washington to discuss it during the week after Thanksgiving.

Thanksgiving Day never came for Jack Kennedy.

There is no need to review the details of that tragic Friday in Dallas when a mentally and emotionally irresponsible misfit senselessly destroyed the life of a young President who had already won his spurs as a statesman and who gave great promise of becoming a real leader of the free world. The assassin's bullet had for the fourth time promoted a man who was second choice into the lonely seat of responsibility that is the presidency of the United States. It was the first time, however, that a stunned nation could participate, vicariously, in the transfer of power and responsibility.

The shocked millions who sat mesmerized before their TV screens to watch Air Force One land at Andrews Air Force Base and roll to a stop were an intimate part of the grim silence which shrouded the November darkness as the howl of engines faded to a whisper and died. The human voice did not violate the reverent stillness as the dead President's casket was carried from the plane to the waiting naval ambulance, followed by the blood-spattered First Lady. And when the new President walked across the field to the microphones to ask the nation's help in the awesome responsibility that had been so brutally thrust upon him, the hearts of his countrymen were with him.

Most Americans liked the solemn humility of his first words as President. They also liked his loyalty to the program of his predecessor as expressed in his first address to Congress: "Let us continue." They smiled wistfully at his pronunciation—"continya"—and realized that their ears were in for some readjustment after Jack Kennedy's "Cuber." And they applauded his whip-cracking performance on Capitol Hill.

Without wishing to detract from Lyndon Johnson's very great political skills, I should like to suggest that Jack Kennedy, alive and dead, had a great deal to do with the passage of his own program. The Eighty-seventh Congress was not actually hostile to Kennedy. If at times both houses seemed to lag behind the President, it was largely a matter of timing. They, like the nation, had not yet adjusted to the climate of the New Frontier. After eight Eisenhower years of stand-pat-ism, Congress, like the country, was in a mood of caution. Legislators were not quite sure the new young President knew what he was doing. As the Kennedy administration neared its tragic end, however, the President was gaining confidence and Congress was gaining momentum.

Most legislators liked Jack Kennedy personally, too, despite his untypical congressional background. His charm transcended his Harvard intellectualism, his inherited wealth, and easy sophistication. His personal warmth carried considerable influence. People did things for Jack Kennedy because they wanted to be his friends.

Some people might do things for Lyndon Johnson because they were afraid of being considered his enemy. He has been an arm twister as well as a hand shaker and an elbow grasper, a politician's politician. While he has a Texas college degree, his real education has been on Capitol Hill.

He speaks the language of the congressmen and he thinks like the congressmen—but always one thought ahead of them. He is not the planner that Kennedy was. James Reston of *The New York Times* says of him: "He came to the Presidency with more Government experience than any man in this century, but personally he is a throwback. He is a link between the Old Frontier of the days of William Jennings Bryan and the New Frontier days of John F. Kennedy. . . . He does not concentrate on thinking programs through but in getting them through."

Nobody can properly appraise how much impact the Kennedy assassination had on the complete rout of opposition to the Kennedy legislative program. Washington observers are certain that the tax cut would have been approved and civil-rights legislation passed before the 1964 elections, had Kennedy lived. They are just as certain that the Kennedy assassination had a great deal to do with the acceleration of the Kennedy program's adoption. Some of the men who fought the Kennedy bills while he was alive felt that they should atone for their hostility to a martyred President by withdrawing their opposition.

Observers also feel that the Kennedy assassination was a factor in Johnson's huge majority over Senator Goldwater in the 1964 election, although how much of a factor we can only guess. The figures do indicate that important forces were at work, and one of them was certainly the great wave of emotion generated by the assassination of a very young and popular President. Jack Kennedy lost Ohio to Nixon in 1960 by some two hundred and seventy-five thousand; Nixon received fifty-three per cent of the vote. Four years later, and less than a year after the Kennedy tragedy, Lyndon Johnson carried Ohio by one million sixty thousand, which represented about sixty-two per cent of the vote. Johnson carried eighty-four of Ohio's eighty-eight counties, including most of the so-called Bible Belt counties. At least some of this difference must be attributed to a mass guilt complex on the part of citizens who had voted against Kennedy because of their religious convictions. And I am certain that part of the Johnson vote was cast by Democrats returning to the fold after having voted Republican for reasons not connected with with political philosophy. It was a repetition of 1928, when Ohio voted against Al Smith, the Democratic candidate for President who happened also to be a Catholic, by a record-breaking majority of almost two to one. Yet only two years later, in 1930, Ohio elected a Democratic governor and a Democratic senator.

I firmly believe that had Kennedy lived he would have been reelected President over Senator Goldwater by a more impressive majority than he scored over Nixon. He had endeared himself to millions who had voted against him in 1960; he had reassured others that the danger of his turning the country over to the Vatican was indeed remote. The nation was beginning to show more support for his legislative program. Moreover, he would have been aided immeasurably by Goldwater's unprepossessing second choice and the inept Republican campaign. By espousing the right-wing elements of his party, by giving the back of his hand to the middle-of-the-roaders who sought party unity even after the triumph of the extremists at the Republican national convention in San Francisco, Goldwater very nearly wrecked the Grand Old Party. By accepting the theses of Congressman William E. Miller, the Republican national chairman (his second choice), and campaign manager Dean Burch, Goldwater showed a dismal misunderstanding of the basic character of the American two-party system, which is not far from Johnson's pet phrase "consensus." By his insistence upon giving the voters a "true choice," Goldwater not only alienated the moderates of his party but created the same sort of internal dissension that caused the disappearance of the Whig party from the national scene a century earlier. Second-choice candidate Miller attacked Johnson's war record (Lieutenant Commander Johnson, while his exploits were less spectacular than those of Lieutenant (j.g.) John Kennedy, had been awarded the Silver Star), and dredged up the old hints of scandal first voiced at the time of his first election to the Senate (which considered the charges, investigated them, and seated Johnson). But nothing could prevent the former Vice-President from running up the greatest plurality in history.

The 1964 landslide, in addition to giving Lyndon Johnson a definite mandate in his own right, also gave him a comfortable majority in both Houses of Congress. His program was still fundamentally the Kennedy program, but, since he had made it his own, its aim was no longer the New Frontier but the Great Society. Moreover, Lyndon Johnson's skill in handling his majority enabled him to realize most of the program. Some previous accidental Presidents, with all the good intentions in the world of carrying out the programs of their predecessors, were balked by hostile legislators. Andrew Johnson, for instance, had inherited and accepted Lincoln's program for Reconstruction "with malice toward none; with charity for all. . . ." His Congress, however, reflected the mood of the northern states, which were determined to punish the South. Harry Truman was a willing heir to the Franklin Roosevelt program, yet was stymied by the "do-nothing" Eightieth on many issues.

Even the Old Master FDR, although he had a majority, sometimes handled it with such surprising awkwardness that he was faced with arched backs, bared teeth, and unfriendly spitting sounds. Johnson's ability to judge the temper of the country therefore may be considered close to genius when we realize that Eighty-ninth Congress enacted more major legislation than even the historic one-hundred-day session of the first Franklin Roosevelt administration. Among the significant measures passed:

*Medicare—national health insurance for the aging, which had been on the agenda of both Truman and Kennedy—and expanded social security benefits.

*Aid to elementary and secondary education (which had struck a snag under Kennedy because parochial schools were not included), as well as college aid, including the first federal undergraduate scholarships.

*Creation of a Cabinet-level Department of Housing and Urban Affairs, a pet project of the Kennedy administration.

*Nearly eight billion dollars in grants and loans for new housing (a rent-subsidy provision was defeated).

*Federal guarantees of voting rights for minorities, supplementing the 1964 Civil Rights Act, and abolishing literacy tests by which some southern states disenfranchised Negroes.

*More than six billion dollars in aid for Appalachia and other depressed areas—LBJ's war on poverty.

*Federal controls to reduce air and water pollution.

*Revision of the Immigration Act, eliminating the discriminatory national-origins basis of the 1924 quota system.

*A proposed constitutional amendment, providing for continuity in the presidential succession (to be discussed in the next chapter). The amendment became effective in 1967.

*Federal funds for medical research.

*Increased federal control over depressant and stimulant drugs.

*Reduction of the gold reserves held by federal reserve banks to cover commercial bank deposits, freeing five billion dollars for international exchange. Reduction of the silver content in dimes and quarters.

*Withholding of some federal road funds from states which permit disfiguring billboards and exposed junkyards along main highways.

*Establishment of a National Foundation for the Arts and Humanities to encourage and subsidize cultural projects.

Lyndon Johnson's uncanny sense of timing and the accuracy with which he has been able to judge the mood of Congress and anticipate problems was never better demonstrated than in the managed delay of his legislative reverses until the end of the Eighty-ninth's long first session. One of his campaign promises—to the labor interests—had been the repeal of Section 14-b of the Taft-Hartley Act, which allows states to outlaw the union shop with so-called "right-to-work" legislation. Sensing that the opposition of minority leader Everett Dirksen of Illinois would meet with a sympathetic response in the Senate, Johnson put off a vote on repeal until the end of the session, when its defeat would not start a chain reaction against priority measures. The proposal to raise the minimum wage to $1.75 an hour was also defeated. So was a late-session bill to give home rule to the District of Columbia, which, as a result, continues to be governed by congressional committee.

The overall result, however, was the greatest triumph in United States history—the adoption almost in toto of the Lyndon Johnson legislative program, which, despite the Texas accent, could very well be mistaken for the Kennedy program.

Although the Texas drawl replaced the Harvard accent to some extent on Johnson's first team of advisers—Johnson has sometimes referred to adviser Jack Valenti as "*my* Harvard man"—a strong Kennedy influence has lingered in the administration. The key Cabinet posts of State and Defense were still, early in 1966, occupied by Kennedy appointees Dean Rusk and Robert MacNamara. The Kennedy secretaries of Interior, Agriculture, and Labor had also survived the first year of Johnson's own administration.

Attorney General Robert Kennedy's resignation was not unexpected, the result of inevitable conflict between two strong-willed men, each secure in his own right. The late President's brother decided to pursue his ambitions by winning a Senate seat from New York.

On the sub-Cabinet level, speech writers Arthur Schlesinger, Jr., and Theodore Sorensen quit to write books about Jack Kennedy. Press secretary Pierre Salinger left to make an unsuccessful bid for a Senate seat from California. Some of the Kennedy economic and scientific advisers returned to the academic life. Their replacements, as well as the Johnson appointments to fill the few vacancies left by Cabinet members returning to the greater opulence of private life, were generally applauded.

Perhaps the most influential Kennedy adviser on foreign affairs—McGeorge Bundy, the Yale-educated Harvard dean—retained almost equal importance in President Johnson's inner circle until he left for greener fields.

In view of the continuity of the policy-making personnel in the field of international affairs, as well as the President's great success in securing the most progressive social legislation since the New Deal, the limited popularity of Lyndon Johnson among the liberal intellectuals is something of a mystery. True, the teach-ins and other professorial protests against Johnson's policies in Vietnam and the Caribbean have been the expression of a small but vocal minority; and the long-haired draft-age demonstrators can hardly be called intellectuals. True, too, the escalation in Vietnam is merely an extension and intensification of the Kennedy policy of containment of communism in Southeast Asia, begun in Laos. And, although Johnson's armed intervention in Santo Domingo may have been too much too soon, it is probable that Jack Kennedy, on the basis of intelligence similar to that obtainable by Johnson, would have taken some sort of action to prevent the possible loss of another Caribbean island to extra-hemispheric influence. Yet among the vast majority of Americans who do support Johnson in his use of American power overseas there are many who do so with crossed fingers. And there has been definite uneasiness among friendly political leaders abroad.

Perhaps this cautious reception of Johnson as an extension of the Kennedy presidency, despite the overwhelming mandate given him in the 1964 election, has been due almost entirely to the differing personalities of the two men, to their backgrounds and to their families. Kennedy was an Easterner, fairly orthodox in his manners, inhibited because his omnivorous reading had made him aware of the historical problems he would have to solve and of the difficulties in their solution because of a world in social and political ferment. Johnson, a rough-and-ready product of the Southwest, wearing the cowboy boots and ten-gallon hat as symbols of the old frontier but anxious to trade the New Frontier for the Great Society because he wanted his own trademark, was uninhibited.

He had found nothing in his reading, confined largely to contemporary documents, to weaken his belief in the steadfast qualities and courage of the American people, the inexhaustible resources of the American continent, and the superiority of the American system of government.

Johnson has been called a pragmatist, but he is religious to the extent that he believes in a God who would look after an America committed to common decency, honesty, justice for all, a concern for the underdog, and private enterprise. He is not happy merely with admiration for his political skill and respect for his statesmanship.

He has wanted to be loved for himself, not for his power or as a Pedernales-brand Kennedy. He made no Kennedy-esque appeal for the affections of the eggheads, the artists, or the artistes, although he did invite a covey of creative people to the White House for the signing of the thirty-six-million-dollar bill establishing the National Foundation for the Arts and Humanities. He has wanted to be, like Jack Kennedy, President of all the Americans, lowbrow as well as highbrow, black and white, labor and management—although whether he showed more finesse in persuading management to hold the line on aluminum prices than Kennedy did on steel is a moot question. Like Kennedy, he is an individualist; like Kennedy, he has been bent on doing things his own way, according to his own habits and natural tendencies.

While Kennedy relaxed by sailing off Cape Cod, Johnson is happy among his livestock on his Texas ranch. Where Kennedy delighted in French cuisine (he installed a cordon bleu in the White House kitchens) and château-bottled Bordeaux, Johnson finds deep satisfaction in barbecued steer, chili, and the wines of California or New York's Finger Lakes. Johnson has bent over backward to be himself. When he felt like pulling a beagle's ears, he pulled them publicly. He did not hesitate, after his 1965 cholecystectomy, to yank up his shirttail and exhibit his surgical scar to the television cameras and the startled millions beyond.

Lyndon Johnson wasted no time in the transition from second fiddle to the conductor's podium. He grasped the baton firmly, and the once-acquiescent team player left no doubt as to who was now the leader. He drove himself as hard as he drove his staff, and wanted the credit for it. He took to television both to make grave declarations of state and to make minor announcements such as other Presidents had left to their press secretaries. The nation got to know every furrow of his frown, every movement of his cleft chin, every twitch of his prominent nose. Television viewers have learned to weigh the thin-lipped presidential smile against the down-to-earth shrewdness of his searching eyes. They have liked what he has said, as a rule, and they generally have liked what he has done. Yet they have never felt very close to him.

Johnson does not radiate the warmth that Jack Kennedy generated.

It is my own feeling that Johnson's own curious inability to communicate his warm and sympathetic concern is at the root of the questioning acceptance of his foreign policy. It is of course too early to judge the final import of his international maneuvers. Future historians, with the perspective of time, will be able to compare the effectiveness of the brief Kennedy skirmishes with friends and enemies abroad and Lyndon Johnson's overseas ventures. There is no question in my mind, however, that American diplomacy was for three years closely dominated by the warmth of Kennedy's personal relationships with the heads of foreign nations. Witness the astonishing number of chiefs of state who flew to Washington to walk behind the flag-draped casket to the chilling rhythm of muffled drums.

Where foreign premiers and potentates have found Lyndon Johnson difficult to understand, Kennedy was able to talk to them confidentially and confidingly, backed by a national prestige that compensated for his youth. He met most major statesmen several times. First meetings served as a basis for personal appraisal. Subsequent meetings were simpler.

He told me that, during his first meeting with Nikita Khrushchev in Vienna, he had tried joking with the Russian dictator.

"What's that decoration the Chairman is wearing?" Kennedy asked the interpreter.

Khrushchev was consulted and replied through the interpreter that it was the Lenin Peace Prize.

"Tell the Chairman," said Kennedy, "that I hope they never have to take it away from him."

Khrushchev scowled. He was far too tense for levity, and, in Kennedy's opinion, inclined to take himself much too seriously. In the late President's own words: "He reminded me of a fellow who had grown up on the wrong side of the tracks, who had made good in a big way, but who was afraid nobody would believe he had achieved importance on his own unless he made them believe it."

Kennedy told me of his admiration and affection for Konrad Adenauer when he was Chancellor of West Germany, and of *Der Alte*'s skill in judging people. Adenauer had a great fondness and respect for Franklin Roosevelt, but could rarely reach agreement with him. On the other hand, he fought constantly with Winston Churchill, but never failed to reach an understanding with him politically. Kennedy's personal warmth enabled him to achieve both respect and political accord. He considered the negotiation of the limited nuclear test ban treaty of 1963 to be one of his major achievements—an important step toward preventing civilization from committing suicide.

World leaders have, in sum, found Lyndon Johnson's personality and approach quite different from his predecessor's—not surprisingly, for Johnson is decidedly different. Whether or not his personality and methods will prevail in the long run is difficult to predict when he has been in the White House such a relatively short time. He is, after all, eligible to serve two full terms on his own.

In any event, he is certain to find heavy going ahead. European statesmen particularly are apt to regard him much as their sophisticated forebears of the early nineteenth century looked down upon the rugged Yankee envoys of a new, upstart nation. American diplomats may no longer be the tobacco-chewing political appointees who once adorned our embassies and legations with brass spittoons, but the pioneering spirit of those shaggy backwoods envoys has somehow carried through to the Lyndon Johnson administration. In the intervening century and three-quarters, the upstart nation has reached the pinnacle of world power, while the more pretentious nations, grown old and tired under their burden of history and glory, have shed their empires and far-flung armadas to withdraw into their shrunken boundaries.

Only time will tell if Lyndon Johnson's foreign policies will succeed. I am inclined to bet on him. He has such a strong personality, such a stubborn will, and such skill and experience in dealing with politicians on a political basis—what successful statesman is not ninety per cent politician?—that I cannot help feeling he will be eternally trading apples for orchards.

The key to President Johnson's character, unlikely though it may seem, appears to lie in his attitude to golf. I once asked an intimate of his if the President had ever played the game. Yes, was the reply, years ago Johnson decided to take up golf. However, when he found that he could only get in nine holes about once a week, he gave it up. Golf required too many hours to develop the skill necessary to become a champion, and, since he could not devote enough time to the game to become an expert, he would rather not play.

Should Lyndon Johnson fail in his mission as President of the United States, he can blame only his own strength. His principal problems in the first years of his presidency have been his complete absorption with the job, a reluctance to delegate responsibility, and an all-consuming fear that his co-workers will not achieve the perfection he demands. It may be that he, too, having grown up on the other side of the tracks and having made good in a big way, wants to make sure that people will believe that he has done it all on his own.

12

NO MORE VACANCIES

After Nearly Two Centuries the Twenty-fifth Amendment Will Keep the Second Spot Always Filled

It has taken one hundred seventy-eight years of nationhood under the Constitution for the American people to get their first hope of a continuity in the office of Vice-President. During this time the vice-presidency has been vacant for a total of nearly thirty-nine years. Seven Vice-Presidents have died in office, leaving a total of more than fourteen years of their terms unfilled. One Vice-President—Calhoun—resigned to fill his old Senate seat. Eight Vice-Presidents, as we have just read, left a total vacuum of nearly twenty-four years behind them when they were elevated to the White House. Yet it was not until July 6, 1965, that Congress decided to do something to make sure there was always a Vice-President on the job.

Then the Senate voted to submit a proposed twenty-fifth constitutional amendment to the states for ratification. The House had already approved. The amendment became effective February 10, 1967, when it was approved by the legislatures of three-fourths of the states—thirty-eight to be exact. The states had seven years in which to complete the ratification, but in view of the overwhelming majorities by which the amendment passed both Houses of Congress, and the obvious need of its adoption, the thirty-eighth state, Nevada, ratified it within nineteen months of its approval by the Senate.

There are four sections of the newest amendment, which is the product of the Senate Subcommittee on Presidential Succession, chaired by Birch Bayh, Democratic senator from Indiana. The first section merely clears up the ambiguity of the original language in Article II—whether the title, as well as "the powers and duties," of the presidency is inherited by the Vice-President. Although nobody has since questioned the precedent set by Tyler in grasping the thistle firmly, the matter is definitely settled once and for all by Section I of the Twenty-fifth Amendment, which declares flatly that "the Vice-President shall become President."

Section II provides that there shall always be a Vice-President. It reads: "Whenever there is a vacancy in the office of the Vice-President, the President shall nominate a Vice-President who shall take office upon confirmation by a majority vote of both houses of Congress."

There was much debate on this subject, and many plans were submitted before the simplest of procedures was adopted. Former Vice-President Richard Nixon, testifying before the Senate Judiciary Committee, proposed reconvening the electoral college to fill a vacancy in the vice-presidency. The proposal had considerable support, but left unanswered a number of questions. What would happen if a closely divided electoral college should change its political complexion between election and the vacancy? Would the President be embarrassed by having to take into his confidence a top-ranking member of the opposition party who might be his opponent in the next election? Until the year 1947, if the President died during a vacancy in the vice-presidency, the succession to the White House passed to the members of the Cabinet in the order of their seniority: State, Treasury, Defense, Attorney General, etc. President Truman, however, believed that an elected officer should be next in line, rather than an appointee, and took the lead in promoting the succession law of 1947, which made the Speaker of the House and the President Pro Tem of the Senate the first and second "nominal vice-president."

When President Truman began plugging for a change in the succession law, his good friend Sam Rayburn was Speaker of the House. By the time the change became law, Truman was saddled with a Republican majority in the Eightieth "Do-nothing" Congress, and Republican Joe Martin was Speaker of the House. The situation seemed incongruous in view of Truman's violent reaction to Senator Fulbright's suggestion, after the 1946 congressional election, that the President resign to make way for a Republican successor.

This former system of succession caused considerable apprehension in many circles following the assassination of President John Kennedy. After all, Vice-President Lyndon Johnson had been riding only a few feet away when the Dallas motorcade came within range of the assassin's fire. If, as the Secret Service at first feared, the whole presidential party was marked for extinction, the contrast between the youth of our youngest elected President and his aging potential successors was something of a shock. Next in line was Speaker of the House John W. McCormack, seventy-two, followed by President Pro Tempore of the Senate, Senator Carl Hayden, eighty-seven.

There were also second thoughts about turning the reins of government over to a member of Congress, whose lifetime may have been spent in the service of a local district or even of one state. Not only might he lack a national viewpoint, but, in view of the congressional seniority system, he is hardly likely to have achieved the office of Speaker of the House before having reached a ripe old age.

The succession system which is provided by the Twenty-fifth Amendment—selection of a Vice-President by the President with the approval of Congress—was advocated by former President Eisenhower before its adoption by Senator Birch Bayh's Subcommittee on Presidential Succession. The procedure parallels the standard practice of our political parties in their selection of vice-presidential candidates by national convention: the delegates merely ratify the choice made by the presidential nominee. No political party would ever think of asking the candidate for President to accept a running mate he regarded as unsatisfactory. In the rare cases when the delegates have risen in apparent revolt, they were rebelling against the party bosses, not the presidential candidate. Theodore Roosevelt was their second choice in defiance of Mark Hanna and company after McKinley had refused to indicate his preference. They chose Coolidge over Lenroot because Lenroot had not been picked by Harding but by the senatorial cabal that had picked Harding.

In my opinion the congressional approval called for by the Twenty-fifth Amendment, unless it is intended to be no more than a rubber-stamp ratification of the President's choice, is superfluous. The simple selection of a Vice-President by the President in case of vacancy would within four years face two severe tests—action by the party's national convention and (the soundest democratic judgment of all) the approval or lack of it by the electorate.

The last two sections of the amendment deal with a more complex problem: that of succession in the event of the disability or incapacity of the chief executive to discharge the obligations of office. The contingency is recognized in the original Article II of the Constitution, which calls for the Vice-President to take over in case of the President's "removal, death, resignation, or *inability to discharge the powers and duties*" of his office (italics added), and to "act accordingly until the disability be removed or a President shall be elected." The Founding Fathers did not, however, specify who was to decide that the President was unable to perform his functions, or how the decision was to be made. Neither did Congress, until 1965, spell out any method of implementing the disability provision of the Constitution.

There have been occasions in the past when there has been a shocking need of the Vice-President's assuming power while the President was technically alive but unable to function. During the long agony of President Garfield, Congress was not in session, no Speaker of the House or President Pro Tem of the Senate had been chosen, and Vice-President Arthur remained in New York, unwilling to take over the presidential duties, although the dying Garfield must certainly have been considered in the state of "disability" described in Article II. Although the executive departments continued to function automatically, the country was actually without a head of government for seventy-nine days.

The incapacity of President Woodrow Wilson during the last year and one-half of his second term was even more hair raising. Wilson suffered a cerebral lesion on September 20, 1919, while on a coast-to-coast speaking tour on behalf of the League of Nations. As a result he was completely paralyzed on the left side.

The President's helplessness was carefully concealed from the nation, from the Congress, and even from the Cabinet. He was held practically incommunicado in the White House by Edith Bolling Wilson, his wife; Admiral Cary Grayson, his physician; and Joe Tumulty, his long-time secretary. Mrs. Wilson screened all mail and messages, allowed Wilson to see only those papers she thought would not upset him. She and Grayson made decisions, sometimes without even consulting Tumulty. Sometimes she consulted the President, sometimes not. When Secretary of State Robert Lansing had the temerity to call a Cabinet meeting on his own initiative (he had not seen Wilson since the President was stricken), she asked for his resignation in the President's name. In his place she appointed Bainbridge Colby, a tyro in foreign affairs.

Lansing, who realized that the acting President of the United States was the First Lady rather than the Vice-President, had tried to get Vice-President Thomas Marshall to assert himself and pick up the reins. Marshall refused unless the President were declared medically incapable. This Admiral Grayson, Wilson's close friend, would not do.

The vice-presidency was an ill-fitting cloak that had always hung loosely from Thomas Marshall's shoulders. During his terms of office, he was forced to accept lecture engagements in order to supplement the Vice-President's salary (twelve thousand dollars a year at that time) to meet his standard of living. When Wilson was in Europe to attend the Versailles Peace Conference, Marshall declined to preside over Cabinet meetings: why should he do the President's job without the President's seventy-five-thousand-dollar salary? When he went to New York with the Secretary of State to extend official greetings in the President's name to the King and Queen of the Belgians, the Vice-President and Mrs. Marshall rode the day coach while Secretary Lansing occupied a drawing room on the same train. When, as substitute host for the ailing Wilson, he gave a state dinner for the King and Queen, he was never reimbursed from White House funds for official entertaining.

With all Marshall's quirks and amiable grumbling, had the Twenty-fifth Amendment been in effect in 1919 permitting him to become acting President of the United States, the history of the world might well have been changed. While Marshall was just as enthusiastic about the League of Nations as Wilson, he declared that he would have accepted the Lodge reservations which Wilson stubbornly rejected, and thus might have saved the League from defeat in the Senate. With the power and prestige of the United States prominent in Geneva, would the League have caved in before the bullying actions of Japan in Manchuria, Mussolini in Ethiopia, and Hitler from the occupation of the Rhineland onward? Would there, in fact, have been a Second World War?

And, following World War II, would the precarious peace have been such a shambles if there had been general acknowledgment of the fact that President Franklin Roosevelt was failing mentally and physically for months before his death? FDR's American colleagues at the Yalta Conference have said that the President had difficulty concentrating while great decisions were being made by Stalin, Churchill, and him, and that he apparently agreed to arrangements that would have shocked him a year earlier. Robert Murphy, Roosevelt's diplomatic troubleshooter in wartime Europe and North Africa, in describing his last interview with FDR shortly after his return from Yalta and only a month before his death, tells how shocked he was at the President's appearance.* Murphy found FDR "unable to discuss serious matters, in no condition to offer balanced judgments upon the great questions of war and peace."

Yet if Roosevelt was actually incapacitated, who would have been able to make an authoritative decision that he was not up to carrying on the functions of a wartime President? Roosevelt himself apparently was unaware of his diminished faculties and would have taken violent exception to any suggestion that he step down.

Quite a few political journalists would have agreed with him. Just three weeks before his death, the President attended the annual dinner of the White House Correspondents' Association, and a number of veteran newspapermen remarked on how well he looked after his sea voyage back from Yalta. The difference of lay opinion underlines the need for impartial expert medical advice on the question of a President's state of health.

The whole question of presidential disability is one of great delicacy, involving as it does the fragile web of human relations. More than mere political considerations, the factors to be scrutinized include motivation, character, and lights and shadows of psychology. Is the chief executive's physical and mental competence being questioned as the gambit for a power grab, or is the national welfare really at stake? Is the President suffering from a brief, transitory illness, or will he be disabled for months, during which far-reaching decisions must be made? Is the man who would move into his chair an adventurer and opportunist like Aaron Burr, or an unambitious, self-effacing, small-town Indiana lawyer like Thomas Marshall of Columbia City (pop. 3027)?

When both President and Vice-President are frank and rational human beings capable of judging objectively the facts of mental and physical health, the temporary transfer of power should be a relatively simple affair. In recent years, it has been customary for the President and Vice-President to arrive at an agreement, either orally or in writing, regarding the succession in case of emergency caused by disability. Vice-President Richard Nixon was certainly *de facto* chief executive during the critical periods of President Dwight Eisenhower's heart attack and his surgery for ileitis. Eisenhower himself has told of his self-searching

* *Diplomat Among Warriors* by Robert Murphy (New York: Doubleday)

following the slight stroke that temporarily affected his speech centers: he set a deadline for the trouble to clear up, after which he was prepared to turn the office over to Nixon.

President Kennedy had a private arrangement with Vice-President Lyndon Johnson just as Johnson has with Hubert Humphrey. In this age of atomic weapons, supersonic jets, intercontinental ballistic missiles, and massive retaliation, such a rapport is imperative. The nation cannot be without a responsible chief executive for a single minute. Even for the few hours that President Johnson was under anesthesia for his gall-bladder operation, Vice-President Humphrey had to be in full possession of the code words and procedures setting in motion the machinery to meet an atomic attack. The lead time provided by our early-warning system is something like forty-five minutes. It was essential that the power of acting President be delegated to Humphrey at least while Johnson was on the operating table.

Such an informal agreement has been legalized by Section III of the Bayh (Twenty-fifth) Amendment, which provides that the President has merely to notify in writing the President Pro Tempore of the Senate and the Speaker of the House that he is unable to discharge his duties, whereupon the Vice-President becomes acting President. Written notice that the President is again able is sufficient to reverse the process.

What happens if the President is disabled and refuses to recognize the fact? Or if the President is in perfect health, and the Vice-President, backed by members of the Cabinet, insists he is unfit to carry on the duties of his office? To answer these two questions the Bayh Amendment follows the suggestions of former Senator Kenneth Keating of New York and the recommendations of the American Bar Association: let Congress have the last word, and provide statutory means for determining the ability or disability of the President to function.

In the language of Section IV of the Amendment, whenever the Vice-President and a majority of the Cabinet "or of such other body as Congress may by law provide," notify both houses of Congress that the President is unable to discharge the duties of his office, the Vice-President shall become "Acting President" until the President transmits a written declaration to the contrary.

If the President tries to reclaim his office by informing Congress in writing that his disability no longer exists, and the Vice-President, with a majority of the Cabinet, "or of such other body as Congress may by law provide," disagrees, then Congress must within twenty-one days settle the dispute by a two-thirds vote of both Houses.

The heart of the matter, in my opinion—the turning point upon which the Twenty-fifth Amendment would succeed or fail—lies in the implementation of that ambiguous phrase "such other body as Congress may by law provide." Unless this "body" is made up of impartial and professionally qualified men, we will be no better off than formerly. The question of disability or non-disability is not a political question. Whether or not a President elected by the people is capable of continuing to serve should not be left to the uncertainty of what could become a lengthy and acrimonious congressional debate. The decision should not be left to men running for office in the fall of an election year.

It seems to me imperative that the state of a President's mental and physical capacity should be made solely by men and women qualified to diagnose deviations from the mental and physical norm. The jurors who would sit in judgment on this solemn question should be drawn from the list of deans of the accredited medical schools of the United States. The names of these eminent men of medicine would be placed in a jury wheel, and twelve drawn to constitute the panel. This jury should have free access to the best qualified medical specialists to help them reach a speedy verdict. A majority of two-thirds should determine the decision, which would then be reported to Congress.

Ideally, the decision of such a jury as to the state of the President's health should be binding upon Congress. The Bayh Amendment would leave the final decision to the House and the Senate. We may hope that the prestige of such a jury of medical experts would carry such weight that the legislators would not dare overturn its verdict. Should the contrary prove true, should political considerations outweigh medical opinion in a decision of such importance, we are in for more trouble.

It may be that those critics who say the principal argument against the Twenty-fifth Amendment is that it is an *amendment* have a valid point. The matter of succession could and should be settled by law within the framework of the existing Article II. Congress has the unchallenged right to pass legislation in this field, as it has done with previous succession laws including those of 1886, 1947. A constitutional amendment, say these critics, has a permanence and inflexibility that is unsuited to modern times. What appears to be the acme of wisdom in one generation may seem complete nonsense to the next. Witness the short life of the Eighteenth Amendment (Prohibition). The Noble Experiment had proved ignobly unworkable before the decade was out, but it took fourteen years before we were rid of it. Moreover, it took devious tactics to insure the ratification of the annulling Twenty-first Amendment. To bypass those state legislatures still dominated by professional "drys," Congress specified that ratification should be accomplished by special state conventions.

The Bayh Amendment was ratified in the orthodox manner by the state legislatures, with Nevada, Minnesota, and North Dakota within minutes of each other in racing to be the thirty-eighth and deciding state.

Meanwhile the status of the vice-presidency seems to be emerging from the pariah caste to which it had been relegated by generations of political Brahmins. The spectacle of Vice-President Hubert Humphrey flying around the world on diplomatic chores for President Johnson, speaking in the name of the Johnson administration, and tearing about Washington on one high official errand after another must have glamorized the job. Something extraordinary, certainly, must be taking place for Senator Jacob K. Javits of New York to make a roundabout announcement in March 1966 that he would be a candidate for the Republican nomination for Vice-President in 1968!

The most striking outer symbol of the changing status of the second choice, however, is the news that Congress is out shopping for a vice-presidential mansion—a cozy little nest in the one- or two-million-dollar range along Embassy Row on Massachusetts Avenue. This will be a far cry from the hotel rooms occupied by Calvin Coolidge when he was Vice-President. And while the Veep's new quarters will scarcely rank with the White House, it is highly unlikely that in this period of American history it will ever be called the Dog House.

INDEX

THE AUTHOR AND HIS BOOK

Michael Vincent DiSalle was born on January 6, 1908. Although a native New Yorker, he has spent most of his life in Ohio, with occasional detours to Washington, D.C. Elected Mayor of Toledo, Ohio, in 1948, he was called to Washington in 1950 by President Truman to become the first director of the new Office of Price Stabilization. Two years later he was requested to serve as Administrator for Economic Stabilization.

In 1958 Mr. DiSalle was elected Governor of Ohio. While in office he inaugurated many reforms within the state government. President Kennedy appointed him one of the four governors to serve on the President's Advisory Committee on Intergovernmental Affairs.

A national figure in Democratic Party politics, Mr. DiSalle has been a delegate to every Democratic National Convention since 1944. He is the author of *The Power of Life or Death* (in collaboration with Lawrence G. Blochman), a book attacking capital punishment. He is currently practicing law in Washington, D.C.

Lawrence G. Blochman, his collaborator, has been a newspaperman in many parts of the world, and has served the U.S. Government as wartime chief of the Voice of America, OWI Deputy Director in France, and consultant to the USIA.

A HAWTHORN BOOK